REDUCING BODIES

Reducing Bodies: Mass Culture and the Female Figure in Postwar America explores the ways in which women in the years following World War II refashioned their bodies—through reducing diets, exercise, and plastic surgery—and asks what insights these changing beauty standards can offer into gender dynamics in postwar America. Drawing on novel and untapped sources, including insurance industry records, this engaging study considers questions of gender, health, and race and provides historical context for the emergence of fat studies and contemporary conversations of the "obesity epidemic."

Elizabeth M. Matelski is Assistant Professor of History at Endicott College, USA.

REDUCING BODIES

Mass Culture and the Female Figure in Postwar America

Elizabeth M. Matelski

NEW YORK AND LONDON

First published 2017
by Routledge
711 Third Avenue, New York, NY 10017

and by Routledge
2 Park Square, Milton Park, Abingdon, Oxon OX14 4RN

Routledge is an imprint of the Taylor & Francis Group, an informa business

© 2017 Taylor & Francis

The right of Elizabeth M. Matelski to be identified as author of this work has been asserted by her in accordance with sections 77 and 78 of the Copyright, Designs and Patents Act 1988.

All rights reserved. No part of this book may be reprinted or reproduced or utilized in any form or by any electronic, mechanical, or other means, now known or hereafter invented, including photocopying and recording, or in any information storage or retrieval system, without permission in writing from the publishers.

Trademark notice: Product or corporate names may be trademarks or registered trademarks, and are used only for identification and explanation without intent to infringe.

Library of Congress Cataloging in Publication Data
A catalog record for this book has been requested.

ISBN: 978-1-138-68164-4
ISBN: 978-1-138-68166-8
ISBN: 978-1-315-54566-0

Typeset in Bembo
by Deanta Global Publishing Services, Chennai, India

For my grandmother,
Rosemary

CONTENTS

Acknowledgments   *viii*

     Introduction: Ideal Bodies   1

1   Creating a Cultural Ideal: The Fashion Industry
     and Hollywood   13

2   "We Must, We Must, We Must Increase Our Bust":
     Uplifting the Feminine Breast   32

3   "The Longer the Belt Line, the Shorter the Life Line":
     Insurance Companies and the Medical Community Weigh In   58

4   Re-Shaping America: The Reducing Neurosis   76

5   What Men Want: Men's Magazines and the Girl-Next-Door   91

6   (Big and) Black Is Beautiful: Body Image and
     Expanded Beauty Ideals   108

7   Not over 'Til the Fat Lady Sings: Fighting Fat Stigma   129

8   Barbie Gets a New Body   146

Bibliography   *153*
Index   *172*

ACKNOWLEDGMENTS

This project is the culmination of many years and uncountable hours of study, but it represents a beginning as much as an end. Since the start of my graduate studies at Loyola University in Chicago, I benefitted from the wisdom and the friendship of numerous individuals. I can only begin to thank those who have helped me along the way. First, I would like to acknowledge the assistance of the archival and special collections staff at the American Medical Association, Chicago Public Libraries, especially those at Woodson Regional, Evanston Public Library, Michigan State University, Northwestern University, University of Wisconsin–Madison, and the University of Wisconsin–Milwaukee. Their patience and willingness to retrieve boxes upon boxes and cartful after cartful of periodicals were exceptionally helpful. I am grateful to the Interlibrary Loan staff at Loyola, particularly Beth Andrews, for going above and beyond to help me find sources that would have otherwise gone unseen. This book would not have been completed if not for the financial support of the History Department and the Graduate School at Loyola that allowed me to work uninterrupted as I completed my dissertation. A postdoctoral fellowship in the humanities allowed me funds to travel to the National Library of Medicine on the campus of the National Institutes of Health. I also wish to thank my fellow graduate students, who provided not only intellectual companionship but made my years living in Chicago memorable. Several faculty members at Loyola University in Chicago deserve special mention for their support. Thank you to my teacher mentor, Bob Bucholz, for his passion for undergraduate teaching and his continued interest in my scholarship beyond my years as his teaching assistant. To Lew Erenberg and Susan Hirsch, who provided me with thoughtful and thorough critiques from the genesis of this project through its completion and from whose many excellent graduate courses I benefitted. I am particularly grateful to Tim Gilfoyle, whose graduate course on nineteenth-century America originally sparked my interest in the history of women's body ideals. As my adviser, he provided me with a model of what an academic should be like, and his motto, "the only good writing is rewriting," is advice I'll practice long into my academic career. His guidance and encouragement from research paper to dissertation to book proposal to historical manuscript is what made this possible. Thank you to my parents, who supported my academic endeavors unflinchingly even though the shortest book ever written is *Job Opportunities for History Majors*. I owe a special thank you to Courtney, who endured the mountain of hours I spent poring over *Playboy* magazine in the name of "research." Because of her love and support, I found a balance between life and academia, and for this, I'll always be in her debt. And lastly, I dedicate this to my grandmother, Rosemary Matelski. It is because of her that I first acquired my passion for the past, sitting in her kitchen while she made bread and entertained me with stories about growing up during the Great Depression. But most of all, I dedicate this to her because she loved me best for being "such a good little eater."

INTRODUCTION
Ideal Bodies

In 1954, Dorothy Bradley found herself the focus of a multipage photo essay in *Life* magazine. Bradley was an unlikely candidate for a feature story in what was then the country's leading news magazine. She was not a celebrity of any kind; she had no discernable special skills. But she did have an accomplishment to advertise: she had lost weight—a lot of weight. When Bradley finished high school in 1940, she carried 205 pounds on her five-feet, five-inch frame. According to popular, standardized height–weight tables, she was more than seventy pounds "overweight."[1]

"No boy I'd have would marry me at this size," she lamented to the magazine. Bradley dreamt of being a doctor and worried that her weight would keep her from performing in medical school, so she lost sixty pounds. Down to 155 pounds, *Life* proclaimed her "an attractive Dorothy." But in her disappointment over the compromise of becoming a nurse instead of a doctor, she returned to old eating habits and regained the weight. Bradley went back on the reducing regime, lost sixty-seven pounds this time, earned her degree in nursing, became head nurse at a settlement hospital in Kentucky, and got a date.[2]

Dorothy Bradley's story was not unique in the postwar period, nor is it unfamiliar in our own time. Her yo-yoing tale of weight gain and loss, of failure and accomplishment, exists as a microcosm for the stigma and the discrimination surrounding "overweight" and "obesity" and the reported reward that comes with conquering fat. Bradley's "success" story encapsulates the themes this book addresses, illustrating the ways and reasons why many American women in the years following World War II refashioned their bodies through whatever means necessary—including reducing diets, exercise, and plastic surgery—to fit an accepted cultural and pseudo-biological ideal.

One of my earliest childhood and most lasting memories of my mother is watching her inspect herself in the full-length mirror of our family bathroom. She would stand, twisting and turning, her eyes intensely scrutinizing the curves of her body. Then she would turn to me and simply sigh, "We were born in the wrong decade." Those same eyes that had previously scrutinized her own shape would gaze on me as if to say that I was destined (doomed?) to follow in her footsteps. I would file away her beauty tips and hints and embarrassingly chant, "I must, I must, I must increase my bust" with my fellow middle-school friends, thanks to the influence of young adult author Judy Blume, a woman who experienced her own teen years in the 1950s. My mother was born in 1960. Like many women of a previous generation, she clung to the urban legend that the Hollywood sex symbol of the 1950s, Marilyn Monroe, wore a size 12 dress. She came of age during an era where youth culture placed a cult-like status on Twiggy, a British high-fashion model with a 31-inch bust and 32-inch hips. How had the ideal female body type changed so drastically? How did we go from a society that worshiped full, buxom blondes to child-like waifs in just over a decade?

Exploring the transition from a curvy to a streamlined figure, along with the often-desperate strategies women sought to obtain these body ideals, highlights the persuasive power of the mass media and cosmetic culture. The malleability of feminine body ideals cannot be overstated. Physical appearances have few limitations. Height, for example, can be altered with platform shoes or better posture. You can change the color and texture of your hair, the length of your eyelashes, the shade of red on your lips. Plastic surgery makes it possible to change the contours of one's face, the shape of one's nose, and the size of one's breasts, and to diminish the appearance of wrinkles. But it is weight that has become the target of so many medical, political, and cultural campaigns of image attainability. The absence of "obesity" or the achievement of specific body dimensions has become regarded as feasible. This tyrannical *should*—a belief that one *should* be a certain weight or maintain a specific bust–waist–hip measurement—helped fuel a reducing neurosis in the years after World War II.

From 1945 to 1975, three major cultural shapers influenced what it meant to be an attractive, feminine, and healthy woman in the postwar years: the fashion industry, Hollywood, and, less predictably, insurance companies. In the 1940s and 1950s, high-fashion designers and the movie industry battled for dominance in shaping and defining beauty ideals. But as Hollywood struggled to find gimmicks and movie stars to tear Americans away from their television sets in the suburbs, the movies' influence on how women felt about their bodies had waned by the middle of the 1960s. Women's fashion magazines like *Harper's Bazaar*, *Vogue*, and *Cosmopolitan*, and teen fashion magazines such as *Seventeen* and *'Teen* that catered to the powerful youth market, set body ideals for the latter half of the 1960s and into the 1970s.

Developing at the same time were insurance company standardized tables that suggested the averages of women's weights in relation to age, height, and body type.

Although originally created by health and life insurance companies to determine the risk factor for providing coverage to a potential applicant, by the 1940s actuarial tables became broadly used guides for "ideal" or "desirable" weights. Previous tables had allowed for weight increases with age, but the widely distributed Metropolitan Life Insurance charts suggested that these gains were unhealthy as well as undesirable. As the decades progressed, the "ideal" figure became more and more slender, not just on the glossy pages of high-fashion magazines, but also in medical- and actuary-approved life insurance charts. As a result of this, the ideology of the perfect female figure became more monolithic rather than celebrating a wide array of body shapes and sizes.

Cultural theorist Mike Featherstone defines body maintenance and body appearance within consumer culture as the *inner* and the *outer* body. The inner body refers to one's physical health, while the outer body concerns one's overall appearance.[3] In the postwar years, the inner and the outer body conjoined. Women were instructed to diet and exercise their way toward skinnier, firmer, and trimmer figures, starting in the early 1950s because of a tightened relationship between postwar consumerism, foreign policy, insurance figures, and medical opinion. Christian Dior's "New Look," for example, began a democratization of fashion and declared that thin was "in." Postwar anxieties about Communism also led to concerns about weight and overly masculine women. And, at the same time, faulty medical and insurance actuary data persuaded the American population to believe that not only was "overweight" unattractive, but that it was deadly as well.

Fat Bodies

This book not only explores and explains changing female body ideals over time, it also contextualizes the genesis of the so-called "obesity epidemic." Fat historian Sander Gilman observes that the contemporary "obesity epidemic" launched a "moral panic" that filled the void left by the AIDS panic of previous decades.[4] But America's "war on fat" did not begin with Surgeon General C. Everett Koop in the 1990s or David Satcher's warnings in 2001. As other historians and fat studies scholars have noted, Americans first became concerned with weight loss at the turn of the twentieth century. In the late nineteenth and early twentieth centuries, Americans used a quantified measurement (body size) to qualify identities as varied as one's suitability to the privileges of citizenship. Amy Farrell's *Fat Shame: Stigma and the Fat Body in American Culture* pinpoints a moment in the mid-nineteenth century where the fat body was no longer admired but was instead connected to fears about modernity, civilization, changing gender roles, and race suicide.[5] Other early fat historians like Peter Stearns and Hillel Schwartz agree that fat shame existed long before the boom in consumer culture and the dieting industry in the 1920s.[6] One only has to look to the existence of anorexia nervosa in the mid-nineteenth century as evidence of this. However, women did not progressively become skinnier over the span of the twentieth century. As this book will show, Rubenesque bodies were desirable in the war years through the early 1950s, and they *stayed* fashionable in African American mass culture. In focusing on the postwar period, *Reducing Bodies* examines the role that fashion, the decline of the Hollywood studio system and the rise of television, print media, and cosmetic surgery played on women's shifting body image and the ways in which this period served as the launching pad for what has come to be known as the "obesity epidemic." In new and persuasive ways, fat became linked with politics, insurance, and healthcare over fears about chronic diseases that now had become synonymous with "overweight."

The decision to focus largely on women in the postwar period is purposeful. E. O. Smith's *When Culture and Biology Collide: Why We Are Stressed, Depressed, and Self-Obsessed* argues that women face more pressure to conform to an ideal standard of beauty than men because women learn early on that their future—economic, social, and reproductive opportunities—hinges on their personal appearance.[7] Borrowing Foucauldian language, Dina Giovanelli and Stephen Ostertag refer to the media as a "cosmetic panopticon" which dictates women's clothing, hairstyle, body size, and shape. Women's bodies are constantly under surveillance. By "violating expectations," such as being fat and female, women are subjected to discrimination.[8] Becky W. Thompson's rethinking of women's eating disorders, *A Hunger So Wide and So Deep: American Women Speak Out on Eating Problems*, agrees. Thompson demonstrates that, while men are not immune to fat-based discrimination, "being a fat woman is a far graver 'mistake' than being a fat man." Whether straight or gay, white, African American, Latina, or something else, most girls come of age learning that being thin is valued.[9]

Americans at the time were made aware of reported connections between "obesity" and health and longevity, but it was women—not men—who became the most religious dieters. Polls in 1956 found that 45 percent of women and 22 percent of men wanted to lose weight and that 14 percent of women and 7 percent of men were on diets to do so. Ten years later, those same polls indicated that 42 percent of women and 35 percent of men were concerned about their weight, and 14 percent of women and 6 percent of men were doing something to lose that extra weight. While concern with weight appeared to be on the rise among men, actual reducing behaviors were not.[10] Lynn Luciano's *Looking Good: Male Body Image in Modern America* recognizes that men in this period were not indifferent to their bodies, but that close attention to one's physical appearance was the realm of women, not men. Despite warnings about heart disease and other chronic health issues connected to "overweight," American men shied away from dieting, fearing weight loss would result in a loss of strength and virility, and exercise, while still considered "masculine," was typically no more strenuous than a round of golf. Luciano describes that, in the 1950s, being a stable provider was paramount to any other male attribute. American women reportedly cared little about a man's physical fitness. In a 1951 *Reader's Digest* article, "What Women First Notice about Men," neatness, well-kept hands, and eyes were cited. Moreover, because women prepared the majority of meals, wives became responsible for keeping American men at a manageable weight.[11]

Reducing Bodies contextualizes the current "obesity epidemic," but it is not only concerned with fatness. It expands beyond fat stigma to highlight how biological and cultural forces impacted the mass media's message about women's bodies. In this way, this book relates closely to academic scholarship that concerns itself with the democratic and/or inclusive and exclusive properties of cosmetic and beauty culture.[12] *Reducing Bodies* contributes to this literature of cosmetics and beauty; the examination of beauty culture through the lens of the body, rather than cosmetics, demonstrates an absence of democratic benefits and qualities. While having the "choice" to look one way or not does appear egalitarian, parameters of preferability still exist and are, generally, Caucasian.

The debate as to whether beauty culture is democratic is central to the study of ideal female forms. Do model body types oppress women? Is body image created by men and dictated to women? Activist authors like Naomi Wolf, Susan Bordo, and Joan Jacobs Brumberg have criticized beauty culture for these reasons.[13] Wolf's *The Beauty Myth: How Images of Beauty Are Used Against Women* argues that Americans' perception of beauty is imposed by a patriarchal society to keep women in their place. She argues that the beauty myth not only works against women, but also encourages them to sabotage themselves by trying to achieve impossible standards. Moreover, she ascribes all of modern women's social ills to the beauty myth, including mental illness and the rise in rape during the 1980s.[14] Wolf labels the beauty myth as a political tool that oppresses women. *Reducing Bodies* expands beyond the political to include consumerism and economics. Beauty industries, such as cosmetics, fashion, and even health-related enterprises, thrive on capitalism. And although fashion designers set clothing trends, most of cosmetic culture is reactionary rather than inventive. Moreover, gender scholars have been quick to criticize fashion and the mass media, but slower to question medical experts and news reporting that may also lead to body image issues.[15]

Historian Kathy Peiss dismisses beauty culture critics like Wolf, arguing, "they have overlooked the web of intimate rituals, social relationships, and female institutions that gave form to American beauty culture."[16] Her *Hope in a Jar: The Making of America's Beauty Culture* challenges the feminist notion that a male-dominated industry and the mass media represent the leading cause of women's historical oppression. While not denying the power of corporations, mass media, and advertisements in creating an American beauty myth, Peiss's investigation of beauty culture exposes how the cosmetics industry, a consumer-dependent economy, was largely built by women. Additionally, many of the most successful of these entrepreneurs originated from immigrant or African American working-class backgrounds and contributed to a reinterpretation of conventional standards of twentieth-century beauty and femininity.[17] Many historians who study this topic are celebratory, like Peiss, about the potential for cosmetic culture to create a united female community.[18] But by expanding cosmetic culture beyond makeup and hair dye and studying the body through the lens of diets, exercise, and plastic surgery, *Reducing Bodies* demonstrates that not all beauty culture is democratic or unifying.

Also celebratory of cosmetic culture, Lois Banner's *American Beauty* sees changing beauty ideals as central to American values. She believes the pursuit of beauty, more than any other factor, is responsible for connecting women of different classes, regions, and ethnic groups.[19] Banner asserts that working-class women and even feminists endorsed new styles, proving that fashion came not just from the wealthy elite or from men. Conversely, though, she interprets the varying standards of beauty as important factors that differentiated classes and ethnic groups.[20] Moreover, she argues that "the rigid standardization of physical appearance" was broken in the 1960s with Barbra Streisand's refusal to change her nose and with the first Asian and African American women to make it to the finals of the Miss America pageant.[21] This book similarly acknowledges this expansion of what became "beautiful" in the 1960s. It adds, however, that beauty was defined by youthfulness and slenderness. Mainstream (white) culture began to embrace the possibility of racial and ethnic "beauty," but ideas about the perfect feminine *body* became more monolith and unattainable.

Historians of African American women have also explored the impact of the beauty industry and mass media on black women throughout the nineteenth and twentieth centuries. In this way, these women's historians question the concept of a universal womanhood. Evelyn Brooks Higginbotham observes that African American women historically lived in communities whose behavior resulted not only from learned African American traditions, but also from the values and behaviors of the dominant white society.[22] Black studies focusing on beauty culture highlight the unique role of cosmetics and hair care in African American women's culture.[23] Other authors have focused on the racial and political meanings behind the American beauty industry, especially attaching it to Black Power and Black Nationalism.[24] Even by the middle of the twentieth century, beauty ideals depicted in advertisements and magazine articles in black periodicals continued to favor lighter complexions and hairstyles similar to those that were fashionable among white women. Dorothea Towles, one of the most successful African American models of the 1950s and 1960s, was light skinned and eventually dyed her hair blonde. Important black actresses such as Lena Horne and Dorothy Dandridge were similarly light complexioned. Straightening one's hair was so common in the twentieth century that the procedure was treated as a coming-of-age ritual for young women. Straight hair was not just a beauty standard, however, but also a marker of one's economic and social standing. Despite the attention given to African American women's historical connections to and relationship with cosmetics, hair, and skin color, ideas regarding black women's body image remain largely unstudied. *Reducing Bodies* expands on this scholarship by identifying and analyzing the spectrum of body types celebrated in black culture.

The primary sources for reconstructing ideal body types in the postwar years come largely from print media, diet and exercise literature, and printed medical sources. Medical archives such as those found at the American Medical Association and National Institutes of Health contain unique and unexplored information on postwar diet fads, food faddists, quack plastic surgeons, and miracle cure-alls for "ailments" as diverse as "obesity" to small breasts. As this project does not have access to women's diaries, nor does it depend upon oral histories, the mindset of the average woman or young girl coming of age in the postwar years must be carefully gleaned through periodicals' letters to the editors and in correspondence sent to the American Medical Association (AMA). Largely, however, this is a study of the mass media—particularly magazines, movies, and other genres designed to influence and reflect the desires and fears of specific demographics. Marjorie Ferguson notes that women's periodicals act as a "syllabus" that provides "step-by-step instructions" to socialize the target audience from adolescence to adulthood.[25] Noliwe M. Rooks agrees that women's periodicals have historically served the same purpose for African American women as well.[26] The primary target market for most magazines was a white, female, and middle-class demographic. Beauty advice and diet products were advertised to this population because of assumptions regarding available funds and a lived experience that equated thinness with beauty, whiteness, and socioeconomics. However, other periodicals selected for this study had a more diverse reading audience based on age, race, gender, and sexual orientation.

Chapter 1, "Creating a Cultural Ideal: The Fashion Industry and Hollywood," documents the battle between the high-fashion industry and Hollywood in promoting two very specific and unique body types—a hyper-skinny fashion model and a shorter, more buxom and curvaceous pin-up girl, respectively. French designer Christian Dior's "New Look" demanded slenderness above all and the popularization of ready-to-wear clothing made high fashion accessible to even those with modest purchasing power. Movies and other forms of mass media also instructed American women in how to be beautiful. But the buxom models of the 1950s gave way when Hollywood struggled to find female celebrities to take the place of the previous decades' fading stars. Women's magazines, however, continued to parade waifishly thin young women on their covers. In this way, the cultural creators of body ideals became more homogenous by the mid-1960s.

Chapter 2, "'We Must, We Must, We Must Increase Our Bust': Uplifting the Feminine Breast," explores the "mammary madness" of the immediate postwar era. The compression and reshaping of feminine breasts to fit a fashionable ideal is not new, but the reverence of busty women was unique to postwar America. Contemporaries attributed the preference for large-breasted figures to the infantilization of American men. But favoring women with aggressive mammary glands was also a way to sexualize, maternalize, and minimize women's power, in hopes of shuffling American women back to the kitchen and the bedroom after the war. Even with the popularity of flat-chested fashion models like Twiggy or similarly small-breasted actresses like Audrey Hepburn late in the 1960s, women and their male partners continued to desire larger breasts. The sustained technological advances in plastic surgery are evidence of this. In addition to breast implants, women attempted to take control of their bodies and their marital futures, or so advertisements touted, with the aid of vitamins, lotions, and hand pumps that promised specific results. The privileging of large-bosomed women had a particular effect on teenage girls, who desired the full curves of their favorite cover girls, and on mothers, who lamented the loss of an inflated bust after the birth of a child. But breast augmentation surgery was just one extreme example of the lengths to which women in the postwar years went to resculpt their figures to mirror the celebrated women deemed most beautiful and desirable.

If the fashion industry and Hollywood battled to create one cultural standard of female body size and shape during the 1940s and 1950s, insurance companies created yet another standard—biological. Chapter 3, "'The Longer the Belt Line, the Shorter the Life Line': Insurance Companies and the Medical Community Weigh In," traces the evolution of standardized height and weight tables, with particular interest in the role of Louis I. Dublin, long-time statistician and vice president of the Metropolitan Life Insurance Company, who devoted his professional life to public health and the longevity of the American people. Importantly, this chapter uncovers the flaws in Louis Dublin's statistical data, which suggested that fat was literally killing Americans. But Dublin was only one of many who perpetuated the belief that fat was in direct correlation to heightened mortality risks. Insurance companies, statisticians, and actuaries could not have created the fear of fat without the support of the medical community and the government. Faulty medical and insurance actuary data misled the American population to believe that not only was being "overweight" unattractive, but that now it was deadly as well. Combined, they fueled the reducing neurosis that exploded, particularly for women, in the early 1950s.

The national weight-loss campaign was directed at the general American population, but women, not men, became the most religious dieters. Chapter 4, "Re-Shaping America: The Reducing Neurosis," demonstrates that just as the ideal body shape transitioned from a woman with curves to an androgynous and shapeless silhouette, the strategies to obtain the model figure changed as well. Guide books and women's magazines encouraged moderate physical activity and a nutritionally balanced diet in the years immediately following World War II to create energized, "built-up" women ready to guide the nation into peacetime. By the early to mid-1950s, however, advice columns tilted toward weight loss and slenderizing tactics, reiterating Louis Dublin's pronouncement that "overweight" was killing Americans. Little effort weight-loss schemes such as crash diets, diet pills, and passive exercise salons appealed to a postwar American population rapidly becoming accustomed to instant gratification and immediate results. Promises of effortless weight loss not only sold these products, they also continued the damaging myth that stereotyped fat people as lazy. Mass culture portrayed "overweight" and "obese" women as not simply unattractive or unhealthy; in a country whose historical foundations praised a solid work ethic, perceived indolence was not a desirable trait.

When the topics covered in men and women's magazines overlapped, they exposed a surprising disconnect in discourse. Women's magazines urged their readers to exercise and diet to obtain an ideal form, but their male-aimed counterparts lamented that American women were squandering away their femininity with such activities. Chapter 5, "What Men Want: Men's Magazines and the Girl-Next-Door," exposes how American men opposed the extreme dieting and obsessive techniques their partners subjected themselves to for the sake of fashion and contemporary standards of beauty. Men's magazines interpreted women's desire to be thinner not as a way to please men or to be healthy, but as a way to compete with other women. Moreover, while women's high-fashion magazines published the newest fashion lines shown in Paris every spring, men's magazines bemoaned how women blindly followed trends set by foreign cultural tastemakers.

Chapter 6, "(Big and) Black is Beautiful: Body Image and Expanded Beauty Ideals," explores the African American experience. Black beauty queens and magazine pin-up girls demonstrated to white America that black was beautiful, too. And because the average African American cover girl weighed more and had broader measurements than the typical white model, black periodicals fêted a more realistic body type. More importantly, unlike their white counterparts, the black press openly celebrated "plus-size" models, celebrities, and female athletes who did not conform to or fit white ideals of acceptable femininity. Although African American men and women were exposed to the same genres of persuasive, popular media as their white counterparts—both in print and on the big screen—black periodicals and mass culture provided alternatives to (white) mainstream ideals.

This theme of celebrating fat is carried into Chapter 7, "Not Over 'Til the Fat Lady Sings: Fighting Fat Stigma," which focuses on the burgeoning Fat Acceptance Movement of the late 1960s and early 1970s through the creation of consciousness-raising groups like the Fat Underground and the National Association to Aid Fat Americans (now the National Association to Advance Fat Acceptance). By inserting alternative populations outside of the dominant white, heterosexual norm, this book challenges the belief that the pursuit of beauty ideals has the democratic potential to unite all American women. The inclusion of both African American women and fat activists suggests that while women may have had equal exposure to cosmetic culture and mass media pressure, the response to these beauty myths was not uniform.

Joan Jacobs Brumberg's *The Body Project: An Intimate History of American Girls* nostalgically laments, "In the twentieth century, the body has become the central personal project of American girls. This priority makes girls today different from their Victorian counterparts ... before the twentieth century, girls simply did not organize their thinking about themselves around their bodies."[27] It is not the purpose of this work to be nostalgic about the 1950s, a decade where actresses with more generous curves proliferated mass media. Women in the immediate postwar years still experienced pressure about ideal shapes; it was just a different kind of ideal than that which women desire today. It is also not my intention to engage with health scientists in the debate over weight management and health. Instead, *Reducing Bodies* aims to provide a historico-cultural context for the relationship between body image and weight in post–World War II America as a jumping-off point for the emergence of fat studies.

A look back to a not-so-distant past reveals an American history where slenderness has been *en vogue* for only a short span of time. Throughout the country's history, a variety of body shapes were deemed beautiful. Only with the widespread nature of mass media and the democratization of fashion did a more psychologically coercive and standardized ideal of feminine perfection rule. The principle source of our belief that thin is better and healthier has been life insurance companies, with the collusion of the medical field. By equating health and beauty with weight and size, Americans have embraced the "thin ideal."

Notes

1. Many have recognized that the terms "overweight" and "obesity" are problematic. In her excellent study, *What's Wrong with Fat?* (New York: Oxford University Press, 2013), Abigail C. Saguy examines the contemporary social implications of understanding fatness as a medical health risk, a disease, and a public health crisis. She recognizes that words like "obesity" and "overweight" have been uncritically applied to fat people to the point that most Americans do not understand these terms as a "frame"—in this case, a medical frame. Saguy instead identifies alternative ways of understanding fatness. These "competing frames for fatness"—the Health at Every Size Movement, Fat as Beautiful, and Fat Rights—pose a direct challenge to "blame frames." In other words, what or who is to blame for fat—the food industry, genetics, or overeating? Beyond the introduction, I have chosen to forgo the placement of quotation marks around "obesity" and "overweight" or the repeated use of phrases like "so-called obesity." Please note that I am not ignoring continued conversations surrounding fat-phobic language, but instead have made an editorial decision for the sake of reading clarity.
2. "The Plague of Overweight," *Life*, March 8, 1954, 120–124.
3. Mike Featherstone, "The Body in Consumer Culture" in *The American Body in Context: An Anthology*, edited by Jessica Johnston (Wilmington, DE: Scholarly Resources, 2001), 80.
4. Sander L. Gilman, *Obesity: The Biography* (New York: Oxford University Press, 2010), xii–xiii.
5. Amy Farrell's *Fat Shame: Stigma and the Fat Body in American Culture* (New York: New York University Press, 2011) is an excellent addition to the growing scholarship on fat studies. Farrell provides ample evidence for the antebellum period through the 1920s along with exploring the Fat Acceptance Movement of the 1970s and contemporary figures like Oprah Winfrey, Monica Lewinski, and the Obama family.
6. The engaging and growing field of fat studies includes scholarship from academics, activists, and artists. In the years between dissertation and manuscript, the field of fat studies has grown exponentially from a few sacred texts to having its own peer-reviewed journal and its own academic conferences. This project builds on and complements an exciting, growing field of study. Prior to the twenty-first century, two major texts,

Hillel Schwartz's *Never Satisfied: A Cultural History of Diets, Fantasies, and Fat* (NY: Free Press, 1986) and Peter N. Stearns' *Fat History: Bodies and Beauty in the Modern West* (New York: New York University Press, 1997) stood as the foundational texts. Since then, a variety of useful anthologies such as Esther Rothblum and Sondra Solovay, eds., *The Fat Studies Reader* (New York: New York University Press, 2009) and Elena Levy-Navarro, ed., *Historicizing Fat in Anglo-American Culture* (Columbus, OH: Ohio State University Press, 2010) and other monographs have progressed the discipline.

7   E. O. Smith, *When Culture and Biology Collide: Why We Are Stressed, Depressed, and Self-Obsessed* (New Brunswick, NJ: Rutgers University Press, 2002), 53.
8   Dina Giovanelli and Stephen Ostertag, "Controlling the Body: Media Representations, Body Size, and Self-Discipline," in *The Fat Studies Reader*, eds. Esther Rothblum and Sandra Solovay (New York: New York University Press, 2009), 289–290.
9   Becky W. Thompson's *A Hunger So Wide and So Deep: American Women Speak Out on Eating Problems* (Minneapolis, MN: University of Minnesota, 1997), 11.
10 Johanna T. Dwyer, Jacob T. Feldman, and Jean Mayer, "The Social Psychology of Dieting," *Journal of Health and Social Behavior* 11, no. 4 (December 1970): 269–287.
11 Lynn Luciano, *Looking Good: Male Body Image in Modern America* (New York: Hill and Wang, 2002).
12 For works addressing women's bodies and beauty ideals in nineteenth-century America, see Lois Banner, *American Beauty* (New York: Knopf, 1983); Joan Jacobs Brumberg, *Fasting Girls: The Emergence of Anorexia Nervosa as a Modern Disease* (Cambridge, MA: Harvard University Press, 1988); Frances B. Cogan, *All-American Girl: The Ideal of Real Womanhood in Mid-Nineteenth-Century America* (Athens: University of Georgia Press, 1989); Alison Piepmeier, *Out in Public: Configurations of Women's Bodies in Nineteenth-Century America* (Chapel Hill: University of North Carolina Press, 2004); Valerie Steele, *Fashion and Eroticism: Ideals of Feminine Beauty from the Victorian Era to the Jazz Age* (New York: Oxford University Press, 1985); Nancy M. Theriot, *Mothers and Daughters in Nineteenth-Century America: The Biosocial Construction of Femininity* (Lexington, KY: The University Press of Kentucky, 1996); and Jan Todd, *Physical Culture and the Body Beautiful: Purposive Exercise in the Lives of American Women, 1800-1870* (Macon, GA: Mercer University Press, 1998).
13 For a critique of contemporary beauty culture and body image, see also Susan Bordo, *Unbearable Weight: Feminism, Western Culture, and the Body* (Berkeley, CA: University of California Press, 2004); and Joan Jacobs Brumberg, *The Body Project: An Intimate History of American Girls* (New York: Random House, 1997).
14 Naomi Wolf, *The Beauty Myth: How Images of Beauty are Used Against Women* (New York: Morrow, 1991).
15 Paul Campos, *The Obesity Myth: Why America's Obsession with Weight is Hazardous to Your Health* (New York: Gotham, 2004) and J. Eric Oliver, *Fat Politics: The Real Story Behind America's Obesity Epidemic* (New York: Oxford University Press, 2006), among others, examine the medical evidence associated with the "obesity epidemic." Their collective words point out the ways in which medical information is misread or misunderstood.
16 Kathy Peiss, *Hope in a Jar: The Making of America's Beauty Culture* (New York: Metropolitan Books, 1998), 7.
17 Ibid., 5.
18 For other works on the historical impact of beauty culture in America see Sarah Banet-Weiser, *The Most Beautiful Girl in the World: Beauty Pageants and National Identity* (Berkeley, CA: University of California Press, 1999); Martha Banta, *Imaging American Women: Idea and Ideals in Cultural History* (New York: Columbia University Press, 1987); E. Mary Lisa Gavenas, *Color Stories: Behind the Scenes of America's Billion-Dollar Beauty Industry* (New York: Simon & Schuster, 2007); Dorothy Hoobler and Thomas Hoobler, *Vanity Rules: a History of American Fashion and Beauty* (Brookfield, CT: Twenty-First Century Books, 2000); Kerry Segrave, *Suntanning in 20th Century America* (Jefferson, NC: McFarland

Company, Inc, 2005); and Rachel C. Weingarten, *Hello Gorgeous!: Beauty Products in America, '40s–60s* (Tigard, OR: Collector's Press, 2006).
19 Banner, *American Beauty*, 3.
20 Ibid., 3.
21 Ibid., 290.
22 Evelyn Brooks Higginbotham, "Beyond the Sound of Silence: Afro-American Women's History," *Gender and History* 1 (1989): 50–67.
23 For works concerning African American women's beauty culture, especially in the post–World War II period, see Laila Haidarali, "Polishing Brown Diamonds: African American Women, Popular Magazines, and the Advent of Modeling in Early Postwar America," *Journal of Women's History* 17 (2005): 10–37; Noliwe M. Rooks, *Ladies' Pages: African American Women's Magazines and the Culture That Made Them* (New Brunswick, NJ: Rutgers University Press, 2004); and Susannah Walker, *Style and Status: Selling Beauty to African American Women, 1920–1975* (Lexington, KY: The University Press of Kentucky, 2007). Scholars have paid particular attention to attitudes about African American women's hair. See Julia Kirk Blackwelder, *Styling Jim Crow: African American Beauty Training During Segregation* (College Station: Texas A&M University Press, 2003); Ayana Byrd, *Hair Story: Untangling the Roots of Black Hair in America* (New York: St. Martin's Press, 2001); and Noliwe M. Rooks, *Hair Raising: Beauty, Culture, and African American Women* (New Brunswick, NJ: Rutgers University Press, 1996).
24 Korey Bowers Brown, "Ideals, Images, Identity: *Ebony* Magazine in an Age of Black Power, 1965–1970," MA thesis, Vanderbilt University, 2000; Maxine Leeds Craig, *Ain't I a Beauty Queen?: Black Women, Beauty, and the Politics of Race* (New York: Oxford University Press, 2002); Monika N. Gosin, "The Politics of African-American Women's Beauty in *Ebony* Magazine: The 1960s and 1970s," MA thesis, University of California-San Diego, 2004; Sue K. Jewell, *From Mammy to Miss America and Beyond: Cultural Images and the Shaping of US Social Policy* (New York: Routledge, 1993); and Megan E. Williams, "The Crisis Cover Girl: Lena Horne, the NAACP, and Representations of African American Femininity, 1941–1945," *American Periodicals* 16 (2006): 200–218.
25 Margorie Ferguson, *Forever Feminine: Women's Magazine's and the Cult of Femininity* (Exeter, NH: Heinemann, 1983), 85.
26 Noliwe M. Rooks, *Ladies' Pages: African American Women's Magazines and the Culture That Made Them* (New Brunswick, NJ: Rutgers University Press, 2004), 89.
27 Brumberg, *The Body Project*, 97.

1

CREATING A CULTURAL IDEAL

The Fashion Industry and Hollywood

> *The disposition for looking well is ruining half the young people in the world—causing them to study their glasses, and paint or patch, instead of pursuing that which is lasting and solid—the cultivation of the mind. It is always a mark of a weak mind, if not a bad heart, to hear a person praise or blame another on the ground alone that they are handsome or homely.*
>
> —*Godey's Lady's Book*, 1831

Beauty and its pursuit have not always been considered appropriate topics of discussion. In the early nineteenth century, conversations concerning the body were deemed impolite. Women and girls preoccupied with their appearance were characterized as self-indulgent and vain. Nonetheless, dialogue surrounding ideal body types appeared in a variety of print sources, popular culture, and medical journals, such as concerns about the size of specific body parts.[1]

Women were particularly affected during America's transition into a quantified weight culture, manipulating their figures through diet, fashion, and exercise. Competing models offered a spectrum of ideal body types and varying opinions about the role of fitness and weight management in achieving these desired forms. In the antebellum period, a frail, waifish woman, the subject of historian Barbara Welter's important essay, "The Cult of True Womanhood, 1820–1860," dominated middle- and upper-class circles.[2] Referred to as the "Currier & Ives" woman or the "steel-engraved lady" by others, the ideal white woman was slight, with small hands and feet, and appeared pale and fragile. Food, femininity, and sexual appetite were inexorably linked. Etiquette books advised young women to eat scantily in public; a ravenous appetite indicated moral turpitude. Fat historian Sander Gilman notes that, already by the end of the eighteenth century, the medical community and popular culture attributed fat to a "weakness of will."[3]

Slimness was also a sign of social status; a physically frail and weak woman literally depended on her working husband for her livelihood.[4] So popular was this physical ideal that the mid-nineteenth century witnessed the birth of contemporary *anorexia nervosa*.[5]

Although accounts of women starving themselves can be found as far back as the Middle Ages with the holy ascetics, a new kind of "fasting girl" emerged in the nineteenth century. *Anorexia nervosa* was the result of not only a new authority given to doctors in the period, but also larger changes in bourgeois life. The self-restraint necessary to achieve this body type was a characteristic valued in antebellum society. Food refusal and its accompanying slimness were signs of social status as thin, frail women were unfit for productive work. Additionally, advice books of the era cautioned their female readers to be careful of what and how much they ate. Hunger and gluttonous eating were connected to sexuality and desire; therefore, by demonstrating a modest appetite, a woman exhibited her own sexual virtue. Historian Joan Jacobs Brumberg makes clear that modern *anorexia nervosa* existed well before the mass preoccupation with reducing in the twentieth century.[6] Yet, because prescriptive literature was aimed largely at young, white, middle-class women, this ideal had a limited impact. In the twentieth century this changed, however, when mass media targeted broader audiences, irrespective of class and race.

The "steel-engraving woman" of antebellum America did not command complete hegemony over female forms throughout the nineteenth century; this so-called "Victorianism" was challenged almost as soon as it appeared in the 1850s. A new wave of sensuality in the post–Civil War era brought with it new repression best illustrated by Anthony Comstock and "real" Victorianism. Moreover, a number of popular medical writers claimed that fat promoted health.[7] By the 1860s, a number of alternative prototypes—each presenting a more active, vigorous model—challenged the frail, thin ideal. With the stateside appearance of the burlesque troop the British Blondes in 1868 and the mass popularity of theatrical actress Lillian Russell, a more buxom model of beauty replaced the delicate ideal in the latter half of the nineteenth century. Russell was rumored to weigh 200 pounds, but was probably closer to 165–180 pounds at the height of her career.[8] These figures marked the beginnings of popular culture's influence on women's body esteem, beyond medical advice and prescriptive literature like *Godey's Lady's Book*. The "voluptuous" ideal waned in popularity by the late 1890s in favor of the tall, athletic "Gibson Girl," a patrician woman popularized by the drawings of *Life* illustrator Charles Dana Gibson. A hybrid of the two previous body ideals, the "Gibson Girl" possessed the lithe features of the "steel-engraving lady" with the ample bust and hips of the heartier ideal. Corsets went out of fashion in favor of form-fitting dresses that encouraged slenderness. Historian Lois Banner notes that with Gibson's figure type, America successfully challenged Europe's control over popular standards of beauty and created a new international ideal.[9] The new idyllic woman in 1894 was five foot four inches tall and weighed 140 pounds.[10]

Between 1890 and 1910, middle-class America initiated the battle against body fat when several factors—changing gender roles, consumerism, economic status, medicine, modernity, and mortality—simultaneously collided. Social stigma against fat predated any health concerns about "overweight" and "obesity."[11] The first penny scale appeared in the United States in 1885, transforming the way Americans thought about weight. The new weighing machine debuted in drug and grocery stores and expanded to street corners, movie theaters, banks, office buildings, railroad stations, and subways.[12] With the ability to measure one's body weight to the nearest pound, weight transitioned from a qualitative subject to a quantitative evaluation.[13] Being fat or thin often has little to do with one's shape or size, but rather an assumed identity directly attached to the body. America became a weight-watching culture when people increasingly believed that the body was tied to the self. Criminologists used weight to identify character types, insurance companies and actuaries tied weight to risk and mortality, and the fashion industry used weight as a litmus test for beauty.[14]

In 1908, Parisian designer Paul Poiret introduced a revolutionary silhouette that shifted visual interest to the legs and away from the Victorian hourglass. The result was a new ideal that featured slender, long limbs and a relatively flat chest. Women of the period bound their breasts with "correctors" or "flatteners" in attempts to appear fashionably shapeless and androgynous. Attractiveness was no longer determined by the shape of a woman's torso, but by the appearance of her face and legs. The shortening of hemlines, resulting in a new display of the body, required that fashionable women manage their diets and practice self-discipline. Woods Hutchinson, medical professor and one-time president of the American Academy of Medicine, predicted, "The longed-for slender and boyish figure is becoming a menace, not only to the present, but also the future generations."[15] What would later be referred to as the "Flapper look" had an influence on even the most staunchly middle-class women. Rather than writing letters back home about happy weight gain and plentiful meals, as the previous generation had, young college women instead worried about gaining weight and discussed their various diet plans.[16]

This relatively shapeless body type remained dominant throughout the 1910s and 1920s, particularly with the popularity of boyishly framed movie actresses like Mary Pickford and Clara Bow. The new mass media of the movies disseminated beauty ideals to an even broader audience and had a particularly strong influence among teenagers and white-collar working women. The movies played a crucial role in the development of a teen girl culture that continued through the 1950s by providing feminine role models and promoting standards of fashion, beauty, language, and the body.[17] Moreover, for the first time, popular serial fiction like *Grace Harlow* and *Nancy Drew*, aimed at younger girls, featured a chubby character who served as a comedic foil to the slender, well-liked protagonist.[18] The 1920s also witnessed the advent of another source of beauty ideals—the Miss America pageant. The contest's first winner, Margaret Gorman, stood at five feet one inch and weighed 108 pounds. Sixty years later, Gorman's beauty queen counterparts weighed approximately the same, but were five inches taller with waists three inches smaller.[19]

Hemlines fell and narrow waistlines returned in the 1930s. During the Great Depression, a new, more mature, and less playful beauty ideal came into being and remained popular through the war years, culminating in a return to the voluptuousness that recalled late nineteenth-century fashion. Popular actresses like Jean Harlow, Mae West, and Greta Garbo highlighted the re-emphasis on breast size and curves. By the early 1930s, the basic beauty institutions of American culture had been established—fashion, cosmetics, modeling, beauty contests, and Hollywood. No new medium for disseminating beauty would appear until the mass production of televisions in the 1950s.

In addition to the mass media, the introduction of ready-to-wear clothing and the creation of standardized dress sizes also shaped women's weight consciousness. Paris still dominated design, but American mass-produced imitations made fashionable clothes widely available by the end of World War I.[20] Although most women's clothing remained custom-made well into the 1920s, store-bought clothes contributed to women's anxieties about their bodies. The manufacturers of ready-to-wear clothing standardized specific body shapes with their numerical sizes; if one failed to fit the pre-made patterns, a woman could perceive that there was something wrong with her figure. Between 1939 and 1940, the National Bureau of Home Economics in the Department of Agriculture collected the measurements of more than fifteen thousand white women to help clothing manufacturers better develop their ready-to-wear clothing. Technicians recorded fifty-nine measurements for each female volunteer to ensure the most accurate results. The compilation was the first large-scale scientific study of women's body measurements ever recorded. The results informed manufacturers that the "average" American woman between the ages of 25 and 29 stood just under five feet three inches tall and weighed 124.7 pounds, with a bust-to-waist-to-hip measurement of 34.2–27.3–37.8.[21] Despite the shift to a more voluptuous ideal in the 1930s, this version of the "average" American woman was significantly slimmer than even the Gibson girl ideal at the turn of the century.

It is tempting to attribute the already entrenched influence of beauty culture on the slenderizing of American women in the early decades of the twentieth century. However, manufacturers of ready-to-wear clothing potentially created standardized figures based on skewed data. Participants in the 1939 clothing study were given a nominal fee for volunteering, which may have influenced the overall results. As the country had not yet pulled itself out of the Great Depression, the study's female volunteers originated from the most impoverished populations, using the token compensation toward food for their families. This likely complicated the representative figure of the "average woman" as the social conditions may have distorted the collected data toward underweight body types. However, if the class status of volunteers goes unquestioned, then these figures illustrate how disseminators of beauty culture had already taken a strong hold of American women's body esteem, even prior to World War II. In the 1930s, size 14 became more popular than size 18, and the "dieter's goal" became size 12.[22] In the 1940s, stores increasingly ordered more size 10s than ever before, and by 1956, size ranges began with size 8.[23] In the late 1950s, department-store buyers reported that, since 1939, the "average" woman had shrunk by three to four dress sizes.[24] Men's clothiers, however, continued to sell the same sizes as they had the previous twenty years.[25] In this way, male fashion did not necessitate weight control. Fashion standards had a broader audience in postwar America. By comparison, in the nineteenth century, fashion was generally limited to the upper classes. Until the mid to late nineteenth century, the country's population was largely rural; therefore, local community standards, rather than urban fashionabilty, influenced the majority of women.[26] As standardized ready-to-wear clothing became more available in the postwar years, women now had the time and the money to keep up with the latest fashion trends. Instead of seeing ready-to-wear clothing as a loss of individuality, American women interpreted it as an easy way to stay fashionably up to date.

At the close of World War II, American feminine beauty ideals were in flux. Betty Friedan famously argued that, during this time, American women fell victim to a "feminine mystique" that instructed them to pursue femininity and to avoid situations that threatened to strip them of it. Although the universal validity of Friedan's claims has been challenged, in regard to body image, the author-housewife was not exaggerating.[27] The postwar period saw the re-emergence of feminine ideals similar to the antebellum "Cult of True Womanhood" to combat the paranoia that American women had become overly masculine during the war.[28] Although this was not a complete return to beauty and domestic ideals from the so-called Victorian era, the postwar ideal focused once again on family togetherness with women at the center of the home. Young women married earlier than their mothers had a generation earlier and gave birth to more children in rapid succession. Large numbers of women abandoned higher education or a full-time career and instead sought fulfillment through marriage, motherhood, and housework.[29] In the words of one contemporary writer, "The war was over, and [women] were supposed to sashay back to the kitchen and learn how to make green beans baked with Campbell's cream of mushroom soup."[30] With recent memories of a debilitating economic depression and a world war casting shadows over America, the country's political, economic, and social institutions endorsed this return to domesticity as patriotic and necessary.

This renewed emphasis on domesticity required a rededication to cosmetic standards. As scholar Barbara Coleman notes, "In a society based on strict gender roles, women needed to look like women. They could not resemble Norman Rockwell's *Rosie the Riveter*."[31] Although wartime propaganda had assured the American public that working a "man's job" would not threaten women's femininity or sexuality, reconversion demanded that women forfeit outside employment to stabilize the home.[32] Among the numerous changes expected of

18 Creating a Cultural Ideal

American women to help the country return to tranquility after World War II was a modification in the ideal feminine figure. Women's and teen magazines played a major role in constructing the ideal body type for the "all-American" woman. During the 1950s, five out of six women read at least one magazine every week.[33] Picture-based magazines changed the face of American journalism after the war. Members of a growing middle class increasingly looked to these cultural tools to guide them through their newly acquired social mobility. In a society where television was just taking root in suburban living rooms, magazines offered guidance, disseminated the news, and informed Americans—both men and women—how to think and feel about national and international issues.[34]

When American women looked at the covers of magazines at the grocery store, the drug store, or elsewhere, they were assaulted with a wide variety of feminine forms. Responsible for this were three modeling agencies, appropriately labeled "The Big Three," who dominated the modeling industry in the early postwar years. Each agency maintained a very specific idea about feminine beauty, and none resembled the typical American woman.[35] John Robert Powers, the most established of the three major modeling agencies (founded in 1933), specialized in "high-fashion" models and was therefore more stringent with the figure measurements of the women and girls under his employ. His models adhered to the motto, "Slender, Tender, and Tall."[36] The typical junior models for the Powers agency stood five feet four inches, with 33–23–34 measurements. Powers' adult models were at least four inches taller than his junior prototypes, with the ideal standing five feet nine inches with a 34–24–34 build. Powers recognized that this figure was not realistic for most women, however, and routinely cautioned the readers of fashion magazines to not copy the body types set by his models. Walter Thornton, best known for his pin-up model agency, similarly noted, "The best clothes drape is a tall, willowy woman, built along the lines of a window dummy … a full, curvaceous figure causes fitting problems." He added, however, that this was not a figure that appealed to men. Thornton's pin-up model agency hired women slightly shorter than the high-fashion Powers girls, with more exaggerated dimensions (Table 1.1).[37]

Harry Conover was the newest of the Big Three. His agency specialized in male and child models, but his trademark was Cover Girls. In 1941, when John Powers reportedly rejected hiring the reigning Miss America, claiming she was built too much like a football player, Conover signed her to a modeling contract. Unlike the fashion trade, magazine cover girls were usually picked with the heterosexual, white male ideal of feminine beauty in mind. Fat historian Hillel Schwartz describes Conover's models as "more robust, more wholesome, more middle-class, more Midwestern."[38] At five feet four inches and with average measurements of 33–23–34.5, his cover girls were also shorter than high-fashion and pin-up models.[39] The agency head prophesied in 1947 that the ideal woman of the immediate future would be fleshier than high-fashion models. "The boys home from the wars are looking for something with more curves, someone who is believable,"

TABLE 1.1 "Big Three" models versus the average American woman

	Height	Bust (inches)	Waist (inches)	Hips (inches)
Average American woman (18–80) per US Department of Agriculture Statistics, 1947	5'3.25"	35.5	29.25	38.75
Average American girl (20–24)	5'3.5"	33.9	26.4	37.4
Hazel Space, Powers junior model	5'4"	33	23	34
Barbara Tullgren, Powers model	5'8"	34	24	34
Rita Daigle, Thornton model	5'6.5"	34	21	34
Madelon Mason, Conover model	5'4"	33	23	34.5

he argued, "who looks like the girl next door, only perhaps a little prettier."[40] Conover accurately predicted the tastes and desires of returning soldiers. What he did not foresee, however, was the impact one French designer would have on American women's body ideals.

J'Adore Dior

On February 2, 1947, French designer Christian Dior unveiled a new fashion line that featured an hourglass silhouette with a tiny waist, high-rounded breasts, and curved shoulders. Carmel Snow, editor of *Harper's Bazaar*, dubbed it the "New Look." The design favored a full, flared skirt and an almost obscene amount of textiles, a microcosm of the relaxed postwar restrictions on consumable products. Of his design, Dior noted, "We came from an epoch of war and uniform, with women like soldiers with boxer's shoulders. I designed flower women, soft shoulders, full busts, waists as narrow as liana and skirts as corollas."[41] The popular feminine fashion reflected the combination of social repression and sexual exploitation. Hemlines fell to mid-calf length and flared skirts were held out by starched crinoline petticoats. Dior's silhouette, although heralded as "natural" and "womanly," required women to wear a hidden armory of foundation garments to achieve the hourglass silhouette. Fashion scholar Harold Koda notes that the relative naturalism of the female body from the 1930s until World War II was abandoned with the "New Look" (Figure 1.1). Dior flattened the stomach and buttocks with girdles, and the hips and bust were emphasized with padding or small panniers. This was not simply a return to the corseted past, however. Previous corset silhouettes were vertical or S-curved; the "New Look" featured a forward-jutting pelvis and a concave buttock.[42] "Get yourself a new shape," *Time* magazine announced.[43] And to fit the new designs, that is exactly what American women had to do.

Dior's "New Look" demanded slenderness above all. Although the silhouette featured high-rounded breasts and full hips, these were features that could be simulated with rubber or foam padding. A tiny hand-span waist, however, could not be faked, even with the help of girdles and corsets. Dior reportedly believed

FIGURE 1.1 Bar suit from Dior's "New Look," 1947.

that waists wider than 17 inches were "repulsive" and that for a woman to wear his designs, she must have an "*epée* silhouette"—be as slender as a fencing blade.[44] Slender models, of course, were not unique to the "New Look"; high fashion dating back to the 1910s and 1920s demanded equally svelte figures to fit the popular, curveless silhouette introduced by Parisian designer Paul Poiret. But the models depicted in magazine advertisements in the earlier period were largely drawings—not actual flesh-and-bone women; a female reader could realistically convince herself that the model's slimness was simply of the artist's doing, much like the exaggerated dimensions of calendar art pin-up girls of the 1940s. Muriel Maxwell, a fashion editor and former cover girl herself, observed of Dior's new style, "We wondered where in the world we were going to get models who could get into them. Then out of the woods came these nymphs with no lungs and very little of the flesh that keeps you alive."[45]

Dior's changes to fashion could be seen everywhere, particularly in department stores. The French designer's "Look" was quickly copied by mass manufacturers in the United States. Even store mannequins changed their shape, now mirroring the "New Look" with a tiny waist, full hips, and conical breasts. American media, reporting on the happenings in Moscow, pointed to American superiority and the lack of sophistication of Russian women's fashion, whose clothes mannequins weighed 160 pounds.[46] Dior's "New Look" become so popular that its absence in non-period movies, according to Edith Head, the premier costume designer for Paramount Studios, "was a self-inflicted slap in the face to Hollywood." Films produced in 1946 that had been shelved until the following year looked suddenly dated from a fashion point of view. "Anything less than the New Look was depressing," Head recalled, "a reflection of a war gone by, and nobody wanted it."[47] Films that did not feature Dior's silhouette appalled female moviegoers who went to the movies to view the latest fashions. Hollywood also held a role in making high fashion accessible to the average American woman. Many popular stars' most famous gowns were copied by ready-to-wear manufacturers; women saw the famous designs on screen and could later purchase a copy of a featured dress straight off the rack. For example, Elizabeth Taylor's party dress with the sunflower-covered bust in *A Place in the Sun*, an Edith Head creation, became the most popular high school prom dress in 1951. Although Head designed the majority of Audrey Hepburn's wardrobe for *Sabrina* (1954), Hubert de Givenchy created Hepburn's white-and-black lace gown, which other clothing manufacturers scrambled to recreate. Givenchy also designed Hepburn's black dress in *Breakfast at Tiffany's* (1961); Holly Golightly's iconic "little black dress" is still one of the most essential cocktail attires for women.[48]

The popularity of Dior's "New Look" cannot be explained away by an absence of alternatives. Congruent with Dior's pinched-waist design of 1947 came the "Wrap-Around Look"—a cocoon-like silhouette that similarly utilized a near orgy of material, reflecting the attitudes of the postwar consumer. Fashion critics praised the "droopy" silhouette for its democratic possibilities. Because of the ability to "hide extra weight," the wrap-around style flattered a range of body types.[49] But Dior's "New Look" silhouette refused to be supplanted. Another challenge came in the 1950s, when designer Cristobal Balenciaga for the House of Dior abandoned the hourglass figure for the H-shape, a look that inspired shapeless silhouettes like the Parisian sack dress, the trapeze, and the balloon dress. But unlike the "New Look," the House of Dior's second silhouette did not inspire Americans. The "New Look" remained the basis for American women's fashion well into the 1960s, until trendsetters and tastemakers introduced a new silhouette for the ideal female figure.

Hollywood's Competing Ideal and Alternate Models

At the same time that women's magazines like *Harper's Bazaar* and *Vogue* filled their pages with photo shoots of "Slender, Tender, and Tall" models, whose figures could not compete with Dior's fashions, Hollywood—just as it had in earlier decades—presented its own definition of feminine beauty. Yet, because fashion design houses and the movie industry endorsed different body ideals, two combating figures emerged—the high-fashion model and the pin-up girl. Marilyn Monroe eventually evolved into the reigning box-office queen of the 1950s, but she certainly was neither the first nor the only actress who attempted to build a career from busty sex appeal. MGM Studios touted "Sweater Girl" Lana Turner as the successor to platinum blonde Jean Harlow. Twentieth-Century Fox had Monroe and, later, Sheree North and Jayne Mansfield. Kim Novak's studio, Columbia Pictures, changed her real first name from Marilyn to avoid confusion with and too many comparisons to her Twentieth-Century Fox competition. Universal International heralded Mamie Van Doren as the answer to Monroe's box office success. When asked how a young starlet could become a star, Van Doren responded, "I can only say: be born stacked and pretty. I know of no other advice."[50] Even America's World War II allies had their own version of the blonde sex goddess. England tried to compete with Diana Dors, France had their buxom sex star in Brigitte Bardot, and the Soviet Union participated in the battle of the busts with actress Irina Skobtseva. Despite similarities in bust, waist, and hip ratios, few measured up to Marilyn Monroe. As one journalist for *Colliers* magazine noted, Hollywood's major studios discovered early on that "actresses, like fingerprints, never match."[51] Much has been written about Monroe, both sympathetic and critical. Film historian Molly Haskell remarks "if she hadn't existed we would have had to invent her, and we did, in a way. She was the fifties' fiction, the lie that a woman has no sexual needs, that she is there to cater to, or enhance, a man's needs."[52] Equally enviable and pathetic, Monroe represented the kind of woman that other women feared might be their husband's secretary on nights he had to "work late."

Monroe and her copycats ruled the pin-up magazines, but they did not hold a monopoly over the box office. Popular actresses like Grace Kelly and Audrey Hepburn materialized in conscious and unconscious opposition to Monroe and those like her. Haskell argues that women wanted their daughters to grow up to be like Grace Kelly and Audrey Hepburn. They seemed "safe from the kind of humiliation to which Marilyn Monroe and Jennifer Jones submit."[53] Kelly and Hepburn represented elegance and independence. But while mothers might have hoped their daughters grew up to emulate the slenderly chic actresses of the 1950s, movie magazines warned their female readers that the new gamine girls like Hepburn, with their short-cropped hair and boyish figures, were problematic. In a decade that desired real divides between the genders, androgyny was not yet wholly fashionable nor considered appealing. One Hollywood producer lamented, "where's a woman's sex when you have to wait for her to turn around to reveal her womanhood?" He warned, "Before you rush to the beauty parlor for the shearing and before you starve yourself into a matchstick figure, hear what some of the male authorities in Hollywood have to say about sex appeal."[54] But although Audrey Hepburn and Marilyn Monroe represented two very different types of popular actress in the 1950s, both women's figures were the same variation on the classic hourglass figure. Monroe's 36–24–34 figure to Hepburn's 31.5–22–31 is the same waist-to-hip ratio of 0.70.[55]

Like Hepburn or Grace Kelly, film star Doris Day was another actress who did not appear to mirror the Sweater Girl/Manufactured Starlet prototype. Day, a Big Band singer turned actress, was the most popular film star in the country. While Monroe appealed mostly to men, Day appealed to both genders. In addition to her movie roles, fan magazines fashioned the singer/actress as a no-nonsense, blue jeans-wearing, makeup-eschewing role model.[56] But even the reportedly tomboyish Doris Day actually had a large bust and curvy, yet trim, figure. Both she and Marilyn Monroe stood at five feet five and a half inches and weighed approximately 120 pounds. When Molly Haskell interviewed the reclusive actress in the late 1970s, she revealed her shock that Day was as shapely as the late-Marilyn Monroe. She notes, "[Doris Day] was a tomboy and therefore on one side—my side—of the chasm that separated the 'women' from the 'girls' in the most sexually schizophrenic of decades."[57] In their films and in real life, Monroe and Day represented different sides of the sexual spectrum, but although Hollywood's most popular actresses advertised a varying degree of sexual availability, the studios continued to promote women with similar slender, yet curvy, figures.

Despite the variances of idyllic body types necessitated by the business of high fashion and in the make-believe world of Hollywood, the ideal figure was always a *white* body. Postwar America experienced a break from its ethnic past. Historian Lynn Spigel argues that network television and its programs helped ease the transition as Americans moved from inner city neighborhoods to the homogenized suburbs, severing the ties to their former ethnic backgrounds.[58] Similarly, popular magazines paid scant attention to the ethnic makeup of Hollywood's and television's biggest stars. A telling example is the career of bombshell and pin-up perennial Rita Hayworth. Born Margarita Carmen Cansino in 1918, Rita Hayworth began her Hollywood career in 1935, cast in largely supporting roles. With her distinctive Mediterranean features, Hayworth struggled to convince Columbia Pictures' Harry Cohn to star her in a leading role. The actress eventually agreed to painful electrolysis to recede her low hairline by a full inch and changed her hair color and her name to become a leading lady. Hayworth's popularity peaked in the mid-1940s, and during World War II she was the second most popular pin-up girl after Betty Grable.[59] None of this appeared in the fan magazines, however, and the public was largely unaware of the lengths Hayworth went to in her transformation from starlet to star. As historian Matthew Frye Jacobson observes, Caucasians are made, not born.[60]

An End of an Era

The 1960s was a turbulent time in America, and not safeguarded from this were women's beauty ideals. With Marilyn Monroe's death in August 1962, the era of the busty blonde officially closed. In the months preceding her death, American women had regarded Elizabeth Taylor and Grace Kelly as the most beautiful women in the world. Only 1 percent of unmarried women and less than 1 percent of married women had awarded that title to Monroe.[61] Cultural critic and historian Susan Douglas remembers, "When she died, it seemed to me ... that the seemingly dumb-blond, busty bombshell would no longer exert the cultural or sexual pull that she once did."[62] In 1965, Mamie Van Doren and Jayne Mansfield began filming *The Las Vegas Hillbillys*. Van Doren, regretfully remembered the filming, commenting, "I realized that Jayne and I were quickly becoming anachronisms. The era of the blondes was gone, and we seemed to be futilely trying to hold on to it."[63] Monroe's death may have signaled the end of an era, but it was not only the end of buxom blondes. It was also the conclusion of Hollywood's influence on women's body ideals. The movie industry, like the country itself, struggled to adapt to the revolutions that would become the radical sixties. The creation of new technologies like CinemaScope, Technicolor, 3-D films, and other less successful gimmicks came as a result of dwindling movie attendance. With the mass move to suburbia, Americans' consumption patterns changed; past moviegoers now cut back on outside entertainment when they had a television in their living room. Moreover, the political and cultural environment was particularly unfavorable to Hollywood. Union strikes, a monopoly indictment, investigations by the House Un-American Activities Committee (HUAC), suburbia, and the popularity of television created a hostile environment in which the movie industry struggled to compete.[64]

Along with the decline of the big studio system, Hollywood momentarily lost its position as one of the harbingers of American beauty ideals. One fan wrote to *Motion Picture* lamenting that television celebrities were more "polished and sophisticated" than Hollywood actresses. Calling Jayne Mansfield "a joke," Elizabeth Taylor "haphazard," and teen-queen Annette Funicello stuck "in a little-girl world," her letter to the editor highlights fan disenchantment with the state of movies in the 1960s.[65] Male actors and films about male bonding dominated the box office in the late 1960s and into the 1970s. Faye Dunaway, Jane Fonda, Vanessa Redgrave, and Barbra Streisand became the most bankable female stars, but opportunities for women were few. Film producer Richard Zanuck of Twentieth-Century Fox declared that in the 1960s, even Marilyn Monroe would have had a hard time becoming a star.[66]

Despite the popularity of television, the new media never possessed the same clout as Hollywood in dictating fashion, beauty, and the shape of the ideal female body. A major reason for this was network television's high level of censorship. Many worried the new medium might broadcast inappropriate material directly into American families' living rooms. Lynn Spigel notes that early television, unlike the glamour-girl machine of Hollywood, aimed to present "unthreatening women."[67] A few buxom stars like Dagmar and Faye Emerson snuck onto live sketch comedy and late-night programming, but even Emerson's low-cut dresses faced the threat of censorship. For the most part, women were portrayed as sexless like the matronly Jewish mother Molly Goldberg, or as middle-aged housewives like Margaret Anderson (*Father Knows Best*) and June Cleaver (*Leave It to Beaver*). And while Lucille Ball may have been a glamour girl on the big screen, television programming contained her sexuality as zany housewife Lucy Ricardo.[68]

The Twig and the Tree

Fashion magazines like *Vogue*, *Harper's Bazaar*, and *Cosmopolitan* harbored a near-monopoly on style and beauty without Hollywood to contend with in the mid- to late 1960s. Dior's "New Look" remained the basis for American women's fashion until a new ideal for the female figure was established in the 1960s when hemlines rose, culminating in the micro-miniskirt and the micro-micro.[69] Although this may appear an extended period for a single silhouette to dominate, considering that fashion "changes" every season, American fashion only experiences major silhouette changes in thirty-year cycles. The general form of the skirt has always been the determining factor in major fashion types, and three fundamental silhouetted skirts—the bell shape contour, the tubular contour, and the back-fullness contour—have dominated since the 1760s. Using this repeating pattern, Dior's "New Look" should have remained the prominent silhouette until the 1980s. Instead, the tubular contour of the miniskirt became the more popular fashion in the mid-1960s. This fashion microcosm demonstrates the true turbulence of the decade and how quickly ideals were changing in the postwar period.

Women's magazines continued to look to Paris for the latest fashions in the 1960s, but one British model took the Western world by storm. Part of the British Invasion that brought the Beatles, miniskirts, and pantyhose to American shores also swept in Leslie Hornby—a sixteen-year-old girl who stood five feet six and a half inches and weighed ninety-one pounds, with 32–22–32 measurements. Better known as Twiggy, the emaciated British teen played an important role in the slenderizing of American feminine body ideals. Reports fluctuated on how much the scrawny model actually weighed, ranging from 91 pounds at her lightest to 97 pounds at her heaviest. In comparison, between 1966 and 1970, the average American sixteen-year-old weighed 122.7 pounds and stood five feet three inches high.[70] "Twiggy is called Twiggy because she looks as though a strong gale would snap her in two and dash her to the ground," one fashion journalist remarked. "In a profession where thinness is essential, Twiggy is of such meager constitution that other models stare at her."[71] Standardized height and weight tables from the period suggest that, at Twiggy's height and small build, a healthy woman aged twenty-five and over should have weighed between 126 and 135 pounds.

The model's genesis is memorable. An androgynous pixie haircut changed her life in 1966, turning the waifish teen from a high school dropout to one of the world's most popular models seemingly overnight. Soon, she was on the cover of British *Vogue* and flying to America, where hemlines had continued undisturbed since the end of World War II, to appear on the pages of *Seventeen* and *Vogue*.

But even the in-demand "It" girl was unhappy with her body. "Whether you're thin, fat, small, dark, blond, redhead, you wanna be something else," the model recalled in a 2010 interview. "I wanted a fairy godmother to make me look like Marilyn Monroe. I had no boobs, no hips, and I wanted it desperately."[72]

Twiggy's popularity testifies to the influence of youth culture in the late 1960s. Unlike previous models, she appeared simultaneously on the covers of teen periodicals as well as high-fashion magazines, and was clearly marketed specifically to the powerful, disposable income of the youth market. Teen culture, particularly girl culture, was certainly not invented or discovered in the 1960s. Throughout the postwar period, from hula-hoops to raccoon-skin caps, companies and advertisers were well aware of the almighty teen dollar. When *Seventeen* magazine debuted in September 1944, the first run of four hundred thousand copies sold out in six days. By February 1947, circulation exceeded 1 million and by July 1949, over 2.5 million girls were reading the magazine.[73] Hollywood, too, began to cater to the youth market. In the 1950s, moviemakers began to systematically study audiences for the first time and discovered that young people (Baby Boomers) outnumbered adults. As a result, Hollywood produced a number of low-budget "teen flicks."

Twiggy's American counterpart was Penelope Tree. Tree, the daughter of a well-to-do family, was legendarily first spotted at one of Truman Capote's black-and-white balls at the age of seventeen. The next day, Diana Vreeland at American *Vogue* called, and for the next four years, Tree would be the American "It" girl, her look and her style personifying the late 1960s. In a 2008 interview, Tree laughed at the irony that her boyish hips and hollowed-out cheekbones helped get her work when she was secretly suffering from anorexia. Tree weighed herself every day, watchful to never let her weight dip below 100 pounds, but go not much above that mark either. A skin disease, drugs, and a nervous breakdown ended her modeling career prematurely.[74]

Some have argued that Twiggy was the predecessor to the emaciated models of today.[75] Such observations, however, are misleading; high-fashion models have always been willowy and slight. As historian Lois Banner notes, since the creation of fashion photography, the "canonical" and "best" models have been those whose slender bodies did not compete with the clothes they were paid to wear.[76] Twiggy's matchstick-skinny legs were the perfect mannequin on which to highlight the new mini-dresses and skirts. Twiggy was a novelty, not simply because she was so thin, but because she was androgynous and young. Twiggy and her high-fashion counterparts were "discovered" when they were less than eighteen years old. This tradition has carried on today in high-fashion modeling: many of the most popular supermodels and runway models start their careers early in their teens when curves have not yet filled out their angular frames. Contemporary scholars may point to Twiggy as the downfall of realistic body types in the mass media, but in many ways the model was revolutionary, with her male clothing, short pixie hair, and androgynous body.

Twiggy's popularity among American teens emphasizes the growing gap between postwar women and their Baby-Boomer children. Curvy, "plump," and reproduction-friendly bodies seemed old-fashioned compared with the carefree form of the emaciated youth. Twiggy represented extreme thinness, but hers was a free and modern body that rejected the ideals of the immediate postwar world. Susan Douglas recalls that as she watched "martyrs" like Marilyn Monroe on the big screen, it reminded her of her mother; both women did not seem to have control over their lives. Above all, Douglas notes, "I especially wanted to avoid ending up like Mom."[77] Young women, getting swept into a burgeoning women's movement, witnessed their 1950s mothers adhering to a very specific feminine ideal of beauty. Just as "Flapper girls" of the 1920s revolted against a "Victorian" body that appeared trapped in the home, squeezed into corsets, and built only for reproduction and pleasing men, in many ways, Twiggy was a revolt against the moms and Monroes.

Conclusions

Fashion is rarely designed to fit bodies. Instead, the body must be contoured to fit the garment. Cotton and textiles are more easily manipulated than flesh and bone, yet magazines aimed at both teen and women audiences encouraged their readers to actively reshape their bodies to fit a culturally created ideal. *Vogue* magazine assured readers in 1965 that, even if fashion reverted to cover-up clothes like those of Dior's "New Look," with a slender body, one would still be ahead of the game. "By fitting yourself to the small mould, by tailoring your body to the small proportion of the present," the magazine assured, "you'll always be confident that when it comes to keeping fashionably warm, there is after all nothing like a bikini."[78] Women's fashion, particularly the "New Look" and, later, mini-dresses and skirts, increasingly encouraged reducing.

The victory of the thin ideal over the more curvaceous figures of Hollywood's biggest stars signaled a win for young women taking control of their bodies and picturing a future beyond reproduction and patriarchal control. But the extreme slenderization was not without its damaging consequences. Those who opposed Christian Dior's "New Look" because of the reliance on undergarments that manipulated the body in unnatural ways did not take into account that foundations like corsets, bras, and girdles also allowed women with less than "perfect" figures to appear firmer and more fit. When the 1960s arrived and women threw away bras or turned away from bunchy crinoline dresses in favor of miniskirts, they could no longer hide their "imperfections" beneath undergarment shapers.

Fewer undergarment foundations and more minimalistic clothing meant stricter diet and exercise regimes for women who desired "fashionable" bodies. American designer Bill Blass noted in the *Ladies Home Journal*, "Until now it was fairly easy to find clothes that helped you hide figure faults, sloppy posture. But today's pared-down knee-baring fashions have you out in the open now, and the only thing to do is shape up fast." Designer Rudi Gernreich agreed. If one was not fashionably thin, he argued, "You'll just have to take weight off ... Without that, you really can't look fashionable."[79] For those women for whom the ideal figure did not come naturally, many sought strategies to reshape their bodies. Despite the "freedom" from foundation garments that came with Twiggy-couture, paradoxically, the thin movement demanded that women discipline their bodies even more rigorously to achieve a svelte figure.

Notes

1 For example, possessing "lumbering limbs" could be seen as lower class. Joan Jacobs Brumberg, *The Body Project: An Intimate History of American Girls* (New York: Random House, 1997), xx.
2 Barbara Welter, "The Culture of True Womanhood, 1820–1860," *American Quarterly* 18, no. 2 (Summer 1966): 151–174.
3 Sander L. Gilman, *Obesity: The Biography* (New York: Oxford University Press, 2010), 59.
4 Lois Banner, *American Beauty* (New York: Knopf, 1983), 50–63.
5 Joan Jacobs Brumberg, *Fasting Girls: The Emergence of Anorexia Nervosa as a Modern Disease* (Cambridge: Harvard University Press, 1988).
6 Ibid.
7 Banner, *American Beauty*, 8, 107.
8 For alternatives to the "steel-engraving lady," see Frances B. Cogan, *All-American Girl: The Ideal of Real Womanhood in Mid-Nineteenth Century America* (Athens, GA: The University of Georgia Press, 1989); and Jan Todd, *Physical Culture and the Body Beautiful: Purposive Exercise in the Lives of American Women, 1800–1870* (Macon, GA: Mercer University Press, 1998). For more on the influence of burlesque and early American theater, see Robert C. Allen, *Horrible Prettiness: Burlesque and American Culture* (Chapel Hill, NC: The University of North Carolina Press, 1991).
9 Banner, *American Beauty*, especially chapter 8.
10 E.O. Smith, *When Culture and Biology Collide* (New Brunswick, NJ: Rutgers University Press, 2002), 62.
11 Laura Fraser, "The Inner Corset: A Brief History of Fat in the United States," in *The Fat Studies Reader*, eds. Esther Rothblum and Sondra Solovay (New York: New York University Press, 2009), 13; Amy Farrell, *Fat Shame: Stigma and the Fat Body in American Culture* (New York: New York University Press, 2011), 3–4.
12 Roberta Pollack Seid, *Never Too Thin: Why Women Are at War with Their Bodies* (New York: Prentice Hall Press, 1989), 90.
13 Amanda M. Czerniawski, "From Average to Ideal: The Evolution of the Height and Weight Table in the United States, 1836–1943," *Social Science History* 31, no. 2 (2007): 273.
14 Hillel Schwartz, *Never Satisfied: A Cultural History of Diets, Fantasies, and Fat* (New York: The Free Press, 1986), 9, 147.
15 Woods Hutchinson, "Fat and Fashion," *The Saturday Evening Post*, August 21, 1926, 60.
16 Brumberg, *The Body Project*, 99.
17 Kelly Schrum, *Some Wore Bobby Sox: The Emergence of Teenage Girls' Culture, 1920–1945* (New York: Palgrave Macmillan, 2004), 129. See also Lary May, *Screening Out the Past: The Birth of Mass Culture and the Motion Picture Industry* (Chicago, IL: University of Chicago Press, 1983); and Kathy Peiss, *Cheap Amusements: Working Women and Leisure in Turn-of-the-Century New York* (Philadelphia, PA: Temple University Press, 1986).
18 Brumberg, *The Body Project*, 99, 110.
19 For more on the history of the Miss America pageant, see Banner, *American Beauty*; Maxine Leeds Craig, *Ain't I A Beauty Queen: Black Women, Beauty, and the Politics of Race*

(New York: Oxford University Press, 2002); and Peter N. Stearns, *Fat History: Bodies and Beauty in the Modern West* (New York: New York University Press, 1997).
20 Schrum, *Some Wore Bobby Sox*, 24.
21 Louis I. Dublin, *The Facts of Life: From Birth to Death* (New York: The Macmillian Company, 1951), 361.
22 Note that these sizes are not the same as those of today's manufacturers. Vintage clothing sizes run four to six sizes smaller than clothing sizes today. An "urban legend" claims that Marilyn Monroe was a size 12 or 14. While this is supposed to make women today feel better about their bodies because the sex symbol of the 1950s wore a larger dress size, it was a *vintage* size 12 or 14.
23 "Era of Dieting Causing Female Figure to Shrink," *Chicago Defender*, May 15, 1956, 9.
24 Betty Friedan, *The Feminine Mystique* (New York: W.W. Norton and Company, 2001), 17.
25 "The Big Bulge in Profits," *Newsweek*, July 23, 1956, 63.
26 Seid, *Never Too Thin*, 66–67.
27 For a reassessment of Friedan, see Joanne Meyerowitz, "Beyond the Feminine Mystique: A Reassessment of Postwar Mass Culture, 1946–1958," *Journal of American History* 79, no. 4 (1993): 1455–1482; and Daniel Horowitz, "Rethinking Betty Friedan and The Feminine Mystique: Labor Union Radicalism and Feminism in Cold War America," *American Quarterly* 48, no. 1(1996): 1–42.
28 Found in middle-class prescriptive literature of the antebellum period, the "Cult of Domesticity" or the "Cult of True Womanhood" declared that, to be a "true" woman, one must be pious, virginal, submissive, and domestic. This system of beliefs placed women in the "private sphere," or the home.
29 For more on the changes women experienced prior to, during, and after World War II, see Karen Anderson, *Wartime Women: Sex Roles, Family Relations, and the Status of Women during World War II* (Westport, CT: Greenwood Press, 1981); William Chafe, *The Paradox of Change: American Women in the 20th Century* (New York: Oxford University Press, 1991); Susan M. Hartmann, *The Home Front and Beyond: American Women in the 1940s* (Boston: Twayne Publishers, 1982); Elaine Tyler May, *Homeward Bound: American Families in the Cold War Era* (New York: Basic Books, 1988); and May, *Pushing the Limits: American Women, 1940–1961* (New York: Oxford University Press, 1994).
30 Susan J. Douglas, *Where the Girls Are: Growing Up Female with the Mass Media* (New York: Times Books, 1994), 8.
31 Barbara J. Coleman, "Maidenform(ed): Images of American Women in the 1950s," in *Forming and Reforming Identity*, eds. Carol Siegel and Ann Kibbey (New York: New York University Press, 1995), 10.
32 For more on wartime and reconversion propaganda, see Maureen Honey, *Creating Rosie the Riveter: Class, Gender, and Propaganda during World War II* (Amherst, MA: University of Massachusetts Press, 1984).
33 Dawn H. Currie, *Girl Talk: Adolescent Magazines and Their Readers* (Buffalo, NY: University of Toronto Press, 1999), 23.
34 Currie's *Girl Talk: Adolescent Magazines and Their Readers* (Buffalo, NY: University of Toronto Press, 1999) argues that women internalize the socializing messages of magazines that persuade women that the pursuit of physical beauty, not intelligence, should be their ultimate goal. Similar to de Beauvoir, she also observes that within a sociological discourse, women's magazines are one way in which "bodies become gendered." Not all scholars see women's magazines as a manipulative medium, however. Marjorie Ferguson's *Forever Feminine: Women's Magazines and the Cult of Femininity* (Exeter, NH: Heinemann, 1983) argues that although women's magazines "foster and maintain a cult of femininity," because editors and advertisers target women as a marketable demographic, they award status to women as a group. Moreover, because women's magazines do not provide a homogenous message, Mary Ellen Zuckerman's *History of Popular Women's Magazines in the United States, 1792–1995* (Westport, CT: Greenwood Press,

1998) argues that this demonstrates that women do not passively consume and accept all the content presented to them. Magazine editors instead actively consider what their readership wants to see and read, and creates the periodical with their target audience in mind.

35 According to the U.S. Department of Agriculture in 1947, the average American woman stood 5 feet 3.25 inches tall with measurements of 35.5–29.25–38.75 (Thomas R. Carskadon, "The Female Form and What of It," *Esquire,* March 1947, 42, 130–131).
36 Gilbert Millstein, "The Modeling Business," *Life*, March 25, 1946, 112–113.
37 Ibid.
38 Schwartz, *Never Satisfied*, 231.
39 Ibid.
40 Carskadon, "The Female Form and What of It," *Esquire,* March 1947, 42, 130–131.
41 Quoted in Barbara J. Coleman, "Maidenform(ed): Images of American Women in the 1950s," in *Forming and Reforming Identity*, eds. Carol Siegel and Ann Kibbey (New York: New York University Press, 1955), 9–10.
42 Harold Koda, *Extreme Beauty: The Body Transformed* (New Haven, CT: Yale University Press, 2001), 2–3.
43 "Revolution," *Time*, August 18, 1947, 22.
44 Teresa Riordan, *Inventing Beauty: A History of the Innovations That Have Made Us Beautiful* (New York: Broadway, 2004), 96–97.
45 Gerald Walker, "The Great American Dieting Neurosis," *New York Times Magazine*, August 23, 1959, 12.
46 Hilde Bruch, *The Importance of Overweight* (New York: W.W. Norton, 1957), 54.
47 Edith Head and Paddy Calistro, *Edith Head's Hollywood* (New York: E.P. Dutton, Inc, 1983), 69.
48 Robert W. LaVine, *In a Glamorous Fashion: The Fabulous Years of Hollywood Costume Design* (New York: Charles Scribner's Sons, 1980).
49 "Newest Styles Give Every Woman's Figure a Chance," *Life*, September 22, 1947, 115–125.
50 Mamie Van Doren, *I Swing* (Chicago, IL: Novel Books, 1965), 51.
51 "Math for Marilyn," *Colliers,* April 1954, 30.
52 Molly Haskell, *From Reverence to Rape: The Treatment of Women in Movies* (Chicago, IL: University of Chicago Press, 1987), 255.
53 Haskell, *From Reverence to Rape*, 268.
54 "Hollywood's New Look in Sex," *Photoplay*, September 1954, 62.
55 Riordan, *Inventing Beauty*, 173.
56 "The Heck with Glamor," *Screen Stars*, August 1951, 48–50, 86.
57 Molly Haskell, *Holding My Own in No Man's Land: Women and Men and Film and Feminists* (New York: Oxford University Press, 1997), 32.
58 Lynn Spigel, *Make Room for TV: Television and the Family Ideal in Postwar America* (Chicago, IL: University of Chicago Press, 1992).
59 Albin Krebs, "Rita Hayworth, Movie Legend, Dies," *New York Times,* May 16, 1987, 1.
60 Matthew Frye Jacobson, *Whiteness of a Different Color: European Immigrants and the Alchemy of Race* (Cambridge, MA: Harvard University Press, 1998), 4–7.
61 Gallup Poll, Attitudes of American Women, June–July 1962.
62 Douglas, *Where the Girls Are*, 42.
63 Mamie Van Doren, *Playing the Field: My Story* (New York: G. P. Putnam's Sons, 1987), 207–208.
64 For more on the decline of the Hollywood studio system, see Jonathan Kirshner, *Hollywood's Last Golden Age: Politics, Society, and the Seventies Film in America* (Ithaca, NY: Cornell University Press, 2012); and Ronald L. Davis, *Celluloid Mirrors: Hollywood and American Society Since 1945* (Orlando, FL: Harcourt Brace, 1997).
65 "Interesting Letters," December 1963, *Motion Picture*, 12.
66 Ibid.

67 Spigel, *Make Room for TV*, 151–154.
68 Ibid.
69 "Fashion: Up, Up, and Away," *Time*, December 1, 1967, 70–80.
70 Cynthia Ogden, Cheryl D. Fryar, Margaret D. Carroll, and Katherine M. Flegal, "Mean Body Weight, Height, and Body Mass Index, United States 1960–2002," Centers for Disease Control and Prevention, *Vital and Health Statistics* No. 347, October 27, 2004, 3.
71 Polly Devlin, "Paris: Twiggy Haunt Couture," *Vogue*, March 1967, 64.
72 Leanne Italie, "Twiggy: 'It Could Have Gone Terribly Wrong,'" *Associated Press*, March 29, 2010, http://www.timesfreepress.com/news/local/story/2010/mar/30/twiggy-it-could-have-gone-terribly-wrong/11319/. Accessed January 26, 2017.
73 Schrum, *Some Wore Bobby Sox*, 2.
74 Louise France, "A Rare Interview with Penelope Tree, the Ultimate Sixties It Girl," *The Guardian*, August 3, 2008, http://www.guardian.co.uk/lifeandstyle/2008/aug/03/celebrity.women. Accessed April 2, 2010.
75 Dorothy Hoobler and Thomas Hoobler, *Vanity Rules: A History of American Fashion and Beauty* (Brookfield, CT: Twenty-First Century Books, 2000), 112.
76 Banner, *American Beauty*, 287.
77 Douglas, *Where the Girls Are*, 42.
78 "Beauty Bulletin: What Makes the Body Fit the Fashion?" *Vogue*, February 15, 1965, 120, 124, 146.
79 "Exercise," *Ladies Home Journal*, November 1965, 94.

2

"WE MUST, WE MUST, WE MUST INCREASE OUR BUST"

Uplifting the Feminine Breast

> *"If you ever want to get out of those baby bras you have to exercise," she told us.*
> *"What kind of exercise?" Gretchen asked.*
> *"Like this," Nancy said. She made fists, bent her arms at the elbow and moved them back and forth, sticking her chest way out. She said, "I must – I must – I must increase my bust." She said it over and over.*
> *We copied her movements and chanted with her. "We must – we must – we must increase our bust!"*
> *"Good," Nancy told us. "Do it thirty-five times a day and I promise you'll see results."*
>
> —Judy Blume, *Are You There God? It's Me, Margaret* (1970)

Although fashions and ideal figures have come and gone, perhaps no singular female body part has experienced more shifting and unnatural shaping than breasts. As one scholar has noted, "The history of the chest is as much about its suppression as it is about its augmentation."[1] Just as the ideal feminine figure witnessed various transformations over the past century, so too has the ideal breast. From the 1900s until World War I, the monobosom, a pigeon-like breast, remained fashionable as a result of straight-front corsets. Around 1914, Caresse Crosby, a socialite also known as Mary Phelps Jacobs, received a patent for a bra-like contraption featuring a ribbon and two handkerchiefs. Historians of fashion debate who created the first bra, but it is generally agreed that Crosby's patent most resembled what was perfected in later decades. During the 1920s, suppression rather than support became the function of brassieres. Young women bound their breasts with bands of chiffon, satin, or lace in order to obtain the fashionably boyish silhouette made popular by the "Flapper" girl. The flattened style fell out of popularity in the 1930s when bras once again served a more natural support function.[2]

Large-breasted women became fashionable only after World War II. Helping to usher in this new feminine ideal were the pen and colors of *Esquire* illustrator Albert Vargas, whose calendar art popularized a slightly muscular female figure with rounded breasts. From the 1940s through 1960, the ideal breast size increased, as E. O. Smith observes, "due in no small part to the pen of Albert Vargas."[3] Alfred C. Kinsey's 1953 study of female sexuality reported that American men were more interested in breasts than European men, who preferred the lower half of the female figure. One *Esquire* columnist observed of this phenomenon, "Confronted by such a bulge of blouse or sweater, the American male snorts like a caribou in the spring thaws. When an actress with cantaloupe contours appears on the screen," he continued, "Marines stomp their feet, husbands tug at their leashes, and college boys roll their eyes like Tristains."[4] The American admiration for large-breasted women was globally recognized. Reports surfaced about prostitutes in Asian countries receiving silicone injections into their breasts to better appeal to American soldiers stationed abroad, and Japan became a forerunner in breast augmentation procedures.[5]

America's preoccupation with mammary size baffled and astonished contemporaries. In a satirical anthropological essay about an imaginary tribe, the "Nacirema" ("American" spelled backward), the author observed, "General dissatisfaction with breast shape is symbolized in the fact that the ideal form is virtually outside the range of human variation. A few women afflicted with almost inhuman hypermammary development are so idolized that they make a handsome living by simply going from village to village and permitting the natives to stare at them."[6] John Steinbeck once remarked that the country's fixation on breasts was so intense that aliens from another world would mistakenly believe that "the seat of procreation lay in the mammaries."[7] Moreover, showing the power of naked female sexuality, the Iron Curtain is destroyed in the fictional story "The Breasts of the Durhams" when Allied soldiers befriend civilian Yugoslavs after hiring a burlesque dancer to entertain the men.[8] Beauty and health guides from the period instructed women on the import of the bosom. "The curve of a smooth, velvety breast is particularly attractive; the lack of such a curve not only causes some to make coarse jokes on the subject, but actually repels," one such manual claimed. The author continued, "I have often, in my experience, heard men refer to a girl with some words such as: 'She has a lovely face, but she has no breasts!' And that settles the matter, so far as that man is concerned—and he is in the majority."[9] Mass culture declared that, to find and keep the attentions of men, one needed large breasts. In addition, employment could also be predicated on breast size. "It may be a sad commentary upon our civilization, and upon the efficacy of higher education," one journalist observed, "but in certain employment circles a well-filled sweater is as great an asset as a Phi Beta Kappa key."[10] In specialized beauty guides, to the plethora of men's pin-up magazines that thrived and died, to the sophistication of breast augmentation surgery, large breasts reigned supreme in the decades after World War II.

Nowhere was the country's adulation for large-breasted women more apparent than in Hollywood. While casting directors once made their decisions on the basis of legs, now contracts were decided based on the applicant's bust measurements. With the rare exception of Audrey Hepburn, talent scouts were under orders not to bring around any starlets unless "they're a good thirty-eight."[11] Today, this breathy, buxom, dim-witted blonde made popular in the 1950s is synonymous with Marilyn Monroe. But even before the blonde bombshell made a splash in her first feature films, a buxom brunette was showing up on the walls of military barracks and dormitory rooms—Jane Russell. The actress made her Hollywood debut in Howard Hughes's *The Outlaw* (Figure 2.1). The film finished production in 1941, but censorship concerns about Russell's décolletage prevented a general release until 1946. Because of the actress's mass popularity, presumably based largely on the size of her breasts, Hollywood producers clambered to find an ingénue who could "out-do her lush proportions."[12] Director Billy Wilder had once predicted that gamine actress Audrey Hepburn would "make bosoms obsolete," but not even she could shake America's preoccupation with breasts.[13]

Much speculation existed as to why large breasts had become so desired. Those writing on the subject, male and female, were conscious that this was a new American phenomenon. Many contributed mammary madness as a result of World War II. Viennese psychologist Dr. Nah Brind believed the war-torn years had caused an instinctive desire to return to the security of the maternal breast.[14]

FIGURE 2.1 Jane Russell in *The Outlaw* (1946).

Some worried that this fixation on breasts was an indicator of the infantilization of the American man. Prolific screenwriter Ben Hecht, writing in *Esquire* magazine in 1957, pointed out that a woman's breasts served no sexual function but were instead designed for infant nourishment. According to Hecht, this was "scientific insight into our national mammary worship." The author likened the American obsession with consumption to another sign of male infantilism, calling suburban homes adult "play pens." He continued to argue that men who fixated on breasts similarly gravitated to then-President Dwight Eisenhower as a fatherly figure.[15] In response, *Esquire* readers wrote in to discredit Hecht's theory. One man protested the idea that American men were attracted to breasts because of a continued attachment to their mothers. Men, he argued, "have succeeded in cutting off all apron strings and think of the female breasts as an important part of the allure of a woman." He believed breasts were essential indicators of her "femaleness" and served as an advertisement for her potential as a wife and mother.[16] Psychiatrist Dr. Wladimir G. Eliasberg agreed. In claiming that women themselves had no personal preference for large breasts over small breasts, he argued that bust worship was a man-made creation. Instead of serving as evidence that American men had grown soft, the demand for larger breasts reflected the authoritative position of American men in society.[17]

Scholars in our own time have attempted to make sense of this postwar mammary phenomenon. Historian Beth L. Bailey suggests that, by dating women with large breasts, men showed their wealth; by affording the expenses that went along with maintaining a relationship with a large-breasted woman, they demonstrated fiscal profusion.[18] Another has argued that the aftermath of World War II "frighten[ed] the Western world into a conservative retrenchment that brought back the breast."[19] This theme of breasts acting as a kind of reassuring, nurturing mother is mirrored in a number of other works.[20] The celebration of large-breasted women, however, was not only a way to shelter men after the horrors of World War II. Instead, the popularity of breasts served as a reaction to the growing assertiveness of American women. Women gained power and confidence during the war years; when veterans returned from abroad, at stake was the mythology of women's primary function as mothers and wives. Due to women's involvement in the workforce during World War II, Americans worried about a perceived explosion of female independence and sexuality.[21] Alfred C. Kinsey's publication in 1953, *Sexual Behavior in the Human Female*, mirrored fears that "nice girls" did in fact have sex prior to marriage. Although men desired "well-equipped" mates, women in control of their sexuality produced more dread than desire. Hollywood personified these fears through the dangerous *femme fatales* in *film noir* of the 1940s and 1950s. What made the *femme fatale* so dangerous was not that she was a sexual being, but rather that she knowingly used her sexual allure to manipulate and ruin men. Early in her film career, Marilyn Monroe played a *femme fatale* in films like *Don't Bother to Knock* (1952) and *Niagara* (1953).[22] But she is best remembered for her role as the antithesis to the *femme fatale*—the dumb blonde.

In 1950s mass media, as a woman's breasts got larger, her IQ presumably became smaller. Although the alphabetic labeling of bra cup sizes resembles a school grading system, it at first seems illogical that As would be given to the smallest breasts. However, if one views women with larger cup sizes as less intelligent than small-breasted women, the sizing system suddenly makes sense.[23] When TV personality Dagmar, who had made a career out of being a large-breasted, dumb blonde, lost twenty pounds, whittling away inches from both her waistline and her mammoth bust line, she claimed she could now "think faster."[24] Dumb blondes, in the tradition of 1920s and 1930s chorus girls, helped sanitize female sexuality and make it acceptable and accessible. These busty, blonde women might have been out to ensnare a wealthy "Daddy," but their sexuality was innocent, naïve, and childlike. Movie stars who had once banked on their dancing, singing, or comedic talent suddenly lost their intellectual acumen in the 1950s. In 1953, Marilyn Monroe received top billing over 1940s pin-up girl, Betty Grable, in *How to Marry a Millionaire*. As the film's title suggests, the plot revolves around three women who scheme together to marry rich men. Both Grable and Monroe, the blondes, rely on the intellect of the brunette, Lauren Bacall, to achieve their plan. In 1941, Grable performed this same scheme in *Moon over Miami*, but in the earlier film, Grable's blonde character conceived of the plan herself. In the 1950s film, Grable became just another dumb blonde. Her wisecracking, dancing, and singing skills are reduced in *How to Marry a Millionaire* to comedic misunderstandings surrounding her severe lack of intellect and common sense. With their cartoon-like proportions, sexual abandon, and child-like innocence, "sweater girls" like Marilyn Monroe and her busty, blonde counterparts were Hollywood's attempt to repress the growing assertiveness of American women.

The Monroe type reaffirmed masculinity and male heterosexuality in a decade where women not only challenged gender norms, but where manliness itself suffered a "crisis" and bachelorhood became suspect.[25] One scholar notes the uneasiness regarding gender and sexuality in the era saying, "men had to look and act tough and masculine; women had to appear as soft and pink as a nursery."[26] As the average age of marriage dropped and anxieties about homosexuality elevated, busty women served the same role as men's magazines like Hugh Hefner's *Playboy*.[27] It is no coincidence that the Monroe type and *Playboy* magazine originated in the same decade, or that Monroe was *Playboy*'s first centerfold in December 1953. This masculine desire for extreme femininity helps explain Hollywood's decision to promote busty actresses. Because Hollywood's Production Code forbade exposing more than a few centimeters of visible cleavage, the major studios, in an effort to outdo each other, encouraged their starlets to use padded bras and to strive for sheer size. Even Monroe, who appeared to be "all-natural," reportedly wore breast padding when in bathing suits or strapless gowns designed to compress the bust.[28] Actress Mamie Van Doren remembered, "Eventually, the padded bras built us out to such mammoth dimensions that we felt a little self-conscious. The bullet-shaped cones under our tight sweaters were just short of becoming hazards to navigation."[29] The media's celebration of blonde, busty, and dumb protected and reaffirmed American men's masculinity. In an era where the pressure to marry early and start a family had become overwhelming, Marilyn Monroe and her wannabes created an uncomplicated escape.

Damned If You Have Them—Damned If You Don't

Women were certainly not blind to the mammary madness of the postwar period. Indeed, many were active participants in reifying this masculine desire. One of the most oppressive impacts of this "Uplift Age" was its effect on adolescent girls. Young women reaching the age of puberty compared their chest sizes with and pined to look like the Hollywood celebrities in fan magazines. Girls attached their self-worth to the size of their breasts. Menstruation, as well as breasts, was a sign that a young girl was becoming a woman, but as American journalist and screenwriter Nora Ephron observes, "But you could *see* breasts; they were there; they were visible."[30] Without ample flesh to fill out their sweaters, American teens worried if they would ever find a boyfriend. Would they ever be desirable to men?

Historian Joan Jacobs Brumberg notes that anxiety about breast size, more than any other body part, characterized the teenage experience during this era. Because full breasts were the ideal, young American girls wrote in their diaries of wistfully envying classmates with larger chests. Teens in gym class locker rooms discreetly compared themselves with other girls, noting who wore a bra and who did not.[31] A 1944 teen survey in *Calling All Girls* discovered that 65 percent of readers wore bras, most buying their first between the ages of thirteen and fifteen. By the early 1950s, several styles of "training" bra were available in AA and AAA sizes for girls who did not yet require a bra, but wanted to wear one nonetheless.[32] Nora Ephron self-identified as a tomboy in her adolescence. She could throw a football and climb trees, but instead of reveling in the ability to straddle both worlds, Ephron wanted desperately to be "a definite indisputable girl." And the only way to achieve that, she believed, was larger breasts. She noted, with disbelief, that her mother was actually proud to be flat-chested. "It was incomprehensible to me that anyone could ever be proud of something like that. It was the 1950s, for God's sake," the writer declares. "Jane Russell. Cashmere sweaters. Couldn't my mother see that?" Ephron recalls sobbing hysterically when she realized that her best friend had "shaped up" and grown breasts over the summer. She felt as though her lifelong friend had left her behind.[33] Historian Carolyn Latteier similarly recalls her own adolescence in the mid-1950s. "Being skinny and flat-chested became for me the symbol of my immaturity," she remembers. "I felt the lack of breasts was an impoverishment of my own nature—a deep failure that was my fault."[34] These feelings of failure and inadequacy would be strong enough to entice some to pursue breast augmentation surgery later in life.

Adolescent girls were not only plagued by an absence of breasts; those who hit puberty earlier than other female classmates experienced a different set of anxieties. Ephron remembers her girlfriends, for whom puberty had come early, complaining about the difficulties their breasts caused them. Teen boys snapped their bra straps in class, and they could not sleep on their stomachs. "They were stared at," she recalls, "whenever the word 'mountain' cropped up in geography."[35] Likewise, Latteier recalls two childhood friends who wore bulky clothes to "armor themselves" against other eighth graders; they were just as alarmed by the size of their breasts as the author was to be flat chested.[36] The bra size of teen celebrities came under scrutiny in the same way. From 1955 to 1959, Annette Funicello was the most popular Mouseketeer on the television program *The Mickey Mouse Club*. The early arrival of puberty made Funicello unique amongst the other female Mouseketeers. The teen star's breasts were envied by other girls and lusted after by boys, but they were also the punch line of numerous jokes. Scholar Susan Douglas contends that Funicello taught girls in the 1950s an early, uneasy lesson: "Girls were defined by their bodies," she argues. "Girls were damned if they had big ones and damned if they had little ones."[37]

Laura Danker, the chesty middle-schooler in Judy Blume's *Are You There God, It's Me Margaret*, is evidence of this as well. On the first day at her new school, the novel's main character, Margaret, inaccurately assumes that Laura is the teacher because the unfortunate middle-schooler hit puberty earlier than everyone else in the class. Although Laura has done nothing to provoke it, she is the target of vicious gossip; her classmates assume she is sexually active because she fills out her sweater. When Margaret reveals the rumors about her, Laura is crushed. She challenges the unsympathetic protagonist to imagine what it would be like to have to wear a bra as early as the fourth grade, "and how everybody laughed and how you always had to cross your arms in front of you," the girl cries. "And about how the boys called you dirty names just because of how you looked."[38] Although adolescence is a time of general bodily discomfort, during the postwar years, the size of a young woman's breasts caused more anxiety than any other transitioning body part. But unlike other unalterable body aspects, like the size of one's hands or feet, breast development came to be interpreted as something women could control.

Cashing In: Breast Enlargement Schemes

Mass culture's obsessive focus on women's breasts and their symbolic and erotic import inspired a variety of entrepreneurs to cash in on the country's mammary madness. A brief scan of women's and celebrity fan magazines from the decades reveals ads whose products all promise the same thing—a larger bust for the less-than-fortunate woman. Most advertisements gave little indication of *how* their product produced an inflated bust line, but "before" and "after" illustrations promised potential customers they too could achieve the desired results. To curb the numerous attempts to exploit women's desire for larger breasts, the Food and Drug Administration (FDA) routinely confiscated pills and creams during raids on manufacturing plants, and the United States Post Office charged mail-order companies with mail fraud, invoking criminal charges on those responsible for scam products.

Three categories of bosom-building products—vitamins, bust creams, and hydromassage—filled the back pages of fashion, teen, and fan magazines. Vitamin supplements like "PRO-FORMA" promised to "restore your breasts to feminine beauty" in a mere six to twelve weeks. Ironically, *pro forma* is Latin for perfunctory, meaning to seek a minimum requirement and conforming to conventions. The active ingredient in "PRO-FORMA" was extract of *Galega*, a plant that increases lactation. The fine print on the product's bottle read: "On the basis of their research and experience, our medical advisers have stated that extract of *Galega* has helped some women to make their breasts fuller and firmer. However, the material weight of medical opinion is to the contrary."[39] Officers for Tyler Pharmacal Distributors, Inc., manufacturers of "PRO-FORMA," tangled with the FDA and the Post Office for the better part of a decade when the product was deemed "ineffective."[40] Advertisements for bust creams promised that the dutiful application of their product encouraged the growth of mammary tissue. One lotion, "Formalon," claimed its product to be the greatest invention since the atomic bomb or penicillin.[41] The secret of such creams was small doses of estrogen that temporarily increased a woman's breast size. If application ceased, however, one's bust returned to its original size. These were not just harmless product scams, however. Physicians believed that the prolonged use of estrogenic chemicals affected normal body functions such as a woman's menstruation cycle. Daniel Platt of the Formalon Company pled guilty to charges of "misbranding" in 1948. The "before" and "after" pictures in advertising were discovered to be fraudulent. He was fined $3,000 and given a suspended sentence of three years in jail.[42] Other products, like "Abunda," "Lady Bountiful," "Lady Ample," and "Voluptae," guaranteed larger breasts through hydromassage or the use of a small vacuum. The main device of such products consisted of small plastic cups to which a hose was attached. Printed instructions directed the user to attach the suction cups to her naked breasts and the hose to a water faucet, which created a vacuum when the tap was turned on. Women were instructed to "exercise" with the device for twenty minutes a day with the false promise that massage would increase blood circulation and encourage tissue growth.[43]

Women did not blindly buy into these mail-order schemes. Their skepticism is apparent in the numerous letters sent to the American Medical Association (AMA) questioning the effectiveness and safety of bust-enhancing products. Oliver Field, director of the AMA's Investigations Bureau, noted, "We have received inquiries by the score on surgical procedures, hand pumps, and even pills put out by those who realize there is gold in them thar [*sic*] hills, particularly those cute little hills."[44] The AMA religiously reported back that no known exercise, preparation, or mechanical device could increase the size of a woman's breasts.[45] Hormone creams helped only women whose sex organs and glands had not reached maturity. Exercise as a bust developer failed, as breasts contain no muscles; one could only "build up" the muscle wall directly behind the breast. Massage could, in fact, injure delicate breast tissue. Moreover, suction cups and cold water treatments that brought a temporary flush of blood to the skin's surface might give overeager women the impression that their breasts were growing and swelling, but this was not the case.

No "grand deceiver," however, received as much attention as "falsies." In 1948, Americans purchased more than 4.5 million pairs of falsies, turning bra inserts into a multimillion-dollar industry. In addition to plush padding came the introduction of the "Very Secret" in 1952, a bra with inflatable cups. But the "secret" would only remain as long as its wearer avoided sharp objects and the hands of an eager partner. *Esquire* contributor Victor Warren Quayle argued that falsies created "equality" for flat-chested women.[46] As another *Esquire* author described, "A type for every personality is provided, ranging in dimensions from the coy and cute Tip Toe Through the Tulips to the Stop, Look and Listen number, favored by ladies who live near dangerous railroad crossings."[47] Cultural advisers instructed women not to be embarrassed about the fake padding. Edith Head, top costume designer for Paramount Pictures, told cinema fans, "If you are flatter than you wish you were ... remember, there is nothing wrong with bust pads. It is very stupid to pretend there are no such things."[48] Joan Bennett, an actress and beauty columnist for the fan magazine *Screen Stars*, similarly urged her readers in this "bosom-minded generation" that there was no disgrace in wearing falsies or having a padded bra. She equated the bra cushioning with the shoulder pads of a suit jacket, noting, "There have to be alterations for every figure."[49] Women of all ages wrote in to Bennett in the early 1950s. Many claimed they were satisfied with their figures, with the exception of the size of their breasts. Young teens lamented not filling out 32A cups, and mothers decried losing cup sizes after the birth of their children. Bennett reminded her readers that no exercise could increase one's bra-cup size, but that building up the chest muscles that supported the breast could add inches to one's measurements. Rather than simply relying on falsies, she suggested an exercise like Nancy Walker's "we must, we must" exercise in *Are You There God, It's Me Margaret*. Similar bust-enhancing regimes appeared in other guidebooks and prescriptive literature. "Fold your arms in front of you and grab each arm with the opposite hand just in front of the elbow. Push in with hard, jerky movements," Bennett instructed readers. "You can tell you are doing the exercise correctly because you can feel the breasts move around the muscles tightening." If practiced religiously day and night for ten to fifteen minutes, Bennett claimed one would see results in a few months. And while waiting, she recommended purchasing a Peter Pan bra—with built-in pads stitched into the cups.[50]

Bra padding did not receive universal support in popular periodicals, however. One beauty guidebook advised, "strive for individuality. With false breasts you cannot have individuality. The false bosom is standardized; it is unnatural."[51] Even more problematic, while falsies and other kinds of cushioning might have given self-conscious women a boost of confidence, the specter of discovery held the promise of panic. Embarrassing stories dealing with falsie mishaps littered both men's and women's magazines as well as the literature of the time. One woman's falsies reportedly popped out while swimming, and they floated past other swimmers. Another's escaped the confines of her bra at the movies and landed in the lap of another moviegoer.[52] Nora Ephron's extra padding brought forth anxiety with her first boyfriend in high school. She enjoyed intimacy, but was terrified that the teen boy would discover the extra padding in her bra. Getting jostled could cause the extra foam to poke inward. Ephron marvels, "I think about all that and wonder how anyone kept a straight face about it." She incredulously wondered how no one had ever commented on the padding since she owned three bras, each with a different size cup.[53]

This fear of discovery is mirrored in works of fiction as well. Margaret, Judy Blume's adolescent heroine, stuffs her bra with cotton balls when she attends her first co-ed birthday party. She quickly panics about the extra padding when the party games shift from pin-the-tail-on-the-donkey in favor of more adult games like "7 Minutes in Heaven."[54] Erika Frohman, in Valerie Taylor's *Journey to Fulfillment*, similarly panics when "parking" with her date. When the high-school boy moves his hand closer to the top of her strapless dress, Erika becomes unnerved, fearing he will discover the foam-rubber padding in her strapless bra.[55] Annice, one of the main characters in Taylor's *The Girls in 3-B*, feels like a phony from her attempted beatnik poetry all the way to her falsies. When her boyfriend discovers the bra padding, he teases her: "You don't have much of a milk fund, do you? You wear falsies." Annice is horrified and shields her vulnerability with anger. "It's only slight padding," she insists, "and besides, it's none of your goddam [sic] business." Even after they have sex, Annice's embarrassment continues at the sight of her padded bra on the floor.[56]

Falsies eventually had become less popular by the 1960s. Whereas early in the 1950s the Sears Roebuck catalog had offered over twenty kinds of bra inserts, by 1961 that number had fallen to six; by 1966, only three shapes of falsies were available from the mail-in catalog.[57] One woman declared she would still rather wear falsies than exercise, however: "I'm not going to exercise to get what I can buy."[58] But because of the obvious problems with padded bras, inserts, and inflatable bras, women looked for alternative ways to obtain a more ample bust.

Plastic Surgery

Developing alongside new ways to change the size and shape of one's breasts through diet, exercise, and padded bras, cosmetic surgery became more sophisticated and acceptable to the average American. Plastic surgery was still in its genesis as late as the 1920s; the profession was not strictly defined and its practitioners' place on hospital staffs was questioned. But with the end of World War II and the need to rehabilitate injured GIs, plastic surgery quickly developed as a field and a practice.[59] By the 1950s, corrective procedures were no longer confined to those with physical deformities or only available to Hollywood celebrities. In 1949, 15,000 Americans underwent plastic surgery operations. A decade later, the number increased tenfold, to 150,000, and by 1969 nearly half a million individuals had obtained some form of cosmetic correction.[60]

Throughout the 1950s and 1960s, magazine articles discussed the relative safety, ease, and manageable price of cosmetic surgery, ranging from face-lifts to breast augmentation.[61] Readers were assured that recovery time was minimal and that more common operations were not egregiously expensive. Fashion magazines urged their readership to not be embarrassed to talk about plastic surgery with their doctors. One periodical even proposed confronting the operation like an architect discussing plans for a new building.[62] Teen magazines, unlike women's fashion magazines, did not present a uniform message about plastic surgery. Joan Bennett advocated cosmetic surgery in *Screen Stars*, but only if the patient was at least eighteen years old or if her features were fully matured.[63] Young readers were cautioned not to pursue cosmetic operations without good cause. As one article advised its readers, "If all you want is relief from boredom, go out and join some joggers or form a folk-rock group."[64] Some argued that anxieties about specific body features could manifest in other areas, even if the problem area was surgically corrected. Other articles, however, mirroring more mature publications, noted that plastic surgery was no longer taboo and that it was now possible to have "a nose straightened, or a chin strengthened without ... gossip."[65]

A number of corrective and cosmetic surgeries were perfected in the years immediately following World War II.[66] The advancement of many procedures, particularly facial reconstruction and skin grafts, came as a result of injuries that soldiers had sustained during the war. But one surgical method gained in popularity, unconnected to the aftermath of wartime combat—female breast augmentation. Plastic surgeons recognized that falsies and other attempts to less intrusively correct small breasts were wholly unsatisfactory. Swimsuits and other fashionably scant apparel called for an alternate solution to the small-breasted woman's problems. Moreover, hand creams, hydromassage, exercise, hormone treatments, and vitamins were equally unsuccessful. One of the earliest examples of breast augmentation appeared in the 1890s when Dr. Robert Gersuny of Vienna used paraffin injections to increase women's breast sizes. The practice halted prior to World War I, however, because the paraffin tended to migrate to other places in the body besides the breasts.[67] In the 1920s and 1930s, surgeons began experimenting with a technique called autologous fat transplantation, wherein fatty tissue usually found in the abdomen or buttocks was transferred to the breast. This technique continued into the 1950s. Although the early results of this method were generally satisfactory, the body often reabsorbed the transplanted fat or caused unsightly bulges and cysts that made early breast cancer detection difficult. In addition, the donor site scars on the abdomen or buttocks were objectionable.[68]

During the 1920s, breast reduction procedures achieved popularity to help women suffering from *gigantomastia*—a term used to describe the "malady" of large-breasted women. It seems too coincidental that breast reduction surgery technologies became more sophisticated in a decade largely defined by fashionable women binding their breasts in order to achieve the "Flapper" girl look. In 1919, at a meeting of the thirty-ninth Congress of the German Society of Surgery, Dr. Charles Girard spoke of the painful psychological disturbances that hypertrophy and pendulosity of too-large breasts could cause women. "It is only those who fully understand the psychology of woman," he noted, "who can fully understand what huge deposits of fat mean to the young woman and what effect they have on her psyche."[69] By the 1930s, because of the mental and physical anguish suffered by those with *gigantomastia,* breast reduction surgery was finally accepted in medical circles. Medical literature on the reduction procedure was generally concerned with preserving the lactation function of the breast through nipple transplantation rather than attention to protecting the erotic function.[70] Plastic surgeon H. O. Bames argued that the procedure not only relieved the patient of physical discomfort, but from mental suffering as well. He observed, "the former feeling of depression and inferiority is replaced by heightened morale, happiness and feminine pride."[71] These same themes—happiness and femininity—were later used during the 1950s to justify the need for breast enlargement surgery.

Surgeons after World War II originally displayed little sympathy for small-breasted women. Historian Elizabeth Haiken notes that this attitude quickly changed when a consumer market appeared for the procedure.[72] American women—encouraged by fashion magazines, eager to fill out Dior's "New Look," and inspired by busty movie stars—sought ways to increase their breast size. In 1950, cosmetic surgeon H. O. Bames identified three types of breast "deformities": (1) *hypomastia,* or the underdevelopment of breasts; (2) *hypermastia,* or the overdevelopment of the breast to between two to three times what was considered typical; and (3) *gigantomastia,* which he labeled as when each breast weighed ten or more pounds. Bames noted that the correction of the latter two "diseases" was already receiving consideration from doctors because of the physical distress overly large breasts caused women, but he also observed that *hypomastia* had recently begun to garner attention.[73] Bames did not "invent" these terms—they had been a part of medical literature for centuries—but for the first time, all three "maladies" were now defined as "problems" worthy of medical attention.

Soon after the end of World War II, physicians in the United States began experimentally inserting various kinds of sponges behind women's mammary glands to increase breast size. The postwar zeal for science and technology also encouraged this experimentation. *Vogue* magazine even predicted in 1959 that, with advancements in endocrinology, women would one day be able to take a synthetic steroid to encourage breast development.[74] The very first breast augmentation patients were women whose careers generally depended on breast size—actresses, burlesque dancers, and other kinds of female entertainers. The busiest surgeons were located in Hollywood, where, as one gossip columnist observed, "a correctly-turned bosom is more important to an actress' career than whether she can recite

'Twelfth Night.'"[75] Fan magazines awarded little attention to the plastic surgery stories of celebrities; no one wanted to read that their favorite cover girl was made of plastic. Magazines like *Confession* and *True*, more tabloid than hard journalism, however, did not shy away from the topic. *Confidential* magazine reported that Tallulah Bankhead, Marlene Dietrich, Gloria Swanson, Sara Shane, and Olympic skater-turned-actress Sonja Henie had all gone under the knife. Most of these women were either older actresses trying to compete with younger stars or up-and-coming actresses looking for a title role. When a gossip magazine hinted that actress Paulette Goddard required falsies, she threatened to sue the periodical and called in the aid of a female reporter so she could "prove" that she was all-natural.[76] Box office stars like Audrey Hepburn, Hedy Lamarr, and Marilyn Monroe were rumored to wear falsies.[77] Reports in recent years have surfaced that pioneering plastic surgeon W. John Pangman implanted Ivalon sponges into Monroe or that she had received direct silicone injections just before her death.[78]

By the mid-1950s, female entertainers such as actresses, models, and dancers became a minority among breast enhancement patients. But the number of reported surgeries stayed modest; augmentation technologies remained crude and few doctors had training to perform the surgery. A March 1960 survey sent out to 500 plastic surgeons in the United States and Canada reported a total of 2,008 reduction mammaplasties, compared with 2,516 patients who underwent breast enlargement surgery. A later questionnaire sent out in mid-August of the same year recorded that the majority of physicians had performed only one to fifty breast augmentation surgeries in their career.[79] One doctor, however, reportedly had operated on three thousand women. This surgeon, no doubt, was Dr. Robert Franklyn.

Robert Alan Franklyn, born Frank Mark Eisenberg, graduated from New York University College of Medicine in 1941. Although he was licensed to practice medicine in New York, California, and New Jersey, he was not a member of any specialty group in plastic surgery, nor was he a member of the AMA. He became director of the first licensed teaching institution in California for plastic surgery—the Plastic Surgery Academy and Institute—and was editor of *Aesthetica*, the first annual surgical journal devoted to cosmetic plastic surgery.[80] Franklyn first appeared in medical journals in the 1940s regarding his work with cosmetic facial surgeries. In the early 1950s, however, recognizing the demand for a successful breast implant, he turned his energies to breast augmentation.

Franklyn, who first coined the phrase "augmentation mammoplasty," discovered what he believed to be the perfect breast implant on a trip to Toronto while inspecting reconstruction surgeries done for the Royal Canadian Air Force. A captured German fighter plane was on display in a park for public viewing. Because the Germans had no access to rubber during World War II, they had made an imitation foam rubber while the Americans had made an imitation solid rubber. The seats in the captured plane had been padded with the German artificial rubber. Believing that the material would make an ideal breast implant, Franklyn first tested it in animals and used small slivers of the foam to elevate the scars of his patients. Foam had been previously used to inflate arteries and collapsed lungs, or to elevate small scars, but it had never been used for the purpose of breast implants.[81] Franklyn boasted that his sponge material was lightweight and therefore better than heavy fat or other plastics. The material was flexible enough that surgeons would be able to create the desired shape and size for each patient. He found it extremely durable; he predicted that in a hundred years the only trace of some of his patients would be the two plastic sponges inserted into their bodies. Moreover, it was transparent and would not show up on an X-ray, which might embarrass the patient who did not want others to know about her operation.[82]

In 1953, Franklyn advertised his unique surgery in *Pageant* magazine, a digest-sized periodical that appeared as a Sunday newspaper insert. Franklyn claimed that over four million women suffered from *micromastia* (immature breasts) and "an accompanying sense of deficient femininity." He estimated that one-third of those women experienced "acute psychological disturbances that border on the tragic." The doctor pointed out how other kinds of plastic surgery, exercise, diet, hormone injections, and creams failed to create a realistic natural breast. Franklyn went on to describe his procedure, which he claimed was a relatively easy and inexpensive, twenty-five-minute operation.[83] In reaction to the *Pageant* article, men and women flooded the AMA with inquiries seeking more information about Franklyn or other surgeons who could perform a similar "Breastaplasty" surgery. Interest was so high that the AMA responded in November of that year with a report against Franklyn's ethics and continued to investigate the material he was implanting behind women's pectoral muscles. At first, doctors working in conjunction with the AMA believed that Franklyn used a compound known as Ivalon, a polyvinyl alcohol and formaldehyde sponge originally created at the Mayo Clinic by Drs. John H. Grindley and John M. Waugh.[84] Ivalon had proven fallible as an implant; after surgery, the sponge shrank by as much as 20 percent and often hardened and calcified.[85] Franklyn denied using Ivalon and refused to reveal the origins of his foam insert, intensifying the tenuous relationship between himself and the AMA. Although complications existed for surgeons who used autologous fat transplantation as well as those who preferred foam inserts, the AMA provided the names of plastic surgeons to women who desired breast augmentation. They continued to caution, however, against Dr. Franklyn's "Breastaplasty" surgery.[86]

The search for a more effective implant continued into the 1960s. Doctors identified six characteristics for the ideal implant: (1) chemically and physically inert; (2) must remain soft; (3) no shrinkage; (4) look and feel as natural as possible; (5) not cause fluid formation, inflammation, or infection; and, (6) once inserted beneath the skin, would become firmly attached to body tissues.[87] In 1962, two Houston plastic surgeons, Thomas Cronin and Frank Gerow, in conjunction with the Dow Corning Corporation, developed the first silicone implant prototype. By filling inflatable silicone bags with hospital-grade silicone gel, three sizes of the mold were made: small, medium, and large, the latter being thought only to be desired by burlesque dancers.[88] The Cronin implants, also known as Simaplast, were such a success that women who were dissatisfied with their Ivalon implants because they had shrunken or hardened removed the original implants and had them replaced with silicone.[89] Dow Corning was able to sell the silicone implants without regulation because the FDA did not yet have authority over medical devices.[90]

Although doctors generally viewed silicone gel implants as the safest and the most satisfactory way to augment the size of a woman's breasts, some continued to use other versions of implants. One San Francisco topless dancer, Carol Doda, infamously went overboard with liquid silicone injections, inflating her bust from thirty-six to forty-four inches.[91] The procedure was similar to the earliest paraffin injections, wherein the material was directly injected into the skin rather than a silicone-filled implant being inserted behind the pectoral wall. Silicone injections were deemed "unethical" by the California Society of Plastic Surgeons and were banned by the FDA in 1965. In the face of these restrictions, some surgeons continued to inject their patients, such as Robert Franklyn who used silicone injections to firm the breasts of women who had suffered *ptosis* as a result of breastfeeding. He called his procedure "Cleopatra's Needle." When the silicone injections were not enough, the doctor turned to a new material—Teflon. Franklyn claimed that the material would last 300 years and that the procedure "makes it possible for a 90-year-old woman to have breasts like a teenager."[92] In 1956, Franklyn averaged ten to fifteen "breast platform" operations a week. By 1967, the self-proclaimed "Dr. Beauty" had performed over ten thousand surgeries.[93]

Justifying Surgery

Plastic surgeons agreed that corrective procedures for physical deformities improved one's daily life. Mammaplasty provided a new justification—psychological relief. While surgeries like rhinoplasty, face-lifts, or the correction of a cleft lip could improve a patient's psychological being, breast augmentation stood out because it served no aesthetic function that falsies or a padded bra could not correct. Only the patient and perhaps her significant other would know the truth. Small breasts were a unique concern because they threatened a woman's femininity. Even if a woman had too large of a nose or ears that stuck out, these physical features did not affect her gender identity. At a meeting of gynecologists, Dr. Goodrich Schouffler of the University of Oregon observed that many American women were developing "a highly-dangerous bosom complex."[94] He told colleagues about one attempted suicide and several "serious and total derangements" based on real or imagined breast deficiencies.[95] "Whether one views them as the victims of the attitudes of a crass society, or as uniquely distorted character problems in a psychiatric sense, none-the-less," Dr. M. T. Edgerton wrote, "their lives and often the lives of their husbands and families are made miserable by the development of such conflicts."[96] Blaming advertisements and "questionable publicity," the respected surgeon asserted that many physically "normal" women had developed "an almost paralyzing self-consciousness" and that his patients "were in sad and even neurotic condition" because of their small breasts. He noted that some had even sought psychiatric help.[97] Women with unilateral mammary hypoplasia (one breast larger than the other) chose to make their breasts larger rather than simply reducing the larger breast to match the smaller, further evidence that women believed a bigger bust was more attractive.[98] Another woman, whose doctor believed she had "reasonable breast development," still demanded augmentation. The surgeon believed that the correction would result in a breast size "excessive from an esthetic standard," but the patient stated that anything less would be unacceptable.[99]

Before allowing a woman to elect to undergo the invasive surgery, prospective patients went through a series of evaluations, both physical and emotional, to evaluate the woman's social situation and needs. In fact, many potential patients did not go directly to the surgeon, but were instead referred by a psychiatrist.[100] Small breasts were not seen, unlike other plastic surgeries, as a physical abnormality. Women with small breasts could perform all functions of everyday life. Instead, surgeons who supported the operation saw it as a psychological defect. Women whose doctors did not believe their neurotic tendencies could be alleviated with the procedure or who had not yet met physical maturity were denied the surgery.[101] Dr. T. R. Van Dellen, medical columnist for the *Chicago Tribune*, observed, "if a woman feels she is nothing but her appearance, she will still feel she is nobody even after her breasts have been enlarged."[102] Would-be patients noted in their psychiatric evaluations that the problem was "a life and death matter" and frequently used words and phrases such as "empty inside," "inadequate," "hollow," and "unacceptable" when describing their self-image.[103]

Because of this perceived psychological stress, doctors had few qualms about justifying breast augmentation for adult women. However, they were largely against the procedure for teenage girls. One doctor, writing in *'Teen* magazine, observed, "Styles in body shapes change just as styles in clothes change. There are certainly very few situations in which it's wise to proceed with surgery that increases the size of the breasts." Although this doctor encouraged *'Teen*'s readership to pursue cosmetic surgery to correct nose, chin, and skin blemishes, in regard to breasts, he noted, "the individual natural contours are better left the way they are."[104] Physicians believed that if a teen did not possess emotional maturity or if her Freudian "ego" was not developed, breast augmentation could cause severe anxiety post-operation. One surgeon described a recent teen patient who, after surgery, worried that her implants would "fall out" or "explode."[105]

Mammaplasty patients differed from other groups of patients who sought plastic surgery. Doctors discovered that women who elected to have breast augmentation were more likely than other plastic surgery patients to have had a previous surgical procedure, such as a tonsillectomy or appendectomy, than a woman who desired, for example, rhinoplasty. Moreover, patients seeking breast augmentation had a higher than usual concern for their appearance. Doctors noted, however, that there was no clear uniformity on social position, occupation, religion, or education among the women on whom they operated.[106] The majority of breast augmentation patients were midwestern women, married with children, around twenty-seven years old, and worried that their husbands were losing interest in them. Young women ranging from sixteen to their early twenties made up the second largest group. About two-thirds of patients reported a sense of inadequacy about their breast size, a feeling that had persisted since adolescence. The other one-third experienced dissatisfaction with their breasts after the birth of a child.[107] The motivation for actresses and topless dancers to desire larger breasts may be clear, but what about the needs and desires of average American girls and women? Why would they pursue such experimental surgery? Those who pursued breast augmentation surgery did so for three very specific reasons: First, women believed they were cheating or lying by wearing padding to increase their breast size. Second, patients felt like less of a woman or unfeminine without large breasts. And lastly, and perhaps most importantly, women desired the surgery to find or keep a husband.

Fear of discovery and a feeling of inauthenticity were powerful enough to encourage some women to pursue breast augmentation. Prospective patients noted that padded bras were not only hot and uncomfortable, but the fear that the falsies would slip out and their padding would be discovered negatively affected their self-confidence. Evelyn Golini, a recent widow who found herself thrust into the workforce after the unexpected death of her husband, desired breast surgery because she feared her coworkers knew her bra was padded and laughed at her behind her back. "I must go into the world after thirteen years as a housewife," she wrote, "and I'm terrified."[108] Women worried they would be in a serious accident and their bra padding would be discovered. Surgeons also noted that the idea of "cheating" was present in a large portion of their patients.[109] Small-breasted women felt like "phonies" with their foam inserts, which only exacerbated feelings of inadequacy.

Because breasts are the most visible sexual identifier, women held the belief that without adequate breasts, they were not feminine, and therefore not real women.[110] Referring to her small chest, one potential patient expressed to her doctor, "[how] would *I* feel if I went out with a man and later discovered he wasn't really a *man*?"[111] In Ann Bannon's lesbian pulp fiction novel, *Odd Girl Out* (1957), the main character, Laura, is ashamed of her lack of bust and is horrified when a girl in her sorority suggests she use "falsies." Laura tries to conceal the presence of her breasts as well as hide their size. Bannon writes, "She wished that they were more glamorous, more obviously *there*. In their present shape they seemed only an afterthought."[112] But Laura is not discouraged about her small breasts because she desires looking like a "Sweater Girl"; her lack of breasts is tied to insecurities about not being a real woman. Without large breasts, Laura fears her queerness is written on her body.

This sense of feminine inferiority affected even married women. One husband wrote to the AMA asking for the name of a doctor or hospital that could perform breast-enlarging surgery for his wife. He stated, "She has a definite inferiority complex because of the smallness of her breasts and I feel that an operation to increase their size and contour will be beneficial to her mental health."[113] Many women traced feelings of inadequacy and inferiority back to their teen years, of being shy and embarrassed because of small breast size. They recalled dreading physical education in school as showering and changing clothes in front of other girls provoked anxiety about the size of their breasts. Comparisons, particularly with other women in their families, caused additional frustration.[114] Even late in the 1960s when androgyny had come into vogue, the feminine breast was still of import. "In these times the female breast often seems to be the only distinguishing sign of sex," Dr. Hugh A. Johnson asserted. "Nothing says quite so well, 'I am feminine,' as a nicely formed breast. The flat chested girl is painfully aware of this; with her padded brassieres, she is ridiculed by her more generously endowed sisters."[115] Another contemporary observed, "[b]reasts aren't a fad." Regardless of whether high fashion called for small or large breasts, "to have breasts," the author continued, "*real* breasts, is vitally important to women."[116]

Beyond feelings of inauthenticity, the fear of discovery, and the desire for increased femininity, women often pursued breast augmentation to find a husband or to improve their marriage. Young women, those aged sixteen and older, often refused to date or were afraid to fall in love only to have their partner discover that they had small breasts. One patient described that she went through a phase of feeling so unattractive that she purposely wore oversized and sloppy clothing "so no boys would look at me."[117] Young women reported feeling incapable of loving and being loved and attributed this attitude to their inadequate breast development. Doctors began to take note of the frequency that marital stress motivated their patients to request the elective surgery. Some women whose relationships were in jeopardy believed that by enlarging their breasts, their marriages could be saved.[118] A forty-two-year-old housewife reported that she primarily desired the operation to satisfy the wishes of her husband. In the 1950s, doctors did not consider this a reason to deny her the procedure. By the early 1960s, however, surgeons had changed their criteria and began denying the operation to women who sought the correction predominantly to please others.[119]

Even in legal proceedings, courts interpreted large breasts as integral to finding and keeping a husband and women whose breasts had been compromised because of a faulty surgery were awarded compensation. The New York Supreme Court awarded Migdatia Massato $150,000 in a suit against her cosmetic surgeon, Dr. William Sparer, when complications after her plastic surgery resulted in the loss of both of her breasts. Sparer had directly injected silicone into Massato's breasts in 1964. "Well-shaped breasts are vital in a woman's search for a husband," announced Justice Thomas A. Aurelio. The court decided in Massato's favor; at the "advanced" age of thirty-seven, she was already considered a "spinster" and would now have an even harder time finding a husband "under the present circumstances."[120] In the case of a forty-six-year-old widow, a Miami, Florida circuit court awarded Mrs. Lavon Crawford $13,000 because a breast lift caused a four-inch loss from her bust line. Crawford, a widow who was engaged to be remarried, visited the office of Dr. James G. Robertson to have an ingrown toenail removed. As she sat in the waiting room, Crawford flipped through literature on face-lifts and breast surgery. In her scheduled appointment with the doctor, she discussed and agreed to have a face-lift, breast lift, and the original toe surgery. In her court case against Dr. Robertson, Crawford claimed the doctor did not tell her the surgery would reduce the size of her breasts, and that at thirty-eight inches, she was now "flat as a pancake." She told the circuit court that the operation had caused her to lose her fiancé and that she was still unmarried.[121]

In the written reports of plastic surgeons, one can glean the voices of female patients and their reactions to their respective surgeries. One doctor noted that the final evaluation could not be judged by "geometric measurements," but by the self-esteem boost the surgery had provided for the patient.[122] The idea of being allowed to choose the size of one's breasts proved to be a staggering reality for some women. "I didn't really believe the doctor was telling me I could select my ideal breast," one patient reported. "I didn't know whether to laugh or cry."[123] Most women surveyed reported satisfaction with their post-surgery results, noting that the operation had changed their lives for the better. They told their doctors they were far less breast-centric, less self-conscious, and now enjoyed activities they were unable to before. Others claimed they no longer felt like "an odd or different creature" or "sexually deformed."[124] Comments about improved marital bliss were common, including reports that sexual relations had improved as body self-consciousness no longer existed. One patient recalled the joy and liberation she felt after her surgery in being able to throw away her padded bras and falsies.[125] Still another patient, a doctor's wife, stated, "For the first time I feel like a really complete woman."[126]

Breast augmentation certainly was not without its dangers. Painful blisters regularly formed near the incision site and required drainage. If the breast implant was not properly sterilized prior to insertion, infection could occur. Actress Joan (née Josephine) Dixon filed a malpractice suit against Manhattan plastic surgeon Dr. Manfred von Linde in 1963 when her implants became infected. Dixon, a starlet who had appeared in a handful of films, desired breast augmentation surgery to better play Elizabeth Taylor's body double in the film *Butterfield 8* (1960). She had the surgery on November 4, 1959, and required four subsequent months of treatment to cure an infection that caused "disfiguring scars, substantial loss of body tissue and progressive and permanent loss of hair from her head." A second, corrective breast surgery was required in March 1960.[127]

In numerous accounts, women's bodies rejected the implant altogether and the internal padding had to be surgically removed. Prior to the Simaplast implant, women complained that the Ivalon insert had shrunk or calcified. Even the widely accepted silicone implants were prone to leakage, particularly in patients who desired aggressively large breasts.[128] Other common complaints were that breasts had not been made large enough. One woman, who had hoped her breasts would be double their original size, reported that even after surgery she continued to wear falsies and therefore felt "doubly deceitful." This patient was seen as atypical, however. Her doctor noted that she had "hysterical character tendencies" due to her father's "aggressive interest" in women and her husband's penchant to flirt with other women.[129] In less physical complaints, other patients expressed disappointment that the operation had failed to alleviate marital issues. Doctors noted that the desire to change how others responded to them, rather than affecting their internal feelings, was an unrealistic expectation.[130]

Conclusions

In the film *Will Success Spoil Rock Hunter?* (1957), Rock Hunter's fiancée, Jenny Wells (played by Betsy Drake), realizes that attending college to develop her mind was a serious mistake. She should have been developing her body instead. Fearing that Rock will leave her for the buxom and vapid Hollywood star Rita Marlowe (Jayne Mansfield), Jenny initiates an exercise regime designed to increase her modest bust line. Upon visiting her apartment after work, Rock discovers his fiancée comatose on the ground and frozen in a perpetual push-up. When Rock informs her doctor that the malady was caused by too much exercise—specifically push-ups—the doctor nods knowingly. "Push-ups are a waste of time," the physician tells the advertising executive. "It's really better for women to just go to a store, if you know what I mean." When Rock Hunter returns to his own apartment that night and checks in on his teenage daughter, he finds her sleeping in bed, her arms above the covers in a frozen push-up.

Women with large breasts were no doubt celebrated in the immediate postwar years. One need only look to the most celebrated Hollywood stars of the 1950s to see evidence of this popularity. An actress required little actual performance acumen as long as she could fill out her sweater. The privileging of large-breasted women in the mass media had a particular effect on teenage girls who desired the full curves of their favorite cover girls and on mothers who lamented the loss of an inflated bust after the birth of a child. Why did female consumers of all ages stuff their bras, exercise, and send away for mail-order scams in an attempt to increase their cup size? Claims of increased femininity and self-confidence litter the historical record, but one reason outnumbered all other motivations—they believed it was what men wanted. Women attempted to take control of their bodies and their marital futures with the aid of vitamins, lotions, and hand pumps that promised specific results, but no exercise or special diet plan could create naturally larger breasts.

The compression and reshaping of feminine breasts to fit a fashionable ideal was not new, but the reverence of busty women was unique to postwar America. Remarkably, Americans were highly cognizant of this obsession and its novelty.

Many contemporaries attributed the preference for large-breasted figures to the infantilization of American men, but favoring women with aggressive mammary glands was a way to sexualize, maternalize, and minimize women's power in the hope of shuffling American women back to the kitchen and the bedroom. Even with the popularity of flat-chested fashion models like Twiggy or similarly small-breasted actresses like Audrey Hepburn late in the 1960s, women continued to desire larger breasts. The sustained technological advances in plastic surgery are evidence of this.

In a consumer-driven market, new companies and methods of achieving larger breasts quickly appeared, taking advantage of women's pocketbooks and their strained body image. Monetarily, breast augmentation was expensive. In the 1950s, the surgery cost between $1,000 and $1,500. In the 1960s, the price of the operation dropped to between $750 and $1,250.[131] To put this in perspective, the average family during these years made just over $3,000 in wages. For single women without a man's bank account to tap into, the surgery was even further out of reach. The median income for white women in 1950 was $1,060. In 1960, that average increased to just $1,349.[132] In this way, unlike makeup or hair dye, access to breast enlargement surgery was not democratic. Still, some Hollywood hopefuls went through with the costly surgery, believing that their new body would garner them more roles and eventually pay for itself. Despite the frequency of complications and high cost of the elective surgery, however, no patients reported in post-surgery interviews that they would have preferred to forgo the operation.[133] But breast augmentation surgery was just one extreme example of the lengths to which women in the postwar years went to resculpt their figures to mirror the women that Hollywood and the fashion industry deemed most beautiful and desirable.

Notes

1. Harold Koda, *Extreme Beauty: The Body Transformed* (New Haven, CT: Yale University Press, 2001), 52.
2. For more on the history of the brassiere and undergarments, see Jane Farrell-Beck and Colleen Gau, *Uplift: The Bra in America* (Philadelphia, PA: University of Pennsylvania Press, 2002); Beatrice Fontanel, *Support and Seduction: A History of Corsets and Bras* (New York: Harry N. Abrams, Inc.); Carolyn Latteier, *Breasts: The Women's Perspective on an American Obsession* (New York: The Haworth Press, 1998); Teresa Riordan, *A History of the Innovations that Have Made Us Beautiful* (New York: Broadway, 2004); and Marilyn Yalom, *A History of the Breast* (New York: Alfred A. Knopf, 1997).
3. E. O. Smith, *When Culture and Biology Collide: Why We Are Stressed, Depressed, and Self-Obsessed* (New Brunswick, NJ: Rutgers University Press, 2002), 61.
4. Ben Hecht, "Bosoms Away," *Esquire*, July 1957, 73.
5. Elizabeth Haiken, *Venus Envy: A History of Cosmetic Surgery* (Baltimore, MD: The Johns Hopkins University Press, 1999), 246; Philip J. Hilts, "Strange History of Silicone Held Many Warning Signs," *New York Times*, January 18, 1992, 1.
6. Horace Miner, "Body Ritual among the Nacirema," *American Anthropologist* 58, no. 3 (1956): 506.

7. Quoted in Robert Alan Franklyn, *On Developing Bosom Beauty* (New York: Fell, 1959), 11.
8. G. R. Stevens, "The Breasts of the Durhams," *Esquire*, May 1952, 50, 118.
9. Zenda Daye, *How to Develop the Bust* (Sydney: World Wide Mail Order, 1952).
10. Victor Warren Quayle, "Beauty and the Bust," *Esquire*, June 1954, 85.
11. Robert Franklyn, *On Developing Bosom Beauty* (New York: Fell, 1959), 7–9.
12. "Who Will Fill Jane Russell's Blouse?" *Flirt*, March 1948, 10–11. In a publicity tour for the musical comedy *Gentlemen Prefer Blondes* (1953), Russell and her co-star, Marilyn Monroe, were top contenders in "the battle of the bosoms." The two posed for a photograph so that their measurements could be compared inch by inch. According to general consensus, Russell had prettier legs but Monroe had more provocative eyes. However, as the column's author commented, "Who's looking at *eyes*, anyway," (*Screen Stars*, June 1953, 26).
13. Quoted in Benita Eisler, *Private Lives: Men and Women of the Fifties* (New York: Franklin Watts, 1986), 58.
14. Robert Alan Franklyn, *Augmentation Mammaplasty* (Rome: International Academy of Cosmetic Surgery, 1976), 13.
15. Hecht, "Bosoms Away," *Esquire*, July 1957, 73–74.
16. "The Sound and the Fury," *Esquire*, October 1957, 12.
17. Franklyn, *Augmentation Mammaplasty*, 13.
18. Beth Bailey, *From Front Porch to Back Seat: Courtship in Twentieth-Century America* (Baltimore, MD: The Johns Hopkins University Press, 1989).
19. Latteier, *Breasts*, 37.
20. Fontanel, *Support and Seduction*; Yalom, *A History of the Breast*.
21. See Karen Anderson, *Wartime Women: Sex Roles, Family Relations, and the Status of Women During World War II* (Westport, CT: Greenwood Press, 1981); Susan J. Douglas, *Where the Girls Are: Growing Up Female with the Mass Media* (New York: Times Books, 1994); Elaine Tyler May, *Homeward Bound: American Families in the Cold War Era* (New York: Basic Books, 1988); Joanne Meyerowitz, ed., *Not June Cleaver: Women and Gender in Post-War America* (Philadelphia, PA: Temple University Press, 1994); Joanna Pitman, *On Blondes* (New York: Bloomsbury, 2003), 225.
22. For further discussion of the *femme fatale*, see *Women in Film Noir*, ed. E. Ann Kaplan (London: British Film Institute, 1999).
23. Carolyn Latteier, "Cosmetic Breast Surgery: The Origins, 1945–1968," MA Thesis, Washington State University, 1997, 45.
24. Hal Boyle, "Dagmar Trims Off 20 Pounds: Claims She Can Think Faster with Less Poundage," *The Spokesman-Review*, January 22, 1953, 16.
25. See Allan Bérubé, *Coming Out Under Fire: Gays and Lesbians in World War II* (New York: Free Press, 1990).
26. Latteier, "Cosmetic Breast Surgery: The Origins, 1945–1968," 11.
27. For the role of *Playboy*, anxieties about homosexuality, and the destruction of the "breadwinner ethic," see Barbara Ehrenreich, *The Hearts of Men: American Dreams and the Flight from Commitment* (Garden City, NY: Anchor Press/Doubleday, 1983).
28. Audrey Minor, "Operation Hollywood: Custom Tailored Bosoms," *Confidential*, July 1954, 14.
29. Mamie Van Doren, *Playing the Field: My Story* (New York: G. P. Putnam's Sons, 1987), 71.
30. Nora Ephron, "A Few Words about Breasts," *Esquire*, May 1972, 95.
31. Joan Jacobs Brumberg, *The Body Project: An Intimate History of American Girls* (New York: Random House, 1997), 111–118.
32. Kelly Schrum, *Some Wore Bobby Sox: The Emergence of Teenage Girls' Culture, 1920–1945* (New York: Palgrave Macmillan, 2004), 51.
33. Ephron, "A Few Words about Breasts," 95.
34. Latteier, *Breasts*, 20.

35 Ephron, "A Few Words about Breasts," 158.
36 Latteier, *Breasts*, 20.
37 Douglas, *Where the Girls Are*, 31–32.
38 Judy Blume, *Are You There God? It's Me, Margaret*, (New York: Dell Publishing, 1970) 117.
39 Charles D. Ablard, "In the Matter of the Complaint Against Tyler Pharmacal Distributors, Inc." H. E. Docket No. 4/232, July, 14, 1958, http://www.usps.com/judicial/1958deci/4-232.htm.
40 *Tyler Pharmacal Distributors, Inc., Plaintiff-Appellant v. U.S. Department of Health, Education and Welfare, Defendant-Appellee*. Docket No. 16637, United States Court of Appeals Seventh Circuit, March 5, 1969, http://ftp.resource.org/courts.gov/c/F2/408/408.F2d.95.16637.16643.html.
41 Formalon advertisement, American Medical Association (AMA) archives, Chicago, Illinois, 0287-20.
42 "Misbranding of Formalon Cream." *United States v. Daniel Platt (Formalon Company)* F.D.C. No. 21466. January, 23, 1948. United States National Library of Medicine, http://archive.nlm.nih.gov/fdanj/handle/123456789/11293.
43 Lady Ample files, AMA archives, Chicago, Illinois 0095-06.
44 Letter from Oliver Field to Art H. Cole, Cleveland Better Business Bureau, July 23, 1954, AMA archives, Chicago, Illinois 0095-19.
45 "Facts You Should Know About Health Quackery," Better Business Bureau Educational Committee, December 1971, 7. AMA archives, Chicago, Illinois, 0018-12.
46 Quayle, "Beauty and the Bust," *Esquire*, June 1954, 109.
47 Herb Graffis, "Figures About Females," *Esquire*, February 1951, 75.
48 Edith Head and Paddy Calistro, *Edith Head's Hollywood* (New York: E. P. Dutton, Inc., 1983), 65.
49 Joan Bennett, "Yours for Beauty," *Screen Stars*, February 1952, 47, 92.
50 Bennett, "Yours for Beauty," *Screen Stars*, August 1951, 84.
51 Daye, *How to Develop the Bust* (1952), 3.
52 Quayle, "Beauty and the Bust," *Esquire*, June 1954, 109, 97.
53 Ephron, "A Few Words about Breasts," 96.
54 Blume, *Are You There God? It's Me, Margaret*, 44, 92
55 Valerie Taylor, *Journey to Fulfillment* (New York: Midwood Tower, 1964), 134.
56 Valerie Taylor, *The Girls in 3-B* (New York: Midwood Tower, 1964), 134.
57 Sears Roebuck Catalogue (Chicago, IL: Sears, Roebuck and Co., 1961), 205–226; Sears Roebuck Catalogue – Fall and Winter (Chicago, IL: Sears, Roebuck and Co., 1966), 447.
58 Quayle, "Beauty and the Bust," *Esquire*, June 1954, 109.
59 Gustave Aufricht, "The Development of Plastic Surgery in the United States," *Plastic and Reconstructive Surgery* 1, no. 1 (July 1946): 3, 21–22.
60 Harriet La Barre, *Plastic Surgery: Beauty You Can Buy* (New York: Holt, Rinehart and Wilson, 1970), 1.
61 Ibid., 139–141; "The Perfect Bosom," *Vogue*, July 1968, 91.
62 "Bosom Perfection: New Possibilities," *Vogue*, October 1959, 139.
63 Joan Bennett, "Yours For Beauty," *Screen Stars*, April 1951, 81.
64 "I Hate My Nose," *Seventeen*, September 1968, 131.
65 Arthur Roth, "Do You Need a New Nose?" *'Teen*, December 1959, 20.
66 For a further discussion on the history of cosmetic and plastic surgery, see Sander L. Gilman, *Making the Body Beautiful* (Princeton, NJ: Princeton University Press, 2001); and Elizabeth Haiken, *Venus Envy: A History of Cosmetic Surgery* (Baltimore, MD: The Johns Hopkins University Press, 1997). Both authors are more concerned with a timeline of plastic surgeries—when each was developed, and by whom. While valuable, my work focuses more on the social and cultural meanings and motivations for having large breasts.

67 Haiken, *Venus Envy*, 233.
68 Michael Gurdin and Gene A. Carlin, "Complications of Breast Implantations," *Plastic and Reconstructive Surgery* 40, no. 6 (December 1967): 530; Haiken, *Venus Envy*, 236.
69 Max Thorek, *Plastic Surgery of the Breast and Abdominal Wall* (Springfield, IL: C.C. Thomas, 1942), 168–170.
70 Jacques W. Maliniac, "Evaluation of Principal Mamaplastic Procedures," *Plastic and Reconstructive Surgery* (July 1949): 359–373.
71 H. O. Barnes, "Reduction of Massive Breast Hypertrophy," *Plastic and Reconstructive Surgery* 3, no. 5 (September 1948): 569.
72 Haiken, *Venus Envy*, 236.
73 H. O. Barnes, "Breast Malformations and a New Approach to the Problem of the Small Breast," *Plastic and Reconstructive Surgery* 5, no. 6 (June 1950): 499–506.
74 "Beauty to Take by [Mouth]," *Vogue*, January 15, 1959, 35.
75 Audrey Minor, "Operation Hollywood: Custom Tailored Bosoms," *Confidential*, July 1954, 14.
76 Franklyn, *Augmentation Mammaplasty* (Rome: International Academy of Cosmetic Surgery, 1976), 10.
77 Ibid., 13-15, 64–65.
78 Joan Kron, "Nipping and Tucking in Tinseltown," *Allure*, May 1995, http://www.facelift.com/1995_niptucktinseltown_home.html; Teresa Riordan, *Inventing Beauty: A History of the Innovations that Have Made Us Beautiful* (New York: Broadway, 2004), 110.
79 Harold I. Harris, "Survey of Breast Implants from the Point of View of Carcinogenesis," *PRS* 28, no. 1 (July 1961): 82.
80 Robert Alan Franklyn, *The Clinical Atlas of Cosmetic Plastic Surgery: A Teaching Manual* (Geneva: International Academy of Cosmetic Surgery, 1976) 7–9.
81 Robert Alan Franklyn, *Beauty Surgeon* (Long Beach, CA: Whitehorn, 1960), 21–23; Franklyn, *The Clinical Atlas of Cosmetic Plastic Surgery*, 29.
82 Franklyn, *Beauty Surgeon*, 21; Franklyn, *The Clinical Atlas of Cosmetic Plastic Surgery*, 30.
83 Robert Franklyn, "Breastaplasty: The Operation that Remolds Flat-Chested Women," *Pageant*, August 1953, 68–75.
84 W. John Pangman, *Southern General Practitioner of Medicine and Surgery* 115, no. 12, (December 1953), np.
85 Surgeons such as Dr. Gustave Aufricht, attending surgeon at New York's Lenox Hill Hospital, continued to favor fat transplantation over Ivalon implants because, as he argued, "It just will not do to have a lump as hard as a baseball inside the breast." "Surgeon Reports Success in Building in Uplifts," *Chicago Defender*, November 6, 1957, 9.
86 Robert Alan Franklyn files, AMA archives, Chicago, Illinois, 0288-13.
87 Benjamin F. Edwards, "Teflon-Silicone Breast Implants," *PRS* 32, no. 4 (November 1963): 519.
88 Latteier, "Cosmetic Breast Surgery: The Origins, 1945–1968," 20.
89 Paule C. Regnault, "Indications for Breast Augmentation," *PRS* 40, no. 6 (December 1967): 526.
90 The Medical Device Amendment to the Federal Food, Drug, and Cosmetics Act gave the FDA authority over medical devices in May 1976, http://www.fda.gov/medical-devices/. Accessed July 24, 2010.
91 Bruce Davidson, "The Naked Luncheon," *Esquire*, March 1966, 99.
92 Hugh Wyatt, "Girls Can Put on Teflon Front Now," *Daily News*, June 27, 1970.
93 Ralph Lee Smith, "All the Twiggies Want to be Sophia," *True*, November 1967, 81–82.
94 Jay Smith, "The Big Bosom Battle," *Playboy*, September 1955, 26.
95 Quoted in Franklyn, *On Bosom Beauty* (New York: Fell, 1954), 14.
96 M. T. Edgerton and A. R. McClary, "Augmentation Mammaplasty," *PRS* 21, no. 4 (April 1958): 279.

97 Ibid., 244; "Surgeon Reports Success in Building in Uplifts," *Chicago Defender*, November 6, 1957, 9.
98 Thomas D. Rees and Christian C. Dupuis, "Unilateral Mammary Hypoplasia," *PRS* 41, no. 4 (April 1968): 309.
99 M. T. Edgerton, E. Meyer, and W. E. Jacobson, "Augmentation Mammaplasty II," *Plastic and Reconstructive Surgery* 27, no. 3 (March 1961): 298.
100 Franklyn, *Augmentation Mammaplasty*, 61.
101 Regnault, "Indications for Breast Augmentation," *PRS* 40, no. 6 (December 1967): 524.
102 Smith, "All the Twiggies Want to be Sophia," 83.
103 Edgerton and McClary, "Augmentation Mammaplasty," 297.
104 Roth, "Do You Need a New Nose?" 22–23.
105 Norman J. Knorr, J. E. Hoopes, and M. T. Edgerton, "Psychiatric-Surgical Approach to Adolescent Disturbance in Self Image," *PRS* 41, no. 3 (March 1968): 251.
106 Edgerton and McClary, "Augmentation Mammaplasty," *PRS* 21, no. 4 (April 1958): 280, 294.
107 Edgerton, Meyer, and Jacobson, "Augmentation Mammaplasty II," Further Surgical and Psychiatric Evaluation, *Plastic and Reconstructive Surgery* 27, no. 3 (March 1961): 296–297.
108 Letter from Evelyn Golini to Oliver Field, June 16, 1954. Robert A. Franklyn files, AMA archives, Chicago, Illinois.
109 Edgerton and McClary, "Augmentation Mammaplasty," 297.
110 La Barre, *Plastic Surgery: Beauty You Can Buy*, 81.
111 Emphasis original. Edgerton and McClary, "Augmentation Mammaplasty," *PRS* 21, no. 4, 297.
112 Bannon, *Odd Girl Out* (1957), 19.
113 Letter from Ben H. Mitchell to Oliver Field, June 14, 1954. Robert A. Franklyn files. AMA archives, Chicago, Illinois.
114 Knorr, Hoopes, and Edgerton, "Psychiatric-Surgical Approach to Adolescent Disturbance in Self Image," *PRS* 41, no. 3 (March 1968): 250.
115 Hugh A. Johnson, "Silastic Breast Implants: Coping with Complications," *Plastic and Reconstructive Surgery* 44, no. 6 (Dec 1969): 588.
116 Emphasis original. La Barre, *Plastic Surgery: Beauty You Can Buy*, 93.
117 Edgerton and McClary, "Augmentation Mammaplasty," *PRS* 21, no. 4, 301–302.
118 Knorr, Hoopes, and Edgerton, "Psychiatric-Surgical Approach to Adolescent Disturbance in Self Image," 249.
119 Edgerton, Meyer, and Jacobson, "Augmentation Mammaplasty II," *PRS* 27, no. 3, 290, 300.
120 M. Cartwright, "$150,000 N.Y. Breast Surgery Suit Recalls Japanese Case," *Chicago Defender*, April 30, 1968, 19.
121 *San Antonio Express*, "Breast Surgery Suit Costs Doctor $13,000," December 1, 1967, 12.
122 H. O. Barnes, "Breast Malformations and a New Approach to the Problem of the Small Breast," *PRS* 5, no. 6 (June 1950): 506.
123 La Barre, *Plastic Surgery: Beauty You Can Buy*, 84.
124 Edgerton and McClary, "Augmentation Mammaplasty," *PRS* 21, no. 4, 289–298.
125 La Barre, *Plastic Surgery*, 87.
126 Edgerton and McClary, "Augmentation Mammaplasty," *PRS* 21, no. 4, 289, 298.
127 *Bridgeport Post*, "Trial Opened in Surgery Suit," February 8, 1963, 52.
128 Johnson, "Silastic Breast Implants: Coping with Complications," *PRS* 44, no. 6 (December 1969): 588–591.
129 Edgerton and McClary, "Augmentation Mammaplasty," *PRS* 21, no. 4, 291.
130 Edgerton, Meyer, and Jacobson, "Augmentation Mammaplasty II," *PRS* 27, no. 3 (March 1961): 296.

131 "Bosom Perfection: New Possibilities," *Vogue*, October 1959, 126, 139, 141; "The Perfect Bosom," *Vogue,* July 1968, 91.
132 US Bureau of the Census, "Income Growth Rates in 1939 to 1968 for Persons by Occupation and Industry Groups, for the United States," *Current Population Reports*, Series P-60, No. 69 (Washington, DC: US Government Printing Office, 1970).
133 Edgerton, Meyer, and Jacobson, "Augmentation Mammaplasty II," *PRS* 27, no. 3, 290–291.

3

"THE LONGER THE BELT LINE, THE SHORTER THE LIFE LINE"

Insurance Companies and the Medical Community Weigh In

In October 1942, the Metropolitan Life Insurance Company (MetLife) published a table of "ideal" weights for women aged twenty-five and over with respect to three different body frame sizes. The table became so popular that MetLife created a corresponding chart for men in 1943. This was not the first height and weight table of its kind, but it was the first that made allowances for various body builds. The MetLife standardized charts were found not only in insurance company offices, but were also distributed to the general population by family physicians, nurses, dieticians, and physical educators. Moreover, popular magazines repurposed the widely accepted tables on the glossy page. For both men and women, height and weight standardized tables became the most popular and trusted source in determining how much an individual should weigh.[1] Fat historian Sander Gilman has argued that the medical community and popular culture have traditionally determined the "boundary" between acceptable and unacceptable bodies.[2] However, one more—albeit unexpected—determinant can be added to that list: insurance companies. While the fashion industry and Hollywood battled to create a cultural ideal for female body size during the 1940s and 1950s, life insurance companies created a physiological standard.

Belgian mathematician Lambert Adolphe Jacques Quételet constructed the first height and weight table in 1836, but because Quételet listed only one average height and weight for Belgian men and women at ages twenty, thirty, forty, fifty, and sixty, the table did not reach a general audience. In 1846, John Hutchinson, a British surgeon, expanded on Quételet's chart, publishing the average weight of thirty-year-old British men ranging from five feet one inch to six feet tall. Incomplete data and medical experience limited these early tables. A more uniform approach was made possible in 1889 with the creation of both the Actuarial

Society of America and the Association of Life Insurance Medical Directors of America (ALIMDA).[3]

Life insurance companies took an early interest in the height and weight of their applicants because they believed these figures were an important indicator of health and, subsequently, a factor in the acceptance or denial of an applicant's petition for insurance. At the end of the nineteenth century, "overweight" continued to be equated with well-being, while medical professionals discouraged "underweight" because of its connection to tuberculosis and pneumonia, the number one killers in America through 1900. In 1895, ALIMDA assigned George R. Shepherd, medical director of the Connecticut Mutual Life Insurance Company, to chair a committee to create a reliable standard height and weight table. Shepherd presented the final product at the ALIMDA annual meeting in 1897. The table was based on the heights and weights of 74,162 accepted male life insurance applicants in North America and afterward became the industry-wide standard. Because of the smaller number of women policyholders, ALIMDA did not develop a women's table until 1912, when the men's table was reconfigured as well. Until then, women's weight standards were inferred from the men's table, continuing a long-standing scientific discourse that used men as the model and viewed women as the same or as an alternate version of men.[4]

Starting around 1912, with the Medico-Actuarial Mortality Investigation, doctors and actuaries began to endorse the preferability of "underweight" to "overweight" in regard to health and long life.[5] Previously, fear of illnesses that caused unhealthy weight loss guided medical opinion about body mass. But as sanitary and medical knowledge improved along with Americans' standard of living, attitudes about "underweight" versus "overweight" shifted. As a result, height and weight tables were subtly adjusted downward between the world wars from average weights toward an "ideal." The architect of this transition was Louis I. Dublin, longtime statistician and vice president for the MetLife Company. First, Dublin tightened the acceptable weight allowances for each height. Previous tables had listed averages instead of Dublin's new "ideal" or "desirable" weights. Data collected from current policyholders enabled Dublin to compile means and median statistics, while input from medical advisers and anthropologists informed the weight ranges for bodies with the lowest rates of mortality. Secondly, Dublin created "ideal" weight spectrums for three different body builds—small, medium, and large. Although the acknowledgment of different body types was progressive, Dublin provided no concrete technique that educated individuals as to which of the three bone structures applied to their own bodies. Finally, the allowance of weight gain for older Americans was discontinued. The 1912 tables that listed average weights had also included an age scale, recognizing that, as individuals age, they also tend to gain weight. The 1942–1943 MetLife tables eliminated the age scale based on actuary data that suggested Americans were healthiest at age twenty-five and younger. A number of fat studies texts have labeled Louis Dublin as "Public Enemy Number One" regarding America's preoccupation with reducing and the collusion of fat with high mortality and chronic health risks.[6] Dublin, however, was just one man among a highly influential group of statisticians and medical advisers who, intentionally or not, misrepresented questionable data that launched the American people, and especially women, into an all-out crusade against "overweight" and fat.

Louis Israel Dublin (1882–1968) studied mathematics at the College of the City of New York and received a doctorate in biology from Columbia University in 1904. He taught for several years before joining the MetLife Company in 1909, when they launched their health and welfare program. Two years later, in 1911, he organized MetLife's Statistical Bureau, where he served as its director and later as vice president of the company until his retirement in 1952. Recognizing his contributions to the profession, in 1961 Dublin was elected into the Insurance Hall of Fame, an institution established in 1957, whose existence, as the Hall of Fame itself declared, was "testimony to the expanding influence of insurance as a social and economic force."[7] Dublin was president or director of a number of public health and welfare institutions, including the American Statistical Association, the American Cancer Society, the American Public Health Association, the National Tuberculosis Association, the National Health Council, and the Population Association of America. Dublin was also a prolific author. In his life, he published a number of books and some 700 papers, along with numerous popular magazine and newspaper articles.[8]

In 1942, diseases of the heart and cancer replaced tuberculosis and pneumonia as the number one and number two causes of death in America. Medical advances had effectively eliminated illnesses associated with childhood, but had been less successful with those occurring later in life. Measured against other countries, the United States lagged behind in preventing these adult-onset diseases, despite the country's high standard of living.[9] But as late as 1944, even after the publication of MetLife's build and weight study, Dublin was not yet campaigning against fat. In a published list of health and welfare predictions that the American people would have to face in the immediate future, Dublin made no mention of weight management or the supposed connection of "overfat" to mortality. He instead focused on eliminating tuberculosis, cleaning up venereal disease, and paying greater attention to mental health.[10]

Starting in 1950, Dublin began reporting a link between overweight and mortality.[11] The next year, he spoke at the annual American Medical Association (AMA) meeting and claimed that overweight individuals were not only at a higher mortality risk but were also more susceptible to chronic diseases like hypertension, diabetes, gallbladder disease, degenerative arthritis, some forms of cancer, joint diseases, gout, hernias, and complications with pregnancy.[12] After his pronouncement before the AMA, Dublin traveled and published extensively, publicly touting the so-called dangers of overweight and obesity. The medical profession had long considered obesity to be unhealthy, but they generally situated their definition of too much fat at the far end of the weight spectrum. Dublin, however, redefined "overweight" as 10 percent above MetLife's "ideal" weights and "obese" as 20–30 percent above it. In doing so, the influential statistician catapulted, overnight, twenty million Americans into the category of "overweight."

In 1952, Dublin spoke on a panel at a nutrition symposium held at the Harvard School of Public Health. He told the assembled medical and health specialists that his life insurance data, without exception, proved that overweight men and women had a higher mortality rate than the "average" and "underweight" person. He added that losing weight would add years to one's life. The other members of the panel, Drs. Howard B. Sprague, Taylor Hunt, and David D. Rutstein, uniformly challenged Dublin's data and methodology. They cited a number of medical studies that indicated obesity and heart disease were not related and argued that the marked weight reduction by an obese person, rather than extending his or her life, actually shortened it. Despite these arguments, however, Dr. Sprague concluded the doctors' remarks with, "I am sure that we shall continue to follow Dr. Dublin's advice in recommending weight reduction for those carrying excess fat. If any of them are unfortunate enough to die, at least they will look better."[13]

The MetLife height and weight charts remained the accepted standard of health-related weight-to-height ideals until 1959, when the Society of Actuaries investigated a possible link between blood pressure and body build. The goal of the study was to determine to what extent hypertension and overweight affected mortality. For these statisticians, correlation implied causation. The only other similar study of mortality among insured North Americans based on blood pressure took place in 1939 and covered the years 1925–1939. Twenty-six insurance companies participated in the 1959 Build and Blood Pressure Study, representing 65 percent of insurance companies in the United States and Canada, with nearly five million policies reported for the build study and just under four million policies for the blood pressure investigation. The report included data from men and women between the ages of fifteen and sixty-nine for policies issued between 1935 and 1953. Because the volume of data was so large, the test's practitioners computed average weights and heights using a stratified sample—290,000 policies for men and 70,000 policies for women.[14]

The Society of Actuaries utilized Dublin's definition of "overweight" (10 percent above ideal weight) and "obesity" (20 percent or more) to ascertain the number of insured Americans who fell under these categories. The study discovered that 20 percent of men and 23 percent of women who had been awarded Standard policies were "overweight." Another 6 percent of men and 11 percent of women who were Standard policyholders were considered "obese." "Underweight" women outnumbered men, with 31 percent weighing in at 10 percent or more below the ideal weight, while 23 percent of men were below average.[15] The findings of the Build and Blood Pressure Study prompted the creation of a new MetLife table for men and women. Armed with this new actuarial data, ideal weights were once again reduced for each height and body build. As Table 3.1 highlights, in most cases the low range of the new 1959 table was a full ten pounds less than the low range for the 1942 table. The ranges themselves spanned wider, allowing for a broader weight range at each height, but also listed a skinnier "desired" weight overall for each body frame.

Challenging the Data

The alarm over an "obesity epidemic" at first blush appears justifiable. If being even a few pounds over the average weight for a typical American man or woman was hazardous to one's health—as all of Dublin's reports to the public seemed to suggest—then the "cure" would be a reducing diet and moderate exercise. Doctors and psychologists disagreed about the causes of obesity—mental, medical, or simply eating too much food—but the solution appeared commonplace. However, how reliable were these various mortality studies? How much stock should the American people have placed in these findings in order to inform their choices about weight and health? Just as the early twentieth century standardized height and weight tables had been limited, Louis Dublin's and other actuarial studies similarly relied on questionable methodology. Specifically, limited demographics, flawed height and weight recordings, too small of representative samples, and the oversimplification in reporting findings to the general public all problematized the conclusion regarding the connection between weight and mortality.

MetLife's 1942 height and weight standardized table for women relied on data from life insurance policies held between 1922 and 1934. One could argue the inherent problems of basing a contemporary standard of measure on decades-old research, but more problematic was the use of a specialized sample as representative of an entire population. Simply put, only a limited population purchases life insurance policies; the people whose average heights and weights were recorded to represent the nation's health were not wholly representative. For example, the majority of Dublin's policyholders were of Northern European origin—a group historically taller and leaner than national averages. Female policyholders were largely housewives, factory workers, stenographers, and clerks, and the majority lived on the East Coast.[16] In the 1959 Society of Actuaries' Build and Blood Pressure Study, five large northeastern insurance companies contributed more than half of the data, skewing the findings geographically and therefore population-wise. Moreover, those who invest in life insurance tend to be from a higher social class. Repeated studies indicated a connection between socioeconomic status and weight.[17] Thus, insurance-purchasing populations do not accurately reflect a national population.

Not only was the collected data from a self-selecting population, but the policies actually included in the study were also handpicked. For example, Dublin disregarded outliers. Height measurements of very tall (over six feet) or very short (under four feet eight inches) women were not included. More problematic, MetLife's height and weight table was based only on policies insured at the Standard rate. If one was deemed too "underweight" or too "overweight" to qualify for a Standard premium, they received a Substandard insurance policy and were charged a higher premium based on their weight. Dublin did not include data from Substandard policies in determining the average and therefore "ideal" measures.[18]

Moreover, insurance applicants' weight and height data was haphazardly collected at the time of policy issue. For data used to create the 1942 height and weight table, applicants were weighed and measured with their clothes and shoes on, and at least 20 percent of applicants self-reported their weights and 90 percent their own heights. Dublin himself admitted, "We are dealing very largely with persons whose height and weight were not actually measured at the time of the examination."[19] MetLife had also had a policy since 1925 to round up or down heights ending in half an inch. For example, heights of five feet 3½ inches and five feet 4½ inches were both recorded as five feet 4 inches.[20]

The 1959 Build and Blood Pressure Study, upon which MetLife's revamped standardized height and weight tables were based, was similarly problematic. Weights continued to be measured in "ordinary" indoor clothing and heights recorded with shoes on. As a general observation, men's average weights in 1959 were higher and those for women lower than in both the Medico-Actuarial Mortality Investigation (1912) and the Medical Impairment Study (1929). When postulating as to why the average weight for women was "appreciably lower" than that reported in the earlier investigations, the study's authors noted the "marked reduction" in the weight of women's clothing in 1959 as compared to three decades earlier, and that the height of women's heels had increased along with the current period's "vogue" for slenderness.[21] They themselves recognized the problems of measuring potential policyholders with their clothes and shoes on. The study's authors also noted a disproportionate amount of recorded heights and weights in even inches and weights ending in the digit 0 or 5.[22] This would suggest that the information was self-reported by the person to be insured, not the insurance company itself, or that heights and weights were estimated or rounded.

This lack of uniformity in measuring policyholders, along with the narrow demographic of those insured, is problematic to be sure. But equally if not more challenging was the inclusion of body frames in the 1942 and 1959 MetLife charts. While the body build allowances were meant to accommodate various body types (small, medium, and large), no uniform criteria were ever provided to help individuals decide which frame corresponded to their own. Dublin used anthropometric studies to inform the ranges for small, medium, and large frames, but remained vague in his labeling on the charts themselves. As a result, as one medical expert noted, "Many athletically built women who consider themselves on the horsey side and are desperately trying to lose weight do not really have a single ounce of fat to spare."[23]

Sample size proved to be another issue. When compiling mortality and build tables, Dublin recorded that accurate assessments could only be made when 100 or more deaths had occurred.[24] For women over the age of fifty, policyholders who were 25 percent "underweight" reportedly had the lowest mortality risk;

however, by Dublin's own admittance, this was too small of a sample—only forty-eight deaths—for a conclusive finding.[25] Other studies did not have enough information on women policyholders for an accurate analysis. For example, a MetLife study observed Substandard policyholders over a twenty-five-year period. Those who reduced enough to qualify for the less expensive Standard policy, according to Dublin, lived as long as other Standard policyholders within the acceptable weight range. Dublin's data suggested that those who reduced their weight lived longer than those who remained overweight or obese. The goal of the study was to demonstrate that even a little bit of overweight was unhealthy. However, Dublin noted that his weight-reduction sampling was too small to draw conclusive results for women.[26] In the same way, only the experience of male lives in the reducing study was large enough to "warrant analysis" in the 1959 Build and Blood Pressure Study.[27] Despite inconclusive data, Dublin continued to claim that reducing helped mortality rates.[28] The findings for male Substandard policyholders were advertised as applicable to all, even though conclusive data regarding women was not available.

Perhaps most damning was Dublin's own recognition of the various flaws of his studies: "We readily admit, therefore, that we have not produced the definitive study on overweights," he reported at the annual ALIMDA conference in 1951. "In fact, it may not be possible to do this on the basis of insurance experience alone because our records contain only a few crude measurements, and these frequently are inaccurate."[29] Dublin himself admitted to erroneous and imperfect data, but only to his own colleagues. In popular magazines, however, he and the medical experts who regurgitated his findings failed to recognize the limitations and shortcomings of the studies.

Regardless of these limited demographics, sample sizes, and questionable recording methodologies, the public reporting of these studies' findings to the lay population was far too simplified and skewed. Unexpected findings that went against Dublin's fat bias led to a dangerous simplification in reporting. Simply put, Dublin did not find a direct correlation between fat and mortality. The percentage of overweight did not linearly increase one's risk of death. In fact, it suggested the opposite. Taken from the pages of Dublin's mortality study, for women of all builds under the age of thirty, "underweight" individuals had a higher mortality risk than those of average weight (99 percent) or even 5–14 percent (96.9 percent) and 15–24 percent (97 percent) overweight.[30] Only when a woman was 25–34 percent overweight did mortality risk (108 percent) exceed that of the average weights. This trend continued for women between the ages of thirty and thirty-nine. For women between the ages of forty and forty-nine, those with average weights had nearly the highest mortality rate (114.4 percent); only women 25–34 percent overweight were at a higher risk (116.9 percent). Women 5–14 percent and 15–25 percent overweight both had a significantly lower mortality rate than those of "average" weight (102.6 percent and 107 percent, respectively). Of this discovery, Dublin wrote, "We believe, however, that this finding is purely accidental. At any rate we have not been able to account for it."[31] Despite data that suggested otherwise, Dublin refused to believe that overweight women could be healthier than their average-weighing or underweight counterparts. For women fifty years old and older, the findings were similarly not linear. Although underweight women's mortality risks were slightly lower than the rate of the average-weighing woman, women 15–24 percent overweight had a similar mortality rate—94.6 percent for average and 98.1 percent at overweight. Only when a woman over the age of fifty was 25–34 percent overweight did the mortality risk spike significantly (149 percent).[32] Dublin's preconceived belief that fat was unhealthy biased the interpretation of his findings; when his data challenged his preconceptions, he called it "accidental," even though he and his colleagues could not account for these so-called "anomalies."[33] The 1959 Build and Blood Pressure Study also investigated weight ranges associated with the lowest mortality among men and women. They assigned policyholders to one of five body categories—marked underweights, slightly underweights and average, slightly overweights, moderate overweights, and marked overweights. Researchers discovered a downward trend in mortality among "slightly overweight" women, especially in the fifteen to nineteen age range. Only among "markedly overweight" women—those who exceeded 25 percent above the average weight—did they witness a sharp increase in mortality.[34]

A disconnect existed between the findings that only a specialized audience (i.e., other insurance actuaries and medical advisors) would have read and what they reported to general audience magazines. Like a game of "telephone," the studies' results became diluted with slight modifications even between the actual report and the summarized findings conveyed to other actuaries and medical advisers in professional journals. And when that information was disseminated to a mass population via the mass media, it became even more generalized. The largest problem proved to be the interpretation of results for men as representing all Americans. For example, in proclaiming that any level of elevated blood pressure increased one's mortality, the authors of the 1959 Build and Blood Pressure Study neglected to note in popular magazines that for *women's* blood pressure, only when it exceeded "substantial elevations" did mortality exceed 125 percent. In fact, they recorded a "distinctly lower mortality" for women among those with elevated blood pressure and those slightly or moderately "overweight."[35] Actuaries were concerned about the longevity of Americans, primarily men in their middle and later stages of life. For women and those under forty years old, a small amount of "overweight" showed the lowest mortality rate. But even though data for women was the inverse of findings for American men, this distinction was never mentioned. Instead, data for white, insured men over the age of forty was used as representative of the entire country.

So why should it matter that standardized height and weight tables were based on inaccurate data, which was then misreported to the public? Monetarily, insurance companies used these charts to determine if a potential policyholder should receive a Standard or Substandard policy, that is, if their weight indicated that they should be charged a higher premium because of an assumed health risk. Companies varied in their weight limits for Standard policies, but generally, a person rated "too fat" exceeded 25 percent above the average weight for their sex, height, and age.[36] Physical fitness books also used the findings of MetLife and the 1959 Build and Blood Pressure Study to encourage weight loss as a way to improve one's health.[37] But far more problematic was when popular magazines as diverse as *Sports Illustrated*, *Seventeen*, *Ladies' Home Journal*, and *Vogue* appropriated the tables for their readers to use in the fight against fat. Despite the desire for a uniform and hence "standardized" height and weight table, far too many outlets repurposed and customized the MetLife chart to make it their own. A number of periodicals directly copied the MetLife tables to help their readers set appropriate weight goals, but others completely made up their own "ideal" charts. Some reprints included the three body frame distinctions, while others only reprinted the desirable weights for the "medium" build designation. Some noted that weights were taken in indoor clothing and wearing shoes, while others offered no such designation. In 1959, *Sports Illustrated* republished the "Average Weights of Men and Women" chart from the Build and Blood Pressure Study. In an article titled "If This Fits You, You're Too Fat," the magazine cited the study's director, Dr. Edward Lew, as saying that the average American was twenty pounds "overweight."[38] What the study *actually* showed, however, was that 20 percent of American men, regardless of age or build, were "overweight." At the annual meeting of the ALIMDA in 1959, Lew told colleagues that for men past the age of thirty, the lowest mortality rate was associated with those who were twenty pounds below average weight. He went so far as to proclaim that for men currently twenty pounds heavier than the average male of the same height and age, "we would be on much sounder ground if we described him as weighing forty pounds more than he should."[39] *Sports Illustrated* used the opportunity to gloat, "We've been pointing out for a long time that keeping fit is an important pastime."[40] Comparing the weights of men from the Build and Blood Pressure Study with those weight ranges associated with lowest mortality, however, reveals a different conclusion to that of Lew's generalized report. At every height, weight, and age, the only average-weighing men whose weight put them at a higher mortality risk were those between the ages of forty and forty-nine at six feet to six feet two inches, and six-feet-two-inch men between the ages of fifty and sixty-nine.[41] Weeks later, when readers wrote in to challenge the findings and point out that the chart listed no body types, the magazine continued to uphold Lew's claim.[42]

Similar to the normative gender reporting of actuarial studies, the *Sports Illustrated* report also utilized statistics for American men as applicable to American women. In other words, if the typical American was twenty pounds too fat, then American women were too fat as well. But just as Lew's report that the average American man was twenty pounds too fat, the numbers for average weights and lower mortality risks did not match for women either. Take an example of a thirty- to thirty-nine-year-old woman who stands five feet, four inches in her shoes. On average, according to the Build and Blood Pressure Study shown in Table 3.1, this woman weighed 132 pounds. As Table 3.3 indicates, a woman at that height and age experienced the lowest mortality between 105 and 134 pounds. *Sports Illustrated* (Table 3.2) told this woman she was "too fat." The original study revealed, however, that she was just within her most healthful range.

TABLE 3.1 "Desired" weights of women twenty-five years and older, 1942 and 1959 (weight in pounds according to frame)

Height (in shoes)	Small frame 1942	Small frame 1959	Medium frame 1942	Medium frame 1959	Large frame 1942	Large frame 1959
5'0"	105–113	96–104	112–120	101–113	119–129	109–125
5'1"	107–115	99–107	114–122	104–116	121–131	112–128
5'2"	110–118	102–110	117–125	107–119	124–135	115–131
5'3"	113–121	105–113	120–128	110–122	127–138	118–134
5'4"	116–125	108–116	124–132	113–126	131–142	121–138
5'5"	119–128	111–119	127–135	116–130	133–145	125–142
5'6"	123–132	114–123	130–140	120–135	138–150	129–146
5'7"	126–136	118–127	134–144	124–139	142–152	133–150
5'8"	129–139	122–131	137–147	128–143	145–158	137–154
5'9"	133–143	126–135	141–151	132–147	149–162	141–158
5'10"	136–147	130–140	145–155	136–151	152–166	145–163
5'11"	139–150	134–144	148–158	140–155	155–168	149–168
6'0"	141–153	138–148	151–163	144–159	160–179	153–173

Statistical Bulletin of the Metropolitan Life Insurance Company, 1942 and 1959.

TABLE 3.2 "If this fits you, you're too fat"[43]

Height (in shoes)	Woman's age						
	15–16	17–19	20–24	25–29	30–39	40–49	50–59
4'10"	97	99	192	107	115	122	125
5'0"	103	105	108	113	120	127	130
5'2"	111	113	115	119	126	133	136
5'4"	117	120	121	125	132	140	144
5'6"	125	127	129	133	139	147	152
5'8"	132	134	136	140	146	155	160
5'10"	–	142	144	148	154	164	169
6'0"	–	152	154	158	164	174	180

Sports Illustrated, November 2, 1959, 33.

TABLE 3.3 Weight ranges associated with lowest mortality among females[44]

Height group	20–29	30–39	40–49	50–59
Short	95–104	115–134	105–114	105–134
Medium	115–134	105–134	105–134	105–144
Tall	115–134	115–144	125–144	145–164

Society of Actuaries, Build and Blood Pressure Study, 1959.

Physicians and Fat

Insurance companies, statisticians, and actuaries could not have created a fear of fat without the support of the medical community. And, unique to this period, Americans trusted doctors as experts more than ever before. In a 1969 study regarding trusted sources for knowing how much a person should weigh, insurance company height and weight tables was the top response and the family doctor came in at number two.[45] Insurance men and doctors agreed: being "overweight" shortened one's life and weight loss lengthened it. But doctors concurred with actuary reports not because their own findings resulted in similar conclusions; instead, medical "experts" relied primarily on the actuaries' flawed data. In their own reports to the public, doctors and scientists continually referred to the MetLife and the Build and Blood Pressure studies rather than seeking out independent sources. Representatives from the National Institutes of Health (NIH) specifically cited the MetLife studies' correlation between "overweight," mortality, and chronic health problems in a number of popular magazines.[46] Using a kind of double-speak, Dr. W. H. Sebrell, Jr., director of the NIH and US Public Health Service, noted that "although there is no proof that obesity is the cause of high blood pressure, heart disease, diabetes, and a shortened lifespan, it is associated with all of these."[47] Another medical authority admitted, "We know about as much about overweight as Hippocrates in ancient Greece knew about fever, namely, that in general it seems to be bad."[48] Moreover, the etiology of this "disease" was not always agreed upon. Theories fluctuated between overeating (calorie intake exceeding calorie output), genetics (thyroids, naturally low metabolism), and psychological disorders. In a study of one hundred physicians, the investigators found that "informal experience" rather than "formal medical training" was doctors' primary source of information about the treatment and etiology of "overweight." Moreover, doctors ascribed more negative characteristics to their "overweight" patients—ugly, weak-willed, and awkward—than to their "normal"-weighing patients.[49] Without medical experts to advise them, the American public turned to self-proclaimed experts—fad dieticians and insurance company statisticians. Although they admitted to knowing little on the topic, doctors continued to reassure the public that "underweight" was far more preferable to "overweight."

The medical community was not in universal agreement, however, about the clinical application of actuarial studies. Dr. John Hutchinson, medical director for the New York Life Insurance Company and one of the authors of the 1959 Build and Blood Pressure Study, had mixed advice about the implications of the study. He pointed to evidence that weight reduction resulted in lower mortality, but he worried that the study might result in pressure on doctors to prescribe treatment for their overweight patients, especially the youth.[50] Years later, Hutchinson echoed his misgivings, saying, "the absolute size of some of these variations [in mortality risk] is at times so small, particularly in young people and in association with borderline blood pressures, that they should not be used as criteria for active therapy."[51] Hutchinson urged his fellow doctors to not use actuarial findings to inform treatment for their overweight patients. Other studies directly challenged the causal link between "overweight" and mortality. Dr. Lester Breslow, chief of the Bureau of Chronic Diseases for the California State Department of Health and consultant for Eisenhower's President's Commission on Health Needs of the Nation, conducted a study of nearly 4,000 overweight San Francisco Bay area longshoremen between 1951 and 1956. In his study, he discovered that the men's extra weight did not bring on higher mortality from disease or other causes. Quite the opposite: he found a lower incidence of heart disease and other mortality risks in his study sample than for all California males in comparable age groups. Breslow concluded that the linkage of "overweight" and mortality from heart disease could not be applied equally to all groups. Despite weighing more (Breslow's group was on average 17 percent above Dublin's life insurance standards for weight, and 360 of the 4,000 men were 40 percent or more overweight), the dockworkers' weight did not negatively impact mortality.[52] These kinds of isolated tests, however, were not enough to topple Dublin's widely touted studies.

When Louis Dublin reconfigured the MetLife Standardized Tables using the results of the 1959 Build and Blood Pressure Study, Dr. Carl C. Seltzer warned about the change. Noting that the midpoint of the ranges of "desirable" weights was significantly lower than the average American weights, Seltzer, a member of the Department of Nutrition at Harvard University's School of Public Health, recognized that the use of height–weight categories and the concept of "underweight" and "overweight" was useful for insurance underwriting purposes, but he challenged its reliability for medical and public health uses.[53] Seltzer, instead, proposed an alternative system of measures to replace the height and weight charts. In a reevaluation of the Build and Blood Pressure Study, he suggested measuring one's *ponderal index* (height in inches over the cube root of weight in pounds) instead of height and weight data. When recalculating the 1959 findings using ponderal index, rather than finding a straight-line relation (i.e., the more overweight a person is, the higher their mortality), as the insurance mortality summaries suggested, Seltzer found an *exponential curvilinear relation* in which an excess in mortality ratio did not exist until one's ponderal index was in excess as well. Therefore, rather than determining that *any* amount of "overweight" was dangerous, Seltzer claimed that only those with what he called "frank obesity" had a high mortality rate. His final recommendation was to replace the tables of "ideal" or "desirable" weights with measurements of skinfold thickness in relation to body frame.[54] Measuring tricep skinfold thickness had first been suggested by Seltzer and Dr. Jean Mayer a year before this evaluation.[55] Drs. Seltzer and Mayer became two of the more outspoken and widely published medical experts who called for a more objective definition of "obesity," who fought against the direct causation between "overweight" and disease, and who continually challenged the reliability of statistics and actuarial data in determining mortality risks. A team of medical advisors commissioned by the US Department of Health, Education, and Welfare, which included Mayer, stressed that standardized height and weight charts were not appropriate measures of fatness as these kinds of comparisons assessed weight, not fat. They wrote, "The limitations of the insurance data make it impossible to accept the statistics as unequivocal evidence that obesity predisposes to early mortality."[56] Instead, a ratio of bone structure, musculature, and fat, along with the distribution of fat, was recommended.[57]

But even the most progressive doctors still had their fat phobia. Mayer, then assistant professor of nutrition at Harvard University, and Dr. Ancel Keys, director of the Laboratory of Physiological Hygiene at the University of Minnesota, were asked to serve as members of *Vogue* magazine's "Dieting Authority." Interestingly, *Vogue* invited two of the most outspoken doctors against weight reduction to answer questions such as "How does the woman who wants to lose 10 pounds lose them?" and "How fast is it possible to take off that 10 pounds?" When asked how a woman can know she is "a little too fat," Keys and Mayer offered no objective answer. Keys suggested removing one's clothing and looking in the mirror. "It may be a ghastly sight," he noted, "but the woman who is honest with herself can see whether or not she is too fat." To the same question, Mayer responded, "If somebody looks fat then she usually is fat, and if she doesn't look fat, then she isn't."[58] These are obviously problematic answers, especially for women with poor body esteem, comparing themselves with the models who appeared in *Vogue*. In a later issue of the magazine, Keys called life insurance height–weight tables "unscientific" and "misleading." He disagreed with the widely held belief that excess weight was unhealthy. Yet he emphasized he did not approve of or encourage being fat. "Obesity is esthetically repugnant," he told *Vogue*'s readers. "It is uncomfortable and impedes motion; it is hard on clothes and furniture."[59]

Dr. Ancel Keys introduced the body mass index (BMI) in 1972 in the hope of providing a more reliable indicator of one's fat level to supplant height and weight tables and the ponderal index. Measuring one's BMI had first been suggested by the original height–weight architect, the Belgian statistician Lambert Adolphe Jacques Quételet. Similar to height and weight charts, BMI soon became a misused tool to indicate one's level of "overweight" or "obesity." Keys, who coined the phrase "body mass index," intended for the measure to be used for entire *populations* and warned against its use on an individual basis. Yet today, BMI continues to be the most widely used indicator of fatness and has largely replaced the height and weight tables.[60]

Starting in the mid- to late 1960s, members of the medical community began to reconsider the reliability of insurance data. Men like Drs. Jean Mayer and Carl Seltzer, advocates for the ponderal index and tricep skinfold thickness measurements for "overweight" and "obesity," and Dr. Ancel Keys, who modernized the BMI, challenged the use of standardized height and weight tables. Dr. Paul Scholten, former president of the San Francisco Medical Society, proclaimed, "It is time for the medical profession to point out that moderately plump persons can be in excellent health and to allow patients to eat just about anything they want within reason." Challenging actuarial data that suggested even a little bit of "overweight" was dangerous, he contended, "We can allow ourselves to be plump and contended, rather than neurotic over a few extra pounds."[61] But, equally, the warnings or the allowances of the medical community would not be enough in and of themselves to convince Americans to take off the weight or, conversely, to leave it on.

The "obesity epidemic" gained new importance in the postwar years over fears that Americans were growing bodily and mentally soft and could therefore be more easily influenced by Communist propaganda. On July 11, 1955, Dr. Hans Kraus and Bonnie Prudden presented the findings of a fitness test at a White House luncheon attended by professional athletes and high-ranking government officials, including President Dwight Eisenhower. Results from the Kraus-Weber Tests for Muscular Fitness, which compared American and European students and their ability to perform activities such as leg lifts and sit-ups, revealed that 8 percent of European children failed just one of the six test components; 56 percent of American children failed at least one, and usually more.[62] In the wake of these disturbing results, President Eisenhower called for the Conference on the Fitness of American Youth, which resulted in the creation of the President's Council on Youth and Fitness. This research had a significant impact in the context of the times. A decade after the conclusion of World War II, less than one year after the Korean War, and with former General Eisenhower as president, the Kraus-Weber test raised concerns regarding youth physical fitness levels and readiness for military service. Not only national pride but national security seemed to be on the line. Russia's commitment to athletics appeared very prominently on the world stage at the Winter Olympic Games in 1956. It was a relatively poor showing by Americans while the Soviets dominated, even though it was their very first year competing in the Winter Games. When the Soviet Union proceeded to win the Summer Olympics in that same year, it was a blow to the American psyche and considered the greatest pro-Communist victory since the conclusion of World War II. America had previously held a monopoly on overall medal count since the 1920 Summer Games, with only one exception—in 1936, to Germany. The government's attention to weight and health fed the ever-growing panic that the country was suffering from an "obesity epidemic" far worse than what insurance companies and the medical community had originally suggested. "We've been called 'soft' and our children have been described as physically unfit, inferior in strength and stamina to children of other countries," the *Ladies Home Journal* warned. "Our technology has created a physical void."[63] In a postwar era defined by excess and mass consumption, middle-class America needed to exhibit restraint, not in the consumption of products, but bodily restraint from food and drink.

Conclusions

Louis Dublin devoted his professional life to the public health and longevity of the American people. He concerned himself not only with "overweight," but also with heart disease, suicide, children's welfare, tuberculosis, and accident rates, among many other topical areas. And while the data upon which he relied was flawed, Dublin was only one of many statisticians and medical advisers who perpetuated the belief that fat was in direct correlation to heightened mortality risks. These men aided the dieting neurosis that exploded, particularly among women, in the 1950s, but they certainly were not the only force dictating the use of extreme tactics to reduce pounds. The dominance of the fashion industry combined with the fall of Hollywood had its own role in this.

Insurance actuaries and members of the medical community created a pseudo-biological ideal to promote well-being and to lower the rates of mortality for American men and women. For insurance companies, this was partly an altruistic endeavor, espousing worries about the health of older Americans, but the creation of height and weight tables was originally conceived to ascertain who was less of a health risk to insure. It also benefitted the bottom line to categorize more policyholders as "overweight" or "obese," as these individuals would be awarded Substandard policies—coverage in which the insured person has less than an average life expectancy and therefore must pay more for their insurance plan. Hollywood and the fashion industry created a second standard—a cultural ideal that, in hindsight, appears more stringent than the biological tables. As one scholar has noted, the existence of two ideals is not necessarily problematic, as long as the population understands the differences and behaves accordingly.[64] Unfortunately, however, the pursuit of cultural ideals often trumps the biological, resulting in body image dissatisfaction and, as this chapter has demonstrated, the creation of a biological standard was not without its problems.

In the years immediately following World War II, the gap between the biological and cultural ideal was minimal. Although high-fashion models had always been uncommonly slender, the figures of the most popular Hollywood stars, cover girls, and pin-up models showed little deviation from standardized height–weight tables. At 5 feet, 5½ inches tall, both Marilyn Monroe and Doris Day's 120-pound figures were just under the "desired" weight for a woman with a medium build and were on target for someone with a small frame. This changed in the 1960s. In a 1969 study, high-school girls reported their "desired" weight and their "proper weight"—how much they wanted to weigh versus the weight they thought correlated to good health. The study's authors then compared those numbers with what they currently weighed. On average, the teen girls weighed 126.2 pounds. Their "desired" weight was 115.3 pounds, while they reported a "proper" weight of 118.6 pounds. Both the ideal and what they felt health-wise they should weigh were significantly different than the same measurements for the boys at their school. Teenage girls desired to be more than ten pounds thinner than their current weight while their male counterparts wanted less than a five-pound weight difference.[65] Even though the MetLife height–weight table was reconfigured again in 1959 toward a more slender biological ideal, the divide between culture and reality became more pronounced in the latter half of the 1960s. That cultural-biological gap has steadily widened in the twenty-first century.

Notes

1. A study of nearly 600 high-school boys and girls in a middle- to upper-class suburban Boston community demonstrates the popularity and believed reliability of such tables, even as late as 1969. Coming in at the number one response, 38 percent of teen boys and 33 percent of teen girls indicated they knew how much they should weigh because of insurance company height and weight charts. J. T. Dwyer, J. J Feldman, C. C. Seltzer, and J. Mayer, "Body Image in Adolescents: Attitudes Toward Weight and Perception of Appearance," *Journal of Nutritional Education* 1, no. 2 (Fall 1969): 14–19.
2. Sander L. Gilman, *Obesity: The Biography* (New York: Oxford University Press, 2010), x.
3. *Medico-Actuarial Mortality Investigation, Volume 1* (New York: The Association of Life Insurance Medical Directors and the Actuarial Society of America, 1912), 11–12. For more on the earliest tables, see Amanda M. Czerniawski, "From Average to Ideal: The Evolution of the Height and Weight Table in the United States, 1836–1943," *Social Science History* 31, no. 2 (2007): 273–279.
4. *Medico-Actuarial Mortality Investigation*, 11–12.
5. Louis Dublin and Herbert H. Marks, "Mortality Among Insured Overweights in Recent Years," *Transactions of the Association of Life Insurance Medical Directors of America*, Annual Meeting 35 (1951): 236.
6. J. Eric Oliver, *Fat Politics: The Real Story Behind America's Obesity Epidemic* (New York: Oxford University Press, 2005); Roberta Pollack Seid, *Never Too Thin: Why Women Are at War with Their Bodies* (New York: Prentice Hall Press, 1989); Marilyn Wann, *Fat! So?: Because You Don't Have to Apologize for Your Size* (Berkeley, CA: Ten Speed Press, 1998).
7. "Insurance Hall of Fame," np. Biographical Data, Box 1. Louis I. Dublin papers. 1906–1968. Modern Manuscripts Collection, History of Medicine Division, National Library of Medicine, Bethesda, MD; MS C 316.
8. Biographical information from the Dublin papers, Modern Manuscripts Collection, History of Medicine Division, National Library of Medicine, Bethesda, MD; MS C 316, and Edward A. Lew's obituary in *The American Statistician* 23, no. 2 (April 1969): 33.
9. Dublin, "The Battle Against Disease," *Harper's Magazine*, February 1944, 239; Dublin, "Overweight, America's No. 1 Health Problem," *Today's Health*, September 1952, 18.
10. Dublin, "Huge Tasks Lie Ahead," *Bismark, N.D. Tribune*, September 19, 1944, np.
11. Dublin, "Women are Different," *Your Life*, December 1950, 23–27.
12. Donald B. Armstrong, Louis Dublin, George M. Wheatley, and Herbert H. Marks, "Obesity and Its Relation to Health," *Journal of the American Medical Association* 147, no. 11 (1951): 1007–1014.
13. Louis Dublin, "Fat People Who Lose Weight Live Longer," *Nutrition Symposium Series* 6 (1953): 106–122.

14 Society of Actuaries, *Build and Blood Pressure Study, Volume 1* (Chicago, IL: Society of Actuaries, 1959), 2, 16. Stratified sampling involves the division of a population into smaller groups, known as strata. The most common strata used in stratified random sampling are age, gender, socioeconomic status, religion, nationality, and educational attainment. Researchers have higher precision with this technique in comparison with simple random sampling, and the researcher can sample the smallest subgroups in the population, in this case, insured women.
15 Ibid., 18.
16 Dublin and Marks, "The Build of Women and Its Relation to Their Mortality: A Preliminary Report," 48th Annual Meeting of the Association of Life Insurance Medical Directors of America, October 28–29, 1937, 5.
17 "New Build and Blood Pressure Study—A Preview" *Record of Society of Actuaries* 4, no. 4 (1978): 859.
18 Dublin and Marks, "The Build of Women and Its Relation to Their Mortality: A Preliminary Report," 48th Annual Meeting of the Association of Life Insurance Medical Directors of America, October 28–29, 1937, 10.
19 Ibid., 5.
20 Ibid.
21 Society of Actuaries, *Build and Blood Pressure Study, Volume 1* (Chicago, IL: Society of Actuaries, 1959), 21.
22 Ibid., 23.
23 Whitney Darrow, Jr., "The Wasteful, Phony Crash Dieting Craze," *Life,* January 19, 1959, 104.
24 Dublin and Marks, "The Build of Women and Its Relation to Their Mortality: A Preliminary Report," Read at the 48th Annual Meeting of the Association of Life Insurance Medical Directors of America, October 28–29, 1937, 16.
25 Ibid., 13.
26 Dublin and Marks, "Mortality Among Insured Overweights in Recent Years," *Transactions of the Association of Life Insurance Medical Directors of America,* Annual Meeting 35 (1951): 235-265.
27 Society of Actuaries, *Build and Blood Pressure Study, Volume 1* (Chicago, IL: Society of Actuaries, 1959), 117.
28 Dublin and Marks, "Mortality Among Insured Overweights in Recent Years," *Transactions of the Association of Life Insurance Medical Directors of America* 35 (1951), 254, 259.
29 Ibid., 261.
30 Numbers in parentheses represent mortality risk percentage. Numbers over 100 percent indicate a higher health risk. Numbers below 100 percent indicate less chance of dying.
31 Dublin and Marks, "The Build of Women and Its Relation to Their Mortality: A Preliminary Report," 48th Annual Meeting of the Association of Life Insurance Medical Directors of America, October 28–29, 1937, 17.
32 Ibid., 13.
33 Ibid., 17.
34 Society of Actuaries, *Build and Blood Pressure Study* (Chicago, 1959), 76–77; John J. Hutchinson, "Clinical Implications of an Extensive Actuarial Study of Build and Blood Pressure," *Annals of Internal Medicine* 54, no. 1 (January 1961): 91.
35 "The Build and Blood Pressure Study," *Transactions of Society of Actuaries* 11, no. 31 (1959): 987–988; John J. Hutchinson, "Highlights of the New Build and Blood Pressure Study," *Transactions of the Association of Life Insurance Medical Directors of America,* Annual Meeting 43 (1959), 34–42.
36 John J. Hutchinson, "Clinical Implications of an Extensive Actuarial Study of Build and Blood Pressure," *Annals of Internal Medicine* 54, no. 1 (January 1961): 94.
37 Victor F. Obeck and Isadore Rossman, *Isometrics: The Static Way to Physical Fitness* (New York: Stravon, 1966), x.
38 "If This Fits You, You're Too Fat," *Sports Illustrated,* November 2, 1959, 33.

39 John J. Hutchinson, "Highlights of the New Build and Blood Pressure Study," *Transactions of the Association of Life Insurance Medical Directors of America*, Annual Meeting 43 (1959), 39.
40 "If This Fits You, You're Too Fat," *Sports Illustrated*, November 2, 1959, 33.
41 Society of Actuaries, *Build and Blood Pressure Study, Volume 1* (Chicago, IL: Society of Actuaries, 1959), 17, 47.
42 "19th Hole: The Readers Take Over," *Sports Illustrated*, November 16, 1959, 97.
43 "If This Fits You, You're Too Fat," *Sports Illustrated*, November 2, 1959, 33.
44 Society of Actuaries, *Build and Blood Pressure Study, Volume 1* (Chicago, IL: Society of Actuaries, 1959), 52.
45 J. T. Dwyer, J. J Feldman, C. C. Seltzer, and J. Mayer, "Body Image in Adolescents: Attitudes Toward Weight and Perception of Appearance," *Journal of Nutritional Education* 1, no. 2 (Fall 1969): 14–19.
46 "Obesity is Now No. 1 U.S. Nutritional Problem," *Science News Letter*, December 27, 1952, 408; "Obesity Called Waste of Manpower and Food," *Science News Letter*, June 16, 1951, 377; "Danger of Being Too Fat," *U.S. News and World Report*, November 2, 1951, 19–21.
47 "Obesity Called Waste of Manpower and Food," *Science News Letter*, June 16, 1951, 377.
48 Whitney Darrow, Jr., "The Wasteful, Phony Crash Dieting Craze," *Life*, January 19, 1959, 104.
49 George Maddox and Veronica Liederman, "Overweight as a Social Disability with Medical Implication," *Journal of Medical Education* 44 (1969): 214–220.
50 "The Build and Blood Pressure Study," *Transactions of Society of Actuaries* 11, no. 31 (1959): 992, 997.
51 John J. Hutchinson, "Clinical Implications of an Extensive Actuarial Study of Build and Blood Pressure," *Annals of Internal Medicine* 54, no. 1 (January 1961): 96.
52 "Study Challenges Obesity-Mortality Link," *Science Digest*, November 1957, 16.
53 C. C. Seltzer, "Limitations of Height-Weight Standards," *New England Journal of Medicine* 272 (May 1965): 1132.
54 Carl C. Seltzer, "Some Reevaluations of the Build and Blood Pressure Study, 1959, as Related to Ponderal Index, Somatotype, and Mortality," *New England Journal of Medicine* 274 (February 1966): 254–259.
55 Carl C. Seltzer, Ralph F. Goldman, and Jean Mayer, "The Triceps Skinfold as a Predictive Measure of Body Density and Body Fat in Obese Adolescent Girls," *Pediatrics* 36, no. 2 (August 1965): 212–218.
56 US Department of Health, Education, and Welfare, *Obesity and Health: A Source Book of Current Information for Professional Health Personnel* (Washington, DC: US Government Printing Office, 1966), 30.
57 Ibid., 1–6.
58 "Announcing *Vogue*'s Diet Authority," *Vogue*, February 1956, 64–67, 132–134.
59 Melva Weber, "Health," *Vogue*, May 1, 1974, 101.
60 Ancel Keys, Flaminio Fidanza, Martti J. Karvonen, Noboru Kimura, and Henry L. Tayler, "Indices of Relative Weight and Obesity," *Journal of Chronic Disease* 25 (1972): 329–343.
61 "Shed Guilt, Not Pounds, Doctor Advises Fatties," *Los Angeles Times*, August 6, 1973, 3.
62 Bonnie Prudden, *Is Your Child Really Fit?* (NY: Harper & Brothers, 1956), 7–11.
63 Patricia and Ron Deutsch, "These Five were Cured of Overweight," *Ladies Home Journal*, March 1963, 131.
64 E. O. Smith, *When Biology and Culture Collide: Why We Are Stressed, Depressed, and Self-Obsessed* (New Brunswick, NJ: Rutgers University Press, 2002), 63.
65 Johanna T. Dwyer, Jacob J. Feldman, C. C. Seltzer, and Jean Mayer, "Body Image in Adolescents: Attitudes Toward Weight and Perception of Appearance," *Journal of Nutrition Education* 1 no. 2 (1969): 15.

4

RE-SHAPING AMERICA

The Reducing Neurosis

> *Mama won't let me diet anymore ... This morning I was having my usual half grapefruit for breakfast and she made me eat a slice of whole wheat bread and a scrambled egg and a piece of bacon. That's probably at least 400 calories, maybe even five or six or seven hundred ... I wonder if I could stick my finger down my throat and throw up after every meal? She says I'm going to have to start eating dinner again too, and just when I was getting down where I want to be and I've quit fighting the hunger pains.*
> —Go Ask Alice (1971)

The anonymous author of the published diary *Go Ask Alice* is obsessed with her weight. Her journal is not only a recounting of her daily activities, but of how much weight she has gained or lost. The fifteen-year-old girl avoids chocolate and french fries and equates her new popularity at school with the ten pounds she has recently lost. When she has whittled her frame down to 115 pounds, the teen author wistfully notes her desire to lose an additional 10 pounds. "Mom says I don't want to get that thin," she writes, "but she doesn't know! I do! I do! I do!"[1] Joan Jacobs Brumberg observes that, since the 1960s, the diaries of adolescent girls repeated the same concerns: "I've been eating like a pig," "I've got to lose weight," or "I must starve myself."[2] This seemingly typical teenage reaction was symptomatic of the heightened preoccupation with weight management starting in the early 1950s that affected American white women of all ages, turning into a national obsession.

"Build-Up" Diets

In a reversal of the rhetoric that appeared in periodicals in later decades, women's magazines and beauty guides published in the years immediately following World

War II did not emphasize starving oneself on a reducing diet. Instead, prescriptive literature urged women to build up their bodies to become sturdy, vigorous machines. Historians have long noted the proliferation of propaganda that urged American women to return to their roles as mothers and housewives, but this does not acknowledge that, at the conclusion of the war, women continued to receive messages that their efforts were needed to rebuild the nation. "These days," one beauty guide observed, "women need all their strength to stand up to the strenuous calls upon their system, and food is the only thing to provide that strength."[3] This message was a continuation of wartime attitudes about the female body. "Strictly Personal," an official US War Department training film, stressed the importance of exercise, a balanced diet, and ample sleep to female military volunteers. The omnipresent narrator announces in the film's opening minutes, "In perfect physical shape; yes that's what it takes to do the man-sized job you've picked for yourselves when you volunteered."[4] Even the MetLife Company, while warning of the dangers of "overweight," recommended a balanced diet in the early wartime years, noting the inefficiency of a reducing diet that also reduced one's health.[5] Delicate waifs would not help America win the war, and neither could they help restore the nation after the global conflict. Exercise and a nutritional diet also became coping strategies for young women dealing with the loss of a husband or boyfriend to war. The *Ladies Home Journal* told the story of a recent widow whose unhappiness had shrunk her figure to less than 100 pounds. Rather than allowing her GI husband's premature death to signal the end of her own life, however, she rebounded and rebuilt her figure.[6]

Rather than providing guidance on reducing diets, women's magazines and fan periodicals in the immediate postwar years addressed the plight of "underweight" women. "You don't have glamorous curves; your chest is flat; your legs are like toothpicks; your neck is scrawny," the beauty editor for *Screen Stars* described. "You feel masculine, like a boyish figure, when you want so much to feel feminine."[7] While this look became fashionable in the late 1960s, in the years immediately following World War II, women's magazines celebrated a different body type. "A chubby, well-groomed figure is always attractive," another author advised her female readers.[8] Italian bombshell Sophia Loren gushed to reporters in 1948 how her 38–24–38 figure had not always been so plentiful. She claimed to have been unpopular, scrawny, and unadmired growing up—her playmates taunted her, calling her "The Stick." The actress claimed that a steady diet of spaghetti helped her gain her famous curves, and that by age fifteen, all the men were whistling at her.[9] Because of the popularity of curvy silhouettes, "underweight" women sought ways to add extra pounds. An advertisement for NUMAL, a vitamin that supposedly encouraged appetite, reminded its female readers, "A skinny, scarecrow figure is neither fashionable nor glamorous. Remember, the girl with the glamorous curves gets the dates."[10] Prescriptive literature advised housewives on the best kinds of exercises and food to help them stay energized and "build up" their bodies. Exercise regimes focused on stretching and strengthening muscles without the use of bulky weights; most articles highlighted exercises one could perform to strengthen muscles while simultaneously doing the daily housework.[11]

Magazines for young girls similarly encouraged their readers to develop healthy eating and exercising habits at an early age, but *not* to actually diet. "Don't be alarmed by those little bumps and bulges because it is much better at your age to be 'round' than too 'skinny,'" one author encouraged.[12] *Polly Pigtails* and *Calling All Girls*, the predecessor to *Young and Modern* (*YM*) magazine, reminded readers that they would be growing several inches in the coming years and that their bodies would grow more easily with some fat reserves. "Doctors do not recommend dieting for your age," a journalist noted. "In fact, if you are twelve or under, they say it is even harmful."[13] *Calling All Girls*, created by the publishers of *Parents* magazine in the autumn of 1941, had little interest in reflecting teenage life; its goal was to encourage healthy habits and set a good example for young readers. Instead of printing pages of diet plans, these magazines urged their readers to be physically active and to eat nutritionally balanced meals. Teen magazines published stories geared toward helping the too-skinny girl as late as 1963.[14] This same pro-body and nutrition-conscious attitude, however, disappeared from women's magazines in the mid-to-late-1950s.

Weight management gained momentum in postwar media due to the widely held belief that fat was literally killing America. Louis Dublin and his cohorts aimed their anti-fat crusade at the general public, publishing in news magazines like *Life*, *Reader's Digest*, and the *New York Times Magazine*, but it was women, not men, who responded to their words of warning.[15] *Reader's Digest* reported that thirty-four million adults considered themselves "too fat" in 1954, but noted that women were more eager to lose weight than men.[16] In that same year, a Gallup poll discovered that twice as many women worried about their weight than men did and one in three of them dieted, compared with one in seven men.[17] Dublin himself noted, "Apparently the campaigns for weight control, to which women have clearly responded, have had much less impact on men."[18] In postwar America, heart-related diseases became the number one killer of American men over the age of thirty. Insurance actuaries and medical experts had long connected heart disease to "overweight" and "obesity." For women, however, cancer, not diseases of the heart or circulatory system, caused the most deaths.[19] In other words, the population least at risk of heart disease became the most desperate to reduce. Moreover, the motivations for female dieting had little to do with health. A Roper poll reported in 1959 that 66 percent of women dieted to "make their clothes fit better" or to avoid "look[ing] heavy."[20] In a 1967 study of high-school girls, 43 percent dieted because of personal discontent with body appearance and beauty. Only 3 percent reduced for health.[21] "Dior has often succeeded where health education has failed," Dr. Jean Mayer wistfully lamented.[22] Health warnings in and of themselves were not enough to persuade Americans to change their eating habits. Instead, an all-consuming discourse in prescriptive literature, namely women's magazines, demanded thinness above all for fashion and beauty, while the life insurance and medical communities continued to equate health with size.

Slimming Down—A Losing Business

Because of these prescriptive pressures, the reducing industry became a viable economic giant in the 1950s. Between 1950 and 1955, diet soda drink sales increased by 3,000 percent. Low-calorie soft drinks sold fifty thousand cases a year in 1952 and expanded to fifteen million by 1959. Although a reducing diet implies eating *less* food, the food industry profited as well. More than 200 firms produced an estimated quarter of a billion dollars' worth of low-calorie foods every year.[23] A new line of diet foods by Flotill Products, Inc. of California ran a full-page ad in the *New York Times* the day after Thanksgiving in 1951, and the Borden Company, producers of dried skim milk, reported sales of 60 million pounds of nonfat dried milk in that same year, up from only 5 million in 1949.[24] Food substitute products like the chalk-powder drinks Metrecal and the "Rockefeller Diet" were introduced in the 1950s as well. Metrecal's earnings grew from $4 million in the late 1950s to $13 million in 1960.[25] By 1959, ninety-two diet books were in print, and by 1961, 40 percent of all Americans used reduced-calorie products.[26]

In addition to the millions of dollars spent on diet foods and books, reducing support groups, youth "fat camps," and exercise salons became *de rigueur* in the 1950s and 1960s. One of the first national diet support groups, TOPS (Taking Off Pounds Sensibly), originated in Milwaukee, Wisconsin, in 1948. Its creator, Esther S. Manz, first came to the idea while participating in a group session designed to help pregnant women prepare for motherhood. Recognizing the power of mutual support, Manz transitioned the group mentality into a dieter's helpmate.[27] TOPS grew from a club of three friends to an organization with 2,481 chapters by the early 1960s.[28] Other dieting groups like Weight Watchers immediately followed. Weight Watchers grossed $160,000 in 1964; in 1970, business had skyrocketed to earnings of over $8 million.[29]

National weight-reducing chains joined the ranks of high-end reducing salons that had appeared in most major cities by the early 1950s. Three of the most popular were Elizabeth Arden, Slenderella International, and Helena Rubinstein's salons. At Arden's salon, clients were exposed to a number of weight-loss techniques such as dieting, massage, posture correction, and exercise. Machines like the "Shake-A-Way" table were advertised to whittle down too-fleshy hips and thighs. While lying down on a table, two series of rollers "rolled away" at solid fat. Arden's salons were also equipped with the Dewar machine, a spot-reducing contraption that used electronic impulses on the muscles.[30] For those with deeper pocketbooks, Arden also offered a "Maine Chance" facility in Maine and Arizona where, for $400 to $600 a week, women learned to "live in sumptuous starvation." Participants wore blue swimsuits as their daily uniform to encourage the goal of shedding a pound a day. Arden described it as a "magic isle where cares and worries vanish."[31]

The popularity of Elizabeth Arden's "Maine Chance" facilities encouraged the construction of others, like the $2 million Palm-Aire in Florida, the Greenhouse in Texas, and the Golden Door in California. These were not "fat farms" or "fat camps," however. Most women who attended the pricey vacation spas had little weight to lose. When Judy Klemesrud, a writer for the *New York Times*, attended the Palm-Aire health spa for six days, she discovered that most of the women she met had three things in common: bleached blonde hair, middle age, and only a "minor" weight problem. "This latter fact surprised me," she noted. "I had come expecting to be a sylph among slobs; instead, I felt the latter."[32] Health spas were joined by other "fat vacations" like Chandris American Lines, a cruise ship designed for passengers to lose weight, and "The Last Resort Diet," where patrons were promised a ten to twenty pound weight loss over a week of fasting at Pawling Health Manor in Hyde Park, New York.[33] One true "fat camp," Green Mountain Weight Control Community for Young Women, started in 1972 in Poultney, Vermont. Green Mountain was one of the few summer weight-loss facilities of its kind for adult women. Campers earned college credit for the experience and stayed four weeks at a cost of $900 or eight weeks for $1,650. Different from health spas like "Maine Chance," Green Mountain's clients focused on nutrition education and rigorous physical activity, with an attempt to modify eating and exercise behaviors.[34]

Another "exercise" company, Slenderella International, promised its patrons that their program could slim a girl in "all the right places." Formed in 1951 by Missourian Larry Mack, Slenderella operated 170 salons in fifty US cities at its peak and grossed $25 million by 1956.[35] Advertisements for the salon defied beliefs that physical health and a trim figure demanded "toil and suffering." Similar to the Elizabeth Arden salons, Slenderella promoted the use of a specially patented machine with rollers designed to "pound away" unwanted inches. While soft music played in the background, vibrating flat leather couches massaged patrons. The company claimed one forty-minute session at two dollars equaled a ten-mile horse ride or thirty-six holes of golf, and that afterward one's shoulders would be straightened, waistline slimmed, and muscles toned and firmed, with improved circulation and relaxation. In addition to these "reshaping" benefits, Slenderella also included a high-protein diet plan for women who desired to lose additional weight. The company claimed that the meal plan was not only enjoyable, but "thoroughly livable." Patrons were also given a supply of vitamin and mineral "mints" to be ingested five times a day to suppress appetite.[36]

For thirty dollars, women could experience "One Day of Beauty" at Helena Rubinstein's salon. Less an exercise facility than even those available at Elizabeth Arden and Slenderella, Rubinstein's salon better resembled a spa retreat where women were cosmetically pampered. Patrons benefited from a private counseling session on diet and exercise and received a supply of Helena Rubinstein "Reduce-Aids," a vitamin-based pill to inhibit appetite. The Rubinstein franchise also offered a "Glamour School," a two-hour-a-day program where, for five days and at the price of twenty-five dollars, women received a condensed version of charm school with instruction on femininity and poise.[37] The selling point for most reducing salons and health spas was minimal effort on the part of the client. "The trouble with exercise is—it's often so much trouble," one women's magazine lamented.[38] The solution was vibrating devices and roller-tables where women relaxed while a machine purportedly did all the work.

For those who preferred the privacy of their homes for passive exercise, for the price of nearly $200, Relax-A-Cizor created the solution. Relax-A-Cizor, like Elizabeth Arden's Dewar system, utilized electricity to promote muscle contraction. The small black vibrating case with pink dials, belts, and other gadgets made its way into 200,000 homes by 1958.[39] Users of these products were instructed to attach small wires to the "problem" areas. Dialing up the appropriate charge of electrical pulse resulted in the erratic and involuntary contracting and relaxing of targeted muscles. One could effortlessly "exercise" at home while reading a magazine or watching a television program.[40] First advocated in 1909 by radiologist Jean-Alban Bergonié, electrification was believed to stimulate the body for overall health and serve as a surrogate for exercise.[41] The Better Business Bureau estimated that the American public spent between $2 and $10 billion for this kind of "medical quackery." The US Post Office concurred, noting that reducing schemes were the most lucrative of such mail-order schemes.[42] Medical and technological advances in plastic surgery certainly precipitated the desire for effortless weight loss as well. Hollywood plastic surgeon Robert A. Franklyn bemoaned to *Esquire* how often he received female patients who weighed over 200 pounds, yet who desired to fit into size 12 dresses. Predicting the impending invention of liposuction, Franklyn noted that rather than make any real effort to lose weight, "they would rather have their stomachs sliced off in a single go."[43]

Vibrating belts, roller-tables, and electrodes were not the only bizarre exercise schemes to come out of the postwar period. Beauty experts widely believed that, by simply pounding away at inches of unwanted fat, the problematic areas would flatten and become streamlined. Even rubbing fleshy areas with a rough bath towel was thought to help "rub away the superfluous inches."[44] Joan Bennett, an actress and beauty contributor for *Screen Stars*, religiously encouraged her readers to roll across the floor 50 to 100 times every morning to reduce inches from their hips and derrieres. Another exercise that she called "the thumper" consisted of lying on the floor, using one leg as a lever to raise the body and dropping back down on fatty spots. She also recommended picking up marbles with the toes every day for twenty minutes to build up calf muscles.

Another passive exercise regime—isometrics—became popular in the early 1960s. Invented by two German scientists in 1953, isometrics is exercise in which the muscles exert force against an immovable object or against themselves without movement. And, like the bumping and rolling machines that preceded it, proponents of the "scientific exercise" promised potential users that they could "exercise without moving a muscle." The benefits of isometrics over isotonic exercise (physical activity) was heralded in periodicals as diverse as *Vogue* to *Sports Illustrated*.[45] The appeal of passive exercise is obvious, but medical doctors also possessed a general misunderstanding and underappreciation for isotonic (active) exercise. Dr. Herbert Pollack, a consultant to the Secretary of War, the US Public Health Service, the Surgeon General, and the Department of the Army, most famously observed that a person had to walk thirty-five miles to lose a single pound.[46] Calling isotonic exercise "of very little value," Dr. James M. Hundley, chief of the Laboratory of Biochemistry and Nutrition at the National Institutes of Health, perpetuated that statement, claiming that the only way to reduce was to limit food intake.[47] Even the American Medical Association, as late as 1970, encouraged reducing diets over exercise.[48] Medically sponsored statements that labeled isotonic exercise as ineffective impacted the way Americans attempted to lose weight. In 1950, 14 percent of weight-watchers exercised. That number dropped to 4 percent in 1953. Gallup polls recorded that the majority of Americans who dieted did so through pills, thyroid medicine, and being mindful of food intake.[49]

Passive exercise appealed to American women not only because of the promise of results with little to no effort. Women also avoided isotonic exercises like active sports, jogging, or weight lifting because of the worry that too much would transform their bodies into bulky, masculine, and muscled figures. At least part of this can be attributed to the influence of the Iron Curtain and the beginnings of the Cold War. A fat, passive nation would be unable to compete with or combat Communism. But because Soviet women were active and strong, American women had to be the opposite. Because of this, postwar magazines held a tenuous position in celebrating professional and amateur female athletes.

The Female (Feminine) Athlete

At the beginning of the twentieth century, the debate about women's involvement in sports centered on the potential for exercise to impair a woman's reproductive capacity and to unleash a woman's sexuality. In the 1920s and 1930s, that debate shifted to fears about athletics making women "mannish" and unattractive. This anxiety came to an apex by the 1950s, turning into fears of lesbianism in athletics.[50] One of the most important beauty goals for women after World War II, regardless of body shape or size, was to establish and protect their femininity. For example, an advertisement for "Royal Typewriter" featured a secretary who worried her arms were getting too muscular because of the physical effort it took to work with her ancient typewriter.[51] Experts debated how much exercise was *too* much and female athletes looked for a way to safeguard their femininity and their heterosexuality all while striving to excel in their respective sports.

In October 1954, *Sports Illustrated* asked a panel of "experts" if competitive sports made women less feminine. Marilyn Monroe admitted that she admired the muscles of female athletes, but her husband Joe DiMaggio countered, "Would a man rather take a lovely bit of femininity into his arms or a bundle of muscles?" Italian movie star Gina Lollobrigida agreed that some physical activity made a girl "healthy and graceful," but shunned more "hard" sports because "muscles are good in the kitchen. But they are maybe not good in the evening gown." Another "expert," Louis Pieri, noted that femininity flourished with "masculine protection." The National Hockey League (NHL) general manager continued, "A woman who can trade strokes on the tennis court with most men, for instance, doesn't look like she needs protection."[52] In order to combat the negative stereotype that athletics made women unattractive and masculine, print media celebrated female athletes more for their beauty than their physical accomplishments.

Sports Illustrated, first published in August 1954, frequently profiled female athletes at two ends of the age spectrum—those over sixty years old, or in their early teens. Profiles on junior and senior swimmers, tennis players, and golfers emphasized their record-breaking abilities, not how pretty they were. The magazine indicated it was admissible for young teens and matronly grandmothers to be competitive and singularly focused on sports, but not on women of childbearing age. For the few women in their twenties or thirties that appeared in the magazine, adjectives like "pretty" and "pert" preceded their names, diminishing the seriousness of their athletic accomplishments. Moreover, even the titles of articles highlighting women's achievements often belittled their victory. In 1959, Barbara McIntire won the fifty-ninth women's amateur golf championship. *Sports Illustrated* titled the corresponding column "Miss Dimples Wins the Cup."[53] Rare was the story celebrating a woman in this age category as a pure athlete without referencing her femininity and beauty.

Life magazine portrayed female athletes as competitive, but similarly emphasized their femininity over their physical prowess. Gretchen Merrill, a champion figure skater, was a "winsome, thoroughly feminine and beautiful girl." A fashion organization had even named her the "best dressed woman in U.S. sports."[54] One headline qualified swimmer Jeanne Wilson as "the fastest, prettiest female breaststroke swimmer in the U.S." and gymnast JoAnn Matthews, no doubt in reference to Russia's female competitors, purportedly looked "more like a woman than a woman athlete."[55] Many women whose photographs appeared in the magazine were not necessarily champions in their sports, but instead represented the prettiest stars. Although only ranking fourth nationally in the tennis world, Gertrude Augusta "Gussie" Moran garnered an article in *Life* based on her "lively green eyes, [and] the face and figure of a movie starlet." The author's article boasted, "If good looks could be translated into points on the tennis court, the girl above would probably be the Wimbledon champion this summer."[56] Moran became one of the most famous tennis stars at the time, not for her prowess on the court, but for her undergarments. Moran shocked the tennis world at Wimbledon in 1954 when she showed up for her second match wearing lace-edged panties under her tennis skirt. "[F]rom that day on I found more attention being focused on my backside than on my backhand," the athlete recalled.[57]

Although periodicals like *Life* and *Sports Illustrated* largely avoided stories that showed American female athletes looking less than feminine, the magazines showed a near obsession with Soviet women in the same sports. Numerous photo essays of the "hardy" Russian women appeared in these periodicals. Columns simultaneously masculinized female Russians while making male competitors effeminate, to demonstrate the backwardness of Communism. Editors claimed the female competitors were the "stronger Soviet sex" and that "frail Red males" owed their team victories to their female teammates.[58] These were women to be pitied, however, rather than emulated. One photograph and caption observed that training was so intense that athletes were not allowed to go on dates and therefore danced with each other in the evenings.[59] In contrast to the way Eastern European female athletes were portrayed compared with their American competition, *Sports Illustrated* reported that while the Russian and Hungarian female gymnasts outmatched the "agility and graceful precision" of their US competitors, the American women "drew photographers in droves" and "rated medals in good looks."[60] The column's language and tone privileged neither national team, as though being attractive was equally as valid as actually winning the competition. The media's coverage of physically imposing Communist women while simultaneously celebrating the femininity of American women athletes may seem counterintuitive. Susan J. Douglas notes that because of America's fervent fear of Communism, "*our* women had to be very different from *their* women."[61] She continues, "It was because all their women were dead ringers for Mr. Potato Head that we knew their society was, at its heart, joyless, regimented, and bankrupt."[62] Because of the mixed messages women received from the media about participation in active sports, they looked for less physical ways to lose weight that would not threaten their femininity.

"Lazybones" Weight Loss: Reducing Diets and Diet Pills

"Build-up" diets of the late 1940s and early 1950s focused on energy, health, and vigor as the goal of shaping up. American women wanted to be slim, no doubt, but the definition of "slenderness" changed by the end of the 1960s. The most crucial difference between the immediate postwar years and the beginning of the 1960s was the dieter's goal. In the early to mid-1950s, the ideal woman still had flesh on her bones. For example, the average contestant in the 1954 Miss America Pageant weighed 121 pounds and measured five feet 6.1 inches tall—around 11 pounds less than the national average and just a little below MetLife Insurance's "desirable" height and weight tables.[63] The culture of slimming culminated with the androgynous high-fashion model, Twiggy, in the late 1960s. Therefore, it is more useful to see Twiggy's body type as a bookend rather than a dramatic, overnight change in the aesthetic ideal.

In addition to a new dieter's goal, by the mid- to late 1950s, a new attitude toward weight loss appeared in women's magazines. Prescriptive literature turned away from promoting exercise—active or passive—as a legitimate means to lose weight in favor of easy, effortless diets. Starting in 1958, *Harper's Bazaar's* "Lazybones Diet" promoted a curtailed eating regime in which dieters were urged to spend the Friday-to-Sunday period in complete idleness. The magazine promised a weight loss of two or two-and-a-half pounds over a "quiet summer weekend." The instructions required that "slot is mandatory," due to the daily 800–1,000 caloric intake, which left little energy available to exercise safely.[64] The role that women's magazines played in popularizing fad diets cannot be overstated. Dr. Vincent P. Dole of Manhattan's Rockefeller Institute for Medical Research and creator of the Dextrose diet wrote about his drinkable diet in the *American Journal of Clinical Nutrition*, but it only gained notoriety when mass advertised in *Look* magazine. Another Dole diet, a formula made of corn oil, evaporated milk, and dextrose, appeared in the *Ladies' Home Journal* and was touted in *Vogue* as the "peasant diet." Sales of dextrose at one chain store increased from 400 to 800 pounds a month.[65]

Women's high-fashion magazines like *Harper's Bazaar* and *Vogue* analyzed some of the most extreme, stringent diets of the period. The "Egg and Wine" diet became the latest crash diet popular in the summer of 1964. Designed as a weekend plan to slip off a few pounds in a few days, weight watchers consumed wine and an egg dish at every meal. The wine, erroneously believed to be an amphetamine, would act as an appetite inhibitor. Moreover, the alcohol content made the dieter not care about only eating eggs. The "Starvation Diet" pulled no punches with its name. Dieters burned fat through fasting, consuming nothing but water and vitamin pills. In another extreme diet, the "Rice Diet," participants ate only rice and vegetables garnished with neither butter nor salt. Originally conceived of at Duke University, the first "Rice Diet" testers were required to stay on campus and could only eat their meals at designated "Rice Houses" for observation. The human chorionic gonadotropin (hCG) injection was another controversial diet aid. For thirty to forty days, dieters visited their doctor to receive an injection of hCG, a hormone produced during pregnancy, and were given a strict daily diet of 500–700 calories. It is unclear whether followers lost weight because of the hormone injection or from the abbreviated diet, but the American Medical Association argued that the injection was neither a safe nor an effective way to achieve weight loss.[66]

Most diets reprinted in the various women's and fashion magazines were intended for women who desired to lose five to ten pounds. The extreme calorie cutting, such as that of the "Lazybones Diet," was only recommended for brief spurts of time—a few weeks at most—with some diets then suggesting a secondary "maintenance" diet for when the desired weight loss had been achieved. But no distinctions were ever made between diets for women who wished to shed a few pounds or dieting strategies for women who wanted to lose fifty to a hundred pounds. The majority of women who frequented exercise salons and health spas, similarly, were not "obese." More problematic, while exercise salons, in-home machines, and fad diets advertised the relative ease with which weight loss could be achieved, this fed dangerously into the negative stereotype that "overweight" or "obese" people were lazy and unmotivated. Anyone, these products claimed, could lose weight. America supposedly suffered from an "obesity epidemic" and yet the largest circulated media of diet advice—women's magazines—failed to highlight the realities and difficulties of losing large amounts of weight.

America's obsession with easy weight loss came to an apex with a diet pill scandal in the late 1960s. Diet pills and appetite suppressants were certainly not new. Advertisements for the popular diet pill Ayds promised that users could eat everything they wanted; sales for the "vitamin candy" quadrupled between 1949 and 1955.[67] Ayds was promoted as a "specially made, low calorie candy fortified with health-giving vitamins and minerals." Just by eating one candy prior to every meal, users "automatically" ate less and could lose weight "naturally, safely, and quickly."[68] What was unique in the late 1960s, however, was the mass number and types of pills being prescribed, and consequently the number of "medical doctors" making a generous living off of the rainbow-colored tablets. The Food and Drug Administration (FDA) estimated that between five thousand and seven thousand "fat doctors" treated five to ten million patients every year, sold more than two billion diet pills, and achieved gross earnings close to half a billion dollars.[69]

In 1968, *Life* magazine published an exposé on the diet pills craze. The article began with the story of Cheryl Oliver, a college coed who worried about her weight and ultimately died from taking a lethal combination of diet pills. Commonly prescribed drugs for weight loss included amphetamines to suppress appetite, barbiturates to counter the jitters the amphetamines could cause, thyroid to increase the rate that the body burns calories, the heart drug digitalis, diuretics to flush water from the body, and laxatives. Using diet pills she had received in the mail, Oliver, at age nineteen, went from 160 pounds to 120. The medical examiner attributed the teen's death to an excessive loss of potassium in her body and digitalis poisoning.[70] In the wake of this tragic story, *Life* sent investigative reporter Susanna McBee undercover to ten "obesity" doctors. At the time, McBee was five feet, five inches tall and weighed 125 pounds. According to Met Life's "desirable" weight tables, the reporter was at an ideal weight, and even a little on the skinny side of the spectrum.[71] Of her own body, she stated, "No one has ever called me fat. A little on the hippy side perhaps. But never fat. I am a reliable size 10." Over a six-week period, McBee visited a number of osteopaths and other "fat doctors," posing as a woman who wanted to lose weight. The reporter expected to be rejected by all the health-care professionals as she was neither "overweight" nor "obese." To her surprise, however, all ten doctors welcomed her business and in fact congratulated her for "catching the problem" early on. Among the doctors McBee visited, there was no consensus on diet or exercise. Moreover, she noted that the preliminary physical examinations she received ranged from exotic tests to merely a weight and measurement assessment. "There was consensus though," she wrote, "on one point: pills, pills, pills." Between the ten doctors she visited, McBee was prescribed 1,479 pills.[72]

The Senate Antitrust Subcommittee, headed by Senator Philip Hart of Michigan, began hearings in late January 1968 on what was considered to be a major scandal in American medicine—the "obesity" business. McBee, the undercover *Life* magazine staffer, was a key witness along with several of the doctors whom she had exposed in her investigative report. Most of the doctors defended dispensing the hundreds of rainbow-colored pills to McBee. And even after the *Life* expose, readers wrote to the magazine with continued praise for the potentially deadly pills. One woman who had reduced her body from 198 pounds to 135 pounds wrote, "I would rather live my present, happy, full life for half as long than to prolong a miserable, self-hating half-life of a fat woman." She claimed that due to her weight loss she was now popular and had acquired a new job that doubled her income.[73] For women such as her, the supposed payoff was far too great a temptation, even if her health was jeopardized.

The American love affair with diet pills in the mid- to late 1960s was indicative of the overall change in exercise and diet literature. Although previous reducing salons had advertised what little actual work one had to do, a new emphasis on effortless weight loss appeared in the 1960s. Short-cut slimming attempts were certainly not created during this period, but they did become more of a visible trend in women's magazines. By the late 1960s, even articles that had once reassured teen girls that they would grow into their bodies or that they should eat three balanced meals a day had all but disappeared. Drawing on the protest vernacular of the day, *Seventeen* magazine suggested readers could hold a "Thin-In." The event's guest list would include girls on diets ("and who isn't?" the 1968 magazine pointed out). Decorations would include large pictures of very thin models, entertainment was an exercise period, and food included low-calorie snacks.[74] Similarly, in *'Teen* magazine, a young girl wrote in to the periodical's beauty editor to ask advice about what style of pants she should wear if her lower body was heavy. Instead of suggesting a flattering cut, the *'Teen* editor responded, "We suggested buying any favorite pant style—one or two sizes too small. Or spend your entire month's allowance on a pantsuit that's too small, and you'll find a new supply of willpower for diet and exercise."[75] While teen magazines in the 1940s and 1950s had once urged their readers to build a positive relationship with their bodies, by the 1960s they now mirrored the message of periodicals aimed at an older generation—slenderizing at all costs.

Conclusions

The word "diet" has not always been associated with losing weight, but phrases like "reducing diet" now seem redundant and "build-up diet" has become oxymoronic. Women's magazine articles that had once featured strategies to "build up" bodies were systematically replaced by slenderizing techniques in the early years of the 1950s, congruent to Louis Dublin's pronouncement that "overweight" was killing Americans. Just as the ideal body shape transitioned from a woman with curves to an androgynous and shapeless silhouette in the postwar years, the strategies to obtain the model figure changed as well. Guide books and women's magazines encouraged moderate physical activity and a nutritionally balanced diet in the years immediately following World War II to create energized, "built-up" women ready to guide the nation into peacetime. By the early to mid-1950s, however, advice columns tilted toward weight-loss and slenderizing tactics.

Actuaries and medical doctors headed the war against fat. Aided with statistics, Louis Dublin and others worked to make a correlation between "overweight" and early death; insurance companies and doctors seemed to agree that being heavier than Dublin's standardized height–weight tables would lead to a premature death. Dublin's reports ultimately decreed, however, that no one was ever *too* thin. But it was American women, not men, who took up the mantle in the war against fat. Partly for vanity and less for health concerns, women looked to periodicals for weight-loss advice. Little-effort weight-loss schemes such as crash diets, diet pills, and passive exercise salons appealed to a postwar American population rapidly becoming accustomed to instant gratification and immediate results. Promises of effortless weight loss not only sold these products but also continued the damaging myth that fat people were lazy. "Overweight" and "obese" women were not only seen as unattractive; in a country whose historical foundations praised a solid work ethic, perceived indolence was not a desirable trait.

Notes

1 Anonymous, *Go Ask Alice* (New York: Simon and Schuster, 1971), 7.
2 Joan Jacobs Brumberg, *The Body Project: An Intimate History of American Girls* (New York: Random House, 1997), 119.
3 Stacy Lett Waddy, *Posture and Poise* (Sydney: Dymock's Book Arcade, 1944), 10.
4 "Strictly Personal," United States Army Pictorial Service, 1945. U.S. National Library of Medicine. Digital Collections, http://collections.nlm.nih.gov/vplayer/vplayer.jsp?pid=nlm:nlmuid-9422795-vid. Accessed January 26, 2017.
5 "Ideal Weights for Women," *Statistical Bulletin of the Metropolitan Life Insurance Company*, October 1942, 6–8.
6 Louise Paine Benjamin, "Build-Up Diet," *Ladies Home Journal*, January 1945, 105.
7 Joan Bennett, "Yours for Beauty," *Screen Stars*, December 1951, 63.
8 Maureen Daly, "The Trouble with Women …" *Ladies Home Journal*, August 1946, 8.
9 Kathryn Tate, "The Stick," *Motion Picture*, 1948, 7.
10 Advertisement, "Skinny Girls Are Not Glamour Girls," *Screen Stars*, August 1951, 5.
11 Louise Paine Benjamin, "Three-Way Perspective," *Ladies Home Journal*, April 1945, 140.
12 Ann Williams-Heller, "Why So Fatso?" *Polly Pigtails*, Spring 1953, 97.
13 Victoria Furman, "Everybody's Thin But Me," *Calling All Girls*, March 1963, 34.
14 Rubie Saunders, "Skinny You," *Calling All Girls*, October 1963, 103.
15 Lynn Luciano's *Looking Good: Male Body Image in Modern America* (New York: Hill and Wang, 2002) recognizes that men were not indifferent to their bodies, but printed media indicated that women in postwar America—specifically wives—were responsible for their husband's health. Louis Dublin ("Stop Killing Your Husband!" *Readers Digest*, July 1952, 107) accused American women of "killing" their husbands by cooking meals that contributed to weight gain, by putting undue stress on them to "keep up with the

Jones," and by being too thrifty to hire professionals to take care of household chores that resulted in overweight husbands falling off of ladders.
16 "Meet the Typical American—Male and Female," *Reader's Digest*, February 1954, 34.
17 Gerald Walker, "The Great American Dieting Neurosis," *New York Times Magazine*, August 23, 1959, 12; June 1959—Roper Commercial #111—Food and Eating Habits Primarily of Women.
18 "New Weight Standards for Men and Women," *Metropolitan Company Statistical Bulletin* 40 (November–December 1959): 1–4.
19 Society of Actuaries, *Build and Blood Pressure Study, Volume 1* (Chicago, IL: Society of Actuaries, 1959), 12–13.
20 Peter Wyden, *The Overweight Society* (New York: Willow Marrow, 1965), 9.
21 Johanna T. Dwyer, Jacob J. Feldman, and Jean Mayer, "Adolescent Dieters: Who Are They? Physical Characteristics, Attitudes and Dieting Practices of Adolescent Girls," *American Journal of Clinical Nutrition* 20, No. 10 (1967): 1045–1056.
22 Jean Mayer, "Overweight and Obesity," *The Atlantic* 196, no. 2 (1955): 71.
23 Gerald Walker, "The Great American Dieting Neurosis," *New York Times Magazine*, August 23, 1959, 12.
24 "Insurance Ads Pave the Way for Dietary and 'Health Foods,'" *Business Week*, December 6, 1952, 46.
25 Roberta Pollack Seid, *Never Too Thin: Why Women Are at War with Their Bodies* (New York: Prentice Hall Press, 1989), 106.
26 Walker, "The Great American Dieting Neurosis," *New York Times Magazine*, August 23, 1959, 12; Stearns, Peter N. Stearns, *Fat History: Bodies and Beauty in the Modern West* (New York: New York University Press, 1997), 109.
27 "History of TOPS," *TOPS*, http://www.tops.org/tops/TOPS/History2.aspx?Website Key=a56ba4c3-a91c-4d57-b04a-b38d910feec5. Accessed January 26, 2017.
28 Seid, *Never Too Thin*, 107.
29 Stearns, *Fat History*, 109.
30 "Remaking Your Measurements," *Vogue*, January 15, 1957, 112.
31 "Billions of Dollars for Prettiness," *Life*, December 24, 1956, 123; "The Pink Jungle," *Time*, June 16, 1958, 86–90.
32 Judy Klemesrud, "The Fat Farms—Or, How to Come Home a Real Loser," *New York Times*, January 23, 1972, xx1.
33 Klemesrud, "From New York to the Bahamas on the Low-Calorie Cruise," *New York Times*, October 18, 1972, 52; Klemesrud, "A Week at a Health Manor on the Last Resort Diet: Fasting," *New York Times*, October 29, 1974.
34 Klemesrud," Don't Call It a Fat Camp," *New York Times*, August 4, 1975, 34.
35 Walker, "The Great American Dieting Neurosis," *New York Times Magazine*, August 23, 1959, 12; "Billions of Dollars for Prettiness," *Life*, December 24, 1956, 124.
36 "Program for the Measure of a Beauty," *Harper's Bazaar*, May 1955, 140; "The Pink Jungle," *Time*, June 16, 1958, 86–90.
37 "Remaking Your Measurements," *Vogue*, January 15, 1957, 111.
38 "The Lazy Woman's Guide to Exercise," *Vogue*, March 1, 1954, 80.
39 "The Pink Jungle," *Time*, June 16, 1958, 90.
40 "Remaking Your Measurements," *Vogue*, 55–56, 111.
41 Sander L. Gilman, *Obesity: The Biography* (New York: Oxford University Press, 2010), 87.
42 Steve Singer, "When They Start Telling You It's Easy to Lose Weight," *Today's Health*, November 1972, 47–49.
43 Robert A. Franklyn, "Confessions of a Plastic Surgeon," *Esquire*, June 1951, 111.
44 Stacy Lett Waddy, *Posture and Poise* (Sydney: Dymock's Book Arcade, 1944), 48.
45 "Beauty Bulletin: The Shape Terrific," *Vogue*, February 15, 1964, 120–124; Gilbert Rogin, "Get Strong Without Moving," *Sports Illustrated*, October 30, 1961, 19–21.
46 Whitney Darrow, Jr., "The Wasteful, Phony Crash Dieting Craze," *Life*, January 19, 1959, 112.

47 "Danger of Being Too Fat," *U.S. News and World Report*, November 2, 1951, 20.
48 *Sports and Physical Fitness; JAMA Questions and Answers from 1965–1969 Issues of the Journal of the American Medical Association* (Chicago, IL: Journal of the American Medical Association, 1970).
49 Summer 1950 Poll #1950-0457: *Life*, February 1953.
50 Susan K. Cahn, *Coming On Strong: Gender and Sexuality in Twentieth-Century Women's Sports* (Cambridge, MA: Harvard University Press, 1998).
51 Advertisement, *Life*, January 8, 1945, 33.
52 "Hot Box," *Sports Illustrated*, October 11, 1954, 4–5.
53 "Miss Dimples Wins the Cup," *Sports Illustrated*, December 7, 1959, 34.
54 Oliver Jensen, "Champion Figure Skater: Gretchen Merrill Excels in a Graceful and Complicated Sport," *Life*, March 4, 1946, 65–66.
55 "Breast Stroke: Underwater Photographs Show How Pretty Jeanne Wilson Wins Races," *Life*, April 15, 1946, 51; "Tumbling Queen: A Pretty 98-Pound Girl from Texas is Country's Best Flip-Flap Artist," *Life*, June 14, 1948.
56 "Gorgeous Gussie: Now No. 4 Ranking Tennis Player Would Be No. 1 if Looks Counted," *Life*, April 25, 1949, 91.
57 Deirdre Budge, "Something for the Girls …" *Sports Illustrated*, September 27, 1954, 35–36.
58 "The Stronger Soviet Sex," *Life*, September 18, 1950, 60–61.
59 "'Toil and Sweat' Win Out Over 'Amusement': Hardy Soviet Girls Sweep International Ski Meet," *Life*, January 5, 1954, 128–129.
60 "Wonderful World of Sports," *Sports Illustrated*, January 7, 1957, 38.
61 Susan J. Douglas, *Where the Girls Are: Growing Up Female with the Mass Media* (New York: Times Books, 1994), 47, italics original.
62 Ibid., 22.
63 Miss America statistics in Frank Deford, *There She Is: The Life and Times of Miss America* (New York: Viking Press, 1971), 313–316, 325.
64 "Lazybones Dieting," *Harper's Bazaar*, July 1958, 81.
65 "Crazy About Reducing," *Time*, August 6, 1956, 32.
66 "Beauty Bulletin: 7 Top Diets Explored and Rated by Vogue," *Vogue*, October 1964, 180.
67 "The Big Bulge in Profits," *Newsweek*, July 23, 1955, 61.
68 "Too Fat? Here's an Easy Way to Reduce Says Barbara Hale," *Screen Stories*, April 1953, 25.
69 "Scandal of the Diet Pills," *Life*, January 26, 1968, 22–23.
70 Ibid.
71 At five feet five inches, the "desirable weight" for women aged twenty-five and over was 118–127 pounds for a small frame, 124–139 pounds for a medium frame, and 133–150 pounds for a large frame.
72 Susanna McBee, "A Slender *Life* Reporter Visits 10 'Fat Doctors,'" *Life*, January 26, 1968, 24–27.
73 "Editorial," *Life*, February 16, 1968, 18A.
74 "Streamlines," *Seventeen*, September 1968, 184.
75 "Dear Beauty Editor," *'Teen*, August 1966, 53.

5
WHAT MEN WANT
Men's Magazines and the Girl-Next-Door

> *There's something wrong, either psychologically or glandularly, with some guy who isn't interested in pictures of pretty girls*
>
> —Hugh Hefner[1]

In the 1950s, while mainstream magazines like *Collier's*, *Saturday Evening Post*, *Look*, and *Life* all struggled with subscription numbers, magazines aimed at a white male readership flourished. At their apex, fifty different periodicals not only existed in print, but they also sold in the hundreds of thousands to a significant portion of the male population.[2] *Playboy* magazine, created in 1953, grew to be the eleventh highest-selling periodical in the United States in the postwar years.[3] Men's magazines addressed a number of topics, but one theme overwhelmed all other subjects—the American Woman. Periodicals such as *Playboy*, *Esquire*, and other lesser-known monthlies offered a unique and previously unexamined source regarding female body image in postwar America. While periodicals aimed at white women largely spoke through a united voice about a specific body image, men's magazines catered to a variety of tastes and anxieties when it came to the "softer sex." In numerous and critical ways, the "ideal woman" presented in men's magazines departed dramatically from the beauty goals promoted in women's magazines. In arguing that women's body ideals are imposed on women by women, early fat historian Anne Scott Beller has noted that the models in men's magazines and calendar art concern more "biometrically realistic images and ideals."[4] But although this was a departure from the waifish high-fashion model found on the cover of white women's magazines, the ideal celebrated in men's magazines was not necessarily a realistic alternative.

The Evolution of Men's Magazines and the Girl-Next-Door

The Godfather of men's magazines in the early twentieth century was *Esquire*. Originally published in October 1933, *Esquire* adopted a masculine agenda that embraced consumption, sexuality, style, and taste.[5] With a layout committed to men's fashion, highbrow fiction, and a limited amount of "cheesecake" photography, *Esquire* appealed to the reader who identified with or inspired to be middle or upper class. In similar fashion to *Playboy* magazine decades later, pin-up photography and racy cartoons helped *Esquire* avoid claims that its content was too effeminate. Despite the magazine's mass popularity, *Esquire*'s editorial approach remained singular among a multitude of other men's periodicals. Magazines like *True*, *Flirt*, *Beauty Parade*, and *Glamor Parade* [*sic*] appealed to a male working-class readership, less interested in men's fashion and fiction. Instead of highbrow fiction, these publications offered readers adventure stories. Rather than examining the latest in business-suit fashion, men were instructed how to buy a high-quality hunting rifle or where to find the best fishing.

The creators of workingmen's magazines discovered their pin-up models in burlesque revues and nightclub shows and on casting couches. Pictorials featured women's wrestling, elaborate costumes, and spanking, each catering to specific fetishes rather than trying to appeal to a generalized audience. Models wore binding corsets, fishnet stockings, and skyscraper high heels, with long hair falling well below their cinched waists. Because legs evaded censorship, as Dian Hanson explains, "[they] were exaggerated and glorified, covered in fishnets and propped on the highest heels."[6] But with the creation of *Playboy* magazine in 1953, the fishnets and precariously high-heeled women in magazines like *Beauty Parade* began to look dated. Moreover, readers eventually tired of seeing the same models featured. While perennial pin-ups like Bettie Page or Marilyn Monroe continued to "play havoc with any male's hormone balance," the same cast of actresses and models had found their way into virtually every men's magazine.[7] As Hanson observes, "the bad girls had to give up pages to the Girl Next Door."[8]

Hugh Hefner was not new to the publishing world when he created *Playboy* magazine. In fact, his experience working at various men's magazines inspired him to create what he saw as a unique venture. As a promotional copywriter for *Esquire*, Hefner received an early education from a magazine that favored style, fashion, and intellect in a men's periodical. But when *Esquire* transferred its headquarters to New York City, Hefner stayed in Chicago.[9] He then worked for Publisher's Development Corporation, a publishing house that produced a number of "girlie" magazines, including *Art Photography*, *Modern Sunbathing*, *Sunbathing Reviews*, and *Modern Man*. *Modern Man* was typical of most men's magazines of the early 1950s, focusing on the outdoors as the "male" domain with fishing trips, golf outings, and camping. Due to censorship fears, partially clothed models appeared in these magazines under the guise of high art or articles about photography lessons. Hefner wanted to reclaim the indoors for men. *Playboy*'s first issue, published in

December 1953, sold over fifty-four thousand of its seventy thousand print run.[10] In the magazine's mission statement, Hefner boldly admitted that this periodical was not meant to be a "family magazine." He urged, moreover, that unsuspecting females who picked up the magazine by mistake should pass it along to a man "and get back to your *Ladies' Home Companion*."[11] Eventually, the midwestern man created an empire of "Bunnies" with *Playboy* clubs across the world and even his own late night talk show, *Playboy's Penthouse*, in 1959.

Hefner wanted to get away from the pin-up traditions found in other men's magazines. Rather than finding his Playmates in strip clubs and on casting couches, *Playboy*'s creator sought his centerfolds in everyday life. As Mark Jancovich observes, Hefner worked to "humanize the pin-up concept."[12] The editorial staff strove to assure its readership that potential Playmates did not just exist in the fantasy play-world of Hollywood. Cheesecake photographer Lisa Larsen observed in 1950, "The best way to capture a man's imagination, it seems to me, is to picture reality for him, rather than some figment of a dream world."[13] Starting with Terry Ryan in December 1954, *Playboy* began revealing the name (albeit usually a false stage name) of the woman featured in its pictorial and listed her occupation and hobbies.[14] Black-and-white photos that accompanied the centerfold showed the Playmate performing everyday activities—a format that would be copied by later facsimile magazines. Historian Elizabeth Fraterrigo observes, "The resulting images suggested that 'nice' but somehow sexually self-aware 'girls' disrobed for *Playboy's* cameras, while the accompanying text affirmed that the Playmate existed not in a world apart from the reader, but all around him."[15] Following the December pictorial, with a few celebrity exceptions like Bettie Page and Jayne Mansfield, the magazine's Playmates were overwhelmingly "average" young women. Playmates held various occupations as common as legal secretary or librarian, but the majority were advertised as dancers, models, or aspiring actresses. In July 1955, *Playboy* looked no further than its own administrative offices to find that month's Playmate when they photographed Janet Pilgrim, an employee in their circulation department. The accompanying article boasted, "potential Playmates are all around you: the new secretary at your office, the doe-eyed beauty who sat opposite you at lunch yesterday, the girl who sells you shirts and ties at your favorite store."[16] Pilgrim, "efficient as she is good looking," quickly won the affection of the periodical's readership and continued to be featured in centerfolds as well as pictorial stories over the next few years.

The magazine went to great lengths to highlight how one could find his or her own Playmate. In a clearly staged article, magazine photographers met one young woman, Barbara Cameron, while shopping at a record store. After asking her to pose for nude photography, the magazine noted Cameron's wistful reply: "It would be fun, she admitted, but she couldn't, really she couldn't." Upon turning the page, however, the reader is immediately rewarded with a photograph of Cameron in the buff, apparently having finally surrendered her inhibitions. She is pictured in the shower, a towel around her midsection, her breasts bare but not in direct view of the camera, as if the photographers merely followed her home for the impromptu photo shoot.[17] When readers wrote in, skeptical that the magazine had "convinced" Cameron, the editors responded, "Those are the facts, friend. We just happen to be getting good at talking the nicest of girls into posing as Playmates. Any objections?"[18] If a reader was not convinced that posing nude was proper for an all-American girl, then *Playboy* reassured its readers by describing the blessings of Playmate parents. Janet Pilgrim's mother reportedly first objected to her daughter appearing in the magazine. But—according to the magazine—after seeing the final photo spread, she was taken aback by how beautiful the pictures were and sent copies of the issue to friends and relatives.[19] Miss January 1958, Elizabeth Ann Roberts, was accompanied by her mother to her scheduled photo shoot. Luckily for Hugh Hefner and the magazine, her mother fully approved of the photography—apparently even signing a permission slip—when it was later discovered that Roberts was not yet eighteen years old.[20]

Playboy prided itself on finding average, wholesome girls to grace its pages and readers approved of the "freshness" of their models. "Your February Playmate, Cheryl Kubert, would look sexy in a sleeping bag," one reader applauded. "[Jayne] Mansfield has to resort to nudity. Please stop featuring big-bosomed, expensive Hollywood types. Give us more of 'the girl next door'—like Cheryl."[21] Because of the "realistic" emphasis on their pin-up models, *Playboy* relayed the belief that real men wanted real women, not Hollywood starlets and perennial pin-up models. In this way, the magazine set itself apart from other men's magazines, including *Esquire*. The girl-next-door concept was important, not only to male readers who wanted a "Bunny" of their very own, but to women as well. Women, married and single, wrote in to the magazine and submitted personal photos for consideration. Men, similarly, suggested the names of women they knew in their own lives whom they thought would make appropriate centerfolds.

Hefner's emphasis on the typical pretty girl who could be found in all walks of life could be precarious, however. The woman in the centerfold could not be *too* average. Letters to the Editor demonstrate that while *Playboy*'s readers preferred the girl-next-door to the tired models who reappeared in various other men's magazines, they dismissed slender pin-ups who reminded them not of a cute neighbor, but of their little sister. One *Playboy* reader wrote in, "Cheryl [Kubert] reminds me of my kid sister and Liz Roberts was just as bad. Let's have more buxom, healthy, sexy females."[22] Weighing a hundred pounds and with measurements of 34–22–34, Roberts better resembled a fashion model than the typical Playmate. *Playboy*'s centerfold models were shorter and slimmer than the average men's magazine models in the 1950s, with an average height of five feet five inches and weight of 115.6 pounds, but with similarly exaggerated measurements at 36–23.3–35.4.

Hugh Hefner mastered the girl-next-door concept, but he was not its creator. During World War II, no pin-up star received more fan letters from soldiers than Betty Grable (Figure 5.1). By the end of the war, she was Hollywood's biggest

FIGURE 5.1 Betty Grable—World War II's favorite pin-up star and the highest-paid woman in America. Her popularity surged after she married and had children.

star, earning the largest paycheck of any woman in America. But Grable was not the most attractive or the most sexually explicit of her Hollywood pin-up compatriots. Her popularity was based instead on her wholesomeness and averageness. In fact, the actress became even *more* popular when she wed Big Band leader Harry James in 1943 and had a child a year later. She was the type of girl that GIs, particularly working-class soldiers, imagined returning home to and marrying.[23] Grable's popularity highlighted the anxieties of soldiers abroad. While pin-ups and cheesecake photography provided men with an escape from the horrors of combat, they wanted no reminders that their wives or girlfriends back home might not be faithful. Once GIs returned, however, all of that changed.[24]

"Vital Statistics"—The Most Important Numbers in a Girl's Life

After World War II, Louise Paine Benjamin, beauty editor for the *Ladies Home Journal*, interviewed returning GIs and asked them "what does your ideal girl look like?" From the respondents, Benjamin created an image of the perfect woman. This type of journalism was popular in the postwar years—creating a *Frankenstein/Weird Science* perfect woman, often from disparate pieces of popular actresses and entertainers. The ideal girl, according to Benjamin's 1946 survey, was five feet 5.7 inches tall, had long wavy brown hair, and a slender but curvaceous figure. Men imagined this woman weighed about 118 pounds, but as the editor noted, "That 'figure' may be all right for dream girls, but you'd better allow a 10-pound margin. It *was* curves you said, wasn't it?"[25] Not only was this a "dream girl," however, this was the woman GIs claimed they wanted to marry. Men appeared to have a very specific idea of what the perfect woman looked like, but they were wholly unaware of what women *actually* weighed. Another magazine survey polled college men in 1947 regarding the perfect college girl. This ideal was an inch shorter than the GI's dream girl, at five feet five inches, but she also weighed 118 pounds with measurements of 34–24–34.5.[26] According to the MetLife height and weight tables from the 1940s, the average woman with a *small* frame (let alone medium or large) who stood at that height weighed between 126 and 136 pounds. This disconnect between what men wanted in their ideal partner and what insurance companies had determined was the ideal weight can be attributed to the kinds of models that appeared in men's periodicals. Although the pin-ups in men's magazines carried more weight on their figures than the high-fashion models found in women's magazines, from 1945 to 1949, the average model in *Esquire* stood five feet 6.5 inches tall and weighed 117 pounds with 34.3–23.5–34.9 measurements.[27]

Similar to justifications for breast augmentation surgery, a romantic relationship—finding or keeping a husband—was one of the major reasons for which women claimed to be dieting. And just as there existed a disconnect between reducing for health and reducing for fashion, so too existed a divide between the ideal figure that women wanted for themselves and the figure that men wanted in a wife or girlfriend. This schism is made clear in a study of high school students from a middle-class, white suburban community. Researchers asked the teens in 1969 to choose among six different silhouettes and to identify which body type was "ideal" and "most feminine." Forty percent of girls (the largest majority) labeled the extreme ectomorph—a shapeless silhouette that resembled a high-fashion model—as "most feminine." Only 8 percent of the young men chose the same. An overwhelming 77 percent of teenage boys instead selected the mesomorphic ectomorph as "most feminine"—a silhouette with a discernible waistline and rounded hips.[28]

Men's magazines similarly reveal that their readership was more interested in a woman's proportions than her actual weight. The unwritten rule when it came to cover girls and pin-ups was that the more exaggerated the bust-to-waist-to-hip measurement, the better. In 1954, the H.W. Gossard Company, manufacturers of women's foundation garments, conducted a study to discover what female body type men preferred in order to fashion their undergarments with that ideal in mind. Not surprisingly, the men surveyed most desired women with cartoon-like

36–22–36 measurements. Over 75 percent of men under the age of twenty-four preferred this figure. The study also discovered, however, that the older a man became, the *less* he preferred women with those measurements, perhaps aware of his own limitations. When the Gossard Company probed husbands whether they were "satisfied" with their wife's figure, 100 percent of men with 36–22–36 shaped partners reported to being content. Seventy-six percent of married men were pleased with wives with 35–25–35 dimensions. The quotient of happy husbands dropped to 48 percent when their wives had a 36–29–38.5 figure, and only 38 percent of men reported that they were satisfied with wives that had 34–24–34 measurements.[29] Ironically, 34–24–34 was considered the perfect high-fashion model figure for this time period. Women's magazines universally highlighted this streamlined yet curvy figure as being ideally symmetric.

By the mid-1950s, as large-breasted women became more *en vogue* in Hollywood and in heterosexual male fantasies, the measurements of cheesecake models became more ample as well. *Playboy* featured stories about women like June Wilkinson, a British starlet who had garnered the nickname "The Bosom" for her 43–22–36 measurements. Referring to the buxom late-night television star, George S. Schuyler of the *Pittsburgh Courier* wrote, "I fervently hope that the Dagmar revolution is here to stay."[30] Norman Saunders, an illustrator for the men's magazine *New Man*, recalled a correction his art director had demanded—to make the women in his drawings have larger breasts. When he returned the next day with the "modifications," his boss asked him to go even larger. Saunders reacted with astonishment: "Holy shit, Louie [Queralt], they don't get any bigger than that! They're already the size of watermelons! They don't make 'em as big as washtubs!" He recalled Queralt's eyes lighting up at the unintended suggestion; the art director promptly demanded Saunders readjust the drawing in favor of the "washtub" size.[31]

To be sure, this male preoccupation with large-chested women was not universal. Novelist and sports writer Paul Gallico was particularly critical of the American male fascination with buxom celebrities and how a woman need only this exaggerated anatomy to catapult her to stardom. Ben Hecht, another *Esquire* columnist, agreed, noting, "a bulbous front will make a star quicker than [Russian ballerina Anna] Pavlova's face or [Marlene] Dietrich's pins."[32] Gallico also lamented how fellow journalists, without fail, could not write a column about these women without at least once emphasizing the "sex-body-shape-hip-wiggle-oo-la-la angle."[33] In the world of men's periodicals, however, journalists like Gallico were a minority. At the height of the country's mammary madness, one *Playboy* writer argued that small-breasted women "had never had it so good." Citing Grace Kelly and Audrey Hepburn as two of the most popular Hollywood stars, and pointing out that buxom Jane Russell had yet to win an Oscar, Jay Smith downplayed the importance of breasts in Hollywood. His own personal tastes, however, ran to the curvaceous in claiming that it was his "Constitutional right" to date a large-breasted woman. As the Constitution protects the pursuit of happiness, he noted, "we're never happier than when we're pursuing a fully-developed 100% 38-D American girl."[34]

"Spooks" and Dieting Dilemmas

Although women might have admired the high-fashion models who appeared in their periodicals, men's magazines did not. Referred to as "spooks," women's fashion models were described as "chestless, hipless, and sexless to the ordinary man." They were seen as women who deliberately destroyed their curves by wearing undersized bras and living on "coffee, Melba toast and Benzedrine."[35] Pin-up photographer Lisa Larsen claimed, "A woman should have firm shoulders, rounded breasts, a slender waist, and legs that remind you of a woman rather than a beanstalk."[36] Harry Conover, head of the Conover modeling agency, popular for cover girls, complained that fashion designers were "trying to give America a generation of flat-chested, emaciated, ill-tempered women who will be hard to live with." Contemporary fashions, he added, favored "women [who] look like matchsticks, thus ruining their health and disposition." Purportedly Conover allowed his models to eat whatever they wanted.[37] This, however, seems far-fetched because even though Conover's favored styles of models had wider hips and larger busts than those women found in high-fashion magazines, they also generally had smaller waist measurements that made their silhouettes look more exaggerated.

Women's fashion magazines urged their readers to exercise and diet to obtain an ideal form that would help them catch or keep a husband. Men's magazines, however, lamented that American women were squandering their femininity with such slenderizing tactics. Upon discovering that his wife had been frequenting the local Slenderella salon, one man mailed the reducing company a self-penned poem. His plea is reminiscent of recording artist Sir Mix-a-Lot's 1991 anthem, "Baby Got Back." He wrote:

> Realign the rear
> And I'll not object, my dear.
> But one thing is a must—
> Don't you dare disturb the bust![38]

A 1946 survey asked returning GIs if they approved of their significant others' diet regimes. Two-thirds of the men accepted their partners dieting "if she needs it," but respondents were decidedly against fad diets.[39] Calorie-counting, according to men's magazines, was just one of the reasons why "the female of the species is often a pain in the neck."[40] Cosmetic surgeon Robert Franklyn observed, "Many a newly-trimmed-down *femme* has devoted so much time, energy, and effort to reducing that, in the process she has driven out the man—or the men—in her life." He urged that while improving their figures and their overall happiness, that women not forget about the happiness of their husbands or boyfriends.[41]

Men did not necessarily oppose slender women. In a 1951 *McCall's* article, "Do Husbands Like Plump Wives?" men responded with a resounding no.[42] What they apparently rejected was the drastic measures women took to achieve the svelte form. Part of the married woman's dieting dilemma was how to cook for her family and watch her own food intake at the same time. When a woman prepared dinner, either she made two separate meals or someone had to make concessions. Would her husband eat an unsatisfying salad, or would she gorge on meat and potatoes? "The growing fear of slimmer competition while she steadily loses ground in the battle of the bulge may make a jealous shrew of the sweetest tempered wife," one journalist observed.[43] Studies printed in men's magazines evinced that heavier women were more happily married than model-thin women and that fat women were more sexual than their skinny counterparts.[44] Moreover, a large part of the antipathy towards slenderizing was the belief that women did not diet or exercise to make their partners happy, but rather because their friends were dieting or because they wanted to look like "the women in the ads."[45]

Exacerbating men's frustration over dieting wives, the most amply figured pin-ups and actresses announced in the mass media that they ate whatever they wanted. Marilyn Monroe admitted to stopping most nights at an ice-cream parlor for a hot fudge sundae.[46] Sophia Loren contributed her figure to heaps of pasta. "Everything you are looking at is a result of spaghetti," she proudly broadcast to *Esquire*. "I grew a whole centimeter last year because of spaghetti."[47] Without being told so, readers could surmise on their own that Loren was not referring to an extra centimeter to her waistline. October 1964's *Playboy* Playmate, Rosemarie Hillcrest (41–25–38), was described as "a big girl," with an appetite to match. "She revels in foods from which the calorie-conscious would shrink."[48] Busty blonde actress and perennial *Playboy* cover girl, Jayne Mansfield, announced that the way to her heart was through her stomach.[49] While their wives and girlfriends were preoccupied with counting calories, men read about actresses and centerfolds who reportedly ate whatever they wanted. No doubt, these claims of insatiable appetites also played homage to the traditional connections between food and sexual appetite.

While men's magazines were generally uniform in their dismissal of "spooks" and excessive dieting, they reveal a more complicated reaction to the fashions that women wore. Journalists were not blind to the fact that "for centuries, Dame Fashion and Dame Nature have been at odds."[50] Men's periodicals demonstrated a concern that fashion, rather than enhancing the feminine figure, often stifled female beauty. And although fashion trends dramatically changed over the postwar years, it appeared to these men that the female form had experienced more alterations than the hemline of a skirt. Similar to their critique of women's diets, men's magazines expressed the belief that women dressed to impress other women, not men.[51]

Perhaps no single fashion trend received more attention in men's magazines than Christian Dior's "New Look." Part of the disdain for the "New Look" originated in its Parisian roots. Although France had been an ally during World War II, American men rejected the reality that, after the war, American women continued to look to Paris for the latest fashion designs. Men seemed to appreciate the full bust, hand-span waist, and ample hip measurements that the "New Look" provoked, but these "blessings" had also come with a longer hemline.[52] "There Ought to be a Law" against long skirts, a story in *Beauty Parade* bemoaned.[53] While men's magazines generally favored the "New Look's" emphasis on curves, they re-imaged a world of short skirts in an almost prophetic way. As early as October 1948, columns in both *Beauty Parade* and *Flirt* predicted the miniskirt, the leg-baring fashion that gained widespread popularity in the late 1960s. In *Flirt* magazine, a photo essay featured a pin-up model wearing a fitted dress whose bottom hemline is so short, her garters and the tops of her stockings are visible. Mimicking a political platform, a list of demands is numbered beside the model: "(1) Up with long skirts! (2) Freedom of the sees! (3) America must outstrip all others! (4) The truth, the whole truth, and nothing but the truth!" The platform ends with a play on Christian Dior's famous tagline: "Remember—the longer the skirt, the shorter the Look!"[54] Despite the dramatic changes in feminine fashion in the postwar period, men's magazines did not stray from what they considered ideal—a slightly voluptuous figure, streamlined, yet with full curves and shapely legs from ankle to thigh.[55]

Faking It

Excessive dieting and the sheep-like following of the newest fashions irked the readers of men's magazines because it also reminded them of how inauthentic the female form could be. While society and heterosexual norms pressured couples to wed at earlier ages than ever before in the postwar years, men's magazines adopted a misogynistic strain in regard to marriage. The editors of these magazines believed they were being duped: trapped into marriage and tricked into relationships with women who not only faked their personalities but faked what their bodies actually looked like. Bras, corsets, and girdles not only contained women's sexuality, they also physically manipulated female bodies into ideal shapes. One journalist estimated in 1947 that the average male spent ten days, five hours, and forty minutes a year on grooming and working out. In comparison, he estimated that women spent over two months out of the year on cosmetic maintenance.[56] For one *Esquire* writer, this helped explain why men were so compelled to stare at women's legs: "They know they've got something there. Something that is unfakable [*sic*]."[57] A photo essay in *Flirt* magazine made public that everything on a woman's body, from her hair to her toes, could be artificially manufactured. The magazine labeled each of the model's body parts and to whom the admirer could attribute her "perfection." Purposely misspelling the names of cosmetic and fashion industry companies, the accompanying photo notes that the model's eyes are courtesy of "Maybellinsky," her complexion is by "Max Wacktor," and her large breasts by "Seks 5th Avenue."[58] When insurance agencies like Lloyds of London began insuring women's body parts in the postwar years, it only exaggerated ideas about women as a collection of interchangeable body parts. Betty Grable most famously had her legs insured for $1 million, while topless dancer Carol Doda insured her silicone-injected breasts for $1.5 million.

A disdain for the inauthentic spilled over to the realm of breast augmentation. Although men might have desired women with large breasts, falsies and other methods of breast enhancement were met with much criticism. "What nature has forgotten they stuff with cotton," observed one *Playboy* writer. "If anybody is entitled to squawk it's not the under-endowed girl but the poor guy who married one of them and then discovers that he's been short changed."[59] *Playboy*'s editors similarly discouraged one woman from getting silicone injections to increase her breast size. In March 1970, Miss P. K. from San Francisco wrote to "The Playboy Advisor," asking if she should pursue plastic surgery to inflate her bust measurements. She worried that her boyfriend was "strictly a 'what's up front' type" and she feared losing him. *Playboy* responded with a definitive answer of "No," and noted that the Food and Drug Administration (FDA) had yet to approve liquid silicone injections. In fact, the agency had banned the hospital-grade injections since 1965. The editorial staff added, "In any event, it's unlikely he would chuck your good looks, personality and sex appeal just for a larger chest."[60] This was not the last of the plastic surgery questions to appear in the magazine. A few months later, in August, another reader pointed out that there were many ways to enlarge one's bust through surgery without direct silicone injections. The magazine acknowledged other kinds of mammaplasty augmentation such as silicone implants, but again observed that liquid silicone injections had not been approved by the FDA, except for experimental purposes.[61] Perhaps the magazine's stance on plastic surgery did have to do with considerations for the young woman's overall health, but one can also image the worry over authenticity came into *Playboy*'s response as well.

Advancing technologies created increasing ways for women to present their bodies as "better" than they actually were. With a growing number of women pursuing breast alterations, one *Chicago Defender* journalist lamented that women were becoming "hunk[s] of plastic." "Pity the falsie specialist," he bemoaned, "and the other unsuspecting. Wonder when somebody will discover a substitute for brains?"[62] While men complained about fake breasts, however, journalist Betty South argued that American men had done it to themselves. "If you think you're sick of reading about and looking at falsies," she ranted, "you can be sure that we are. Our torsos are used to sell everything from twenty-five-cent mystery stories about horses to movies dealing with the French Foreign Legion." South argued that if Americans stopped buying commercial items in which breasts were used in the advertising, the country would suffer a financial crash.[63]

Twiggy versus the Swimsuit Model

Despite small-busted fashion models and the continued popularity of the gamine Audrey Hepburn, breasts never went out of vogue. The breast size of *Playboy* centerfolds became more modest during the late 1960s than in previous years, but flat-chested models never took over the glossy pages of men's magazines as they had done in women's fashion periodicals.[64] But while men continued to eroticize large-breasted women, even into the late 1960s, the fashion world promoted a different extreme ideal—an androgynous, slender silhouette whose breasts were minimized. At least one scholar has called this period a time of "aesthetic disjunction."[65] High-fashion models had always been slender in order to better highlight the clothes they were paid to wear, but Twiggy and similar, shapeless models appeared even in non-fashion magazines. The Twiggy couture movement could be interpreted as a return to Flapper fashions of the 1920s, but unlike the twenties, it is clear that American men did not covet high-fashion models as their centerfolds. Calling Twiggy "a fad" and the voluptuous Sophia Loren "eternal," one *True* journalist noted, "Give the average man a choice and he'll take Sophia Loren over Twiggy every time."[66] While American women whittled away at their hips and thighs in order to look like the women (girls) in their magazines, men continued to admire pin-up models that unabashedly revealed their rounded curves.

The creation of *Sports Illustrated*'s "Swimsuit Issue" is further evidence of this. *Sports Illustrated* published its first "Swimsuit Issue" on January 20, 1964. Sandwiched between articles on fishing, boating, and where to go on vacation, the original photo spread previewed the latest fashions in women's sporty swimwear. Each subsequent year, the Swimsuit Issue produced animated conversations in the Letters to the Editor section. Men and women wrote in to the magazine both complaining about and praising the new winter feature. Some claimed the inclusion of the swimsuit models was unnecessary; the magazine was a sports periodical, these critics pointed out, not a "girlie picture" magazine. Other readers, resembling "Dear *Playboy*" responses, requested more personal information about the swimsuit models. Jules Campbell, fashion writer for the sporting magazine, was in charge of choosing the models for the swimsuit issues. Similar to Hugh Hefner, the fashion editor embraced the "girl-next-door" philosophy when vetting potential models. "I just look for a girl who seems the type my husband would like," Campbell explained. "The girl," she continued, "has to look healthy, has to be the kind men turn around to stare at, has to have visible spirit and should be athletic."[67] Although the swimsuit column featured the latest resort and beachwear, Campbell chose models whose measurements would have been too aggressive to appear in an average fashion magazine. "I always used California girls in the early days," she said. "They were bigger, healthier and more natural."[68] Campbell also published the models' names beside their photos—a rare practice in fashion modeling, but not in pin-up art.

In 1969, the swimsuit models strayed from Campbell's "healthy California look" and readers took note. One observed, "With this latest issue *SI* seems to have abandoned this formula in favor of a style and format more suited to *Vogue*, and I believe I am not alone in asking you to return to the 'fundamentalism' that made the first issues so appealing."[69] In later years, *Sports Illustrated* returned to

FIGURE 5.2 Marilyn Monroe lifting barbells. Photography of the Hollywood star actively working on her figure did not appear in mainstream magazines.[70]

their previous "formula" due to the many requests of like-minded readers. From Hugh Hefner's *Playboy* Playmates to *Sports Illustrated*'s swimsuit models, men's magazines continued to profit so long as they recognized the kind of woman their readers most desired. A tension existed, more so than at any other time in the nineteenth and twentieth century, between what men wanted and the idyllic figure highlighted in women's magazines. Perhaps never again would both American men and women agree on what constituted femininity and physical beauty; certainly not in the same way that Marilyn Monroe and her blonde, busty counterparts had influenced the country a decade earlier (Figure 5.2).

Conclusions

Women looked to magazines for advice about everything, from cooking recipes, to housekeeping tips, to relationship advice. Their fashion and lifestyle magazines similarly provided instruction on how to diet, exercise, and dress in order to attract and keep a husband. Men's magazines, rather than serving as a "How To" guide to masculinity, often simply complained about the opposite sex or heralded the newest Hollywood starlet. Magazines like *Esquire* and *Playboy*, and in some ways *Sports Illustrated*, suggested ways in which a man might reclaim his masculinity, but certainly not with the same aggressive focus that women's magazines promoted femininity.

When the topics covered in men and women's magazines overlapped, they exposed a surprising disconnect in discourse. While women's magazines urged their readers to exercise and diet to obtain an ideal form, their male-aimed counterparts lamented that American women were squandering their femininity with such activities. Men did not necessarily object to slender wives and girlfriends; more often they simply opposed the extreme dieting and other techniques their partners subjected themselves to for the sake of fashion and beauty. They interpreted women's desire to be thinner not as a way to please men, but as a way to compete with other women. Comparing extreme weight loss tactics to the "never-never land of fads" like mah-jongg, chain letters, and quiz shows, one male reporter noted, "It would appear that weight reducing and dieting have gone far beyond the bounds of science and logic." He continued, "What can we talk about, and why should our friends sympathize with and admire us, if we merely walk around the block twice a day and substitute an apple for our usual layer cake? Where is the glamour? Where are those spectacular if temporary coups of 10 pounds in 10 days?"[71] Moreover, while high-fashion magazines published the newest fashion lines displayed in Paris every spring, men's magazines bemoaned how women blindly followed trends set by foreign cultural tastemakers. Women and men's magazines did more than promote contradictory messages about dieting and high-fashion models, however; they displayed a paradox more complex than simply a gender binary. "High-fashion" during these years was the product of male designers, and "anti-spook" journalism—columns in men's magazines that rallied against the popularity of ultra-thin fashion models—exposed a power struggle between two groups of men—the international fashion houses of designers like Christian Dior and the homegrown preferences of American men. Similarly, Twiggy and her multiple facsimiles did little to impress American men. They found few things appealing about the flat-chested, androgynous pixie model and begrudged her influence on American fashionability. For men, the importance of high-fashion models stopped at the newsstands; they desired the girl-next-door.

Notes

1 Quoted in Elizabeth Fraterrigo's Playboy *and the Making of the Good Life in Modern America* (New York: Oxford University Press, 2009), 41.
2 Max Allan Collins, *Men's Adventure Magazines in Postwar America: The Rich Oberg Collection* (Los Angeles, CA: Taschen, 2004), 8.
3 Bruce Lohof, *American Commonplace: Essays on the Popular Culture of the United States* (Bowling Green, OH: Bowling Green University Popular Press, 1982).
4 Anne Scott Beller, *Fat and Thin: A Natural History of Obesity* (New York: Farrar, Straus, and Giroux, 1977), 59.
5 For more on the history of men's magazines in the twentieth century, see Dian Hanson, *Dian Hanson's The History of Men's Magazines*, Volume II (Los Angeles, CA: Taschen, 2004); Elizabeth Fraterrigo, Playboy *and the Making of the Good Life in Modern America* (New York: Oxford University Press, 2009); and Tom Pendergast, *Creating the Modern*

Man: *American Magazines and Consumer Culture, 1900–1950* (Columbia: University of Missouri Press, 2000).
6   Hanson, *Dian Hanson's The History of Men's Magazines*, 44.
7   "Letters to the Editor," *Playboy*, April 1956, 7.
8   Hanson, 186.
9   Biographical information from Russell Miller's *Bunny: The Real Story of* Playboy (New York: Holt, Rinehart, and Winston, 1984); Fraterrigo, Playboy *and the Making of the Good Life in Modern America; Hugh Hefner: American Playboy*. DVD. Directed by Kevin Burns (Los Angeles, CA: Foxstar Productions, 1996).
10   Hanson, 216.
11   "Mission Statement," *Playboy*, December 1953, 1.
12   Mark Jancovich, "The Politics of *Playboy*: Lifestyle, Sexuality, and Non-conformity in American Cold War Culture," in *Historicizing Lifestyle: Mediating Taste, Consumption and Identity from the 1900s to 1970s*, eds. David Bell and Joanne Hollows (Burlington, VT: Ashgate Publishing, Co., 2006), 83.
13   Lisa Larsen, "The Woman Behind the Camera," *Esquire*, May 1950, 50.
14   In the magazine's inaugural issues, Playmates appeared anonymously. Readers wrote in to the editorial staff begging for names, addresses, marital status, and body proportions of the stars of the centerfold. In May 1954, Hefner relented and began publishing the name of his centerfolds. Joanne Arnold, Miss May, was a model who had previously appeared in the magazine in March for the pictorial, "Sex Sells a Shirt." Unlike later Playmates, Arnold's name and biographical sketch did not appear next to her centerfold pictorial, but rather in the editorial notes on the magazine's opening page.
15   Fraterrigo, Playboy *and the Making of the Good Life in Modern America*, 42.
16   "Playboy's Office Playmate: Janet Pilgrim, subscription manager," *Playboy*, July 1955, 27.
17   "Meet Barbara Cameron," *Playboy*, November 1955, 30.
18   "Letters to the Editor," *Playboy*, March 1958.
19   "December Playmate Janet Pilgrim—What's Her Parent's Reaction?" *Playboy*, March 1956.
20   "The Naked Truth," *Time*, February 3, 1958.
21   "Letters to the Editor," *Playboy*, May 1958, 7.
22   Ibid.
23   Robert Westbrook, "'I Want a Girl, Just Like the Girl that Married Harry James': American Women and the Problem of Political Obligation in World War II," *American Quarterly* 42, no. 4 (December 1990): 587–614.
24   Dian Hanson, *Dian Hanson: The History of Men's Magazines*, Volume I (Los Angeles, CA: Taschen, 2004), 296.
25   Louise Paine Benjamin, "The Girl I Would Like to Propose To," *Ladies Home Journal*, June 1946, 179.
26   Dawn Crowell, "One and a Half Million College Men Can't be Wrong," *Ladies Home Journal*, September 1947, 68–69, 257.
27   By the early 1950s, *Esquire* no longer listed the measurements of the models in its pages, perhaps as an attempt to separate itself from 'nudey' magazines.
28   J. T. Dwyer, J. J. Feldman, C. C. Seltzer, and J. Mayer, "Body Image in Adolescents: Attitudes Toward Weight and Perception of Appearance," *Journal of Nutrition Education* 1, no. 2 (Fall 1969): 14–19.
29   Charles Armstrong, "One Man's Meat," *Playboy*, June 1954, 11–12.
30   "Boost for Big Busts," *Jet*, November 1, 1951, 30.
31   Quoted in Adam Parfrey, *It's a Man's World: Men's Adventure Magazines: The Postwar Pulps* (Los Angeles, CA: Feral House, 2003), 46.
32   Ben Hecht, "Bosoms Away," *Esquire*, July 1957, 73, 74.
33   Paul Gallico, "This Man's World," *Esquire*, October 1956, 50, 130.

34 Jay Smith, "The Big Bosom Battle," *Playboy*, September 1955, 26, 42.
35 Henry Lee, "Sex is Here to Sell," *Esquire*, March 1952, 72–74.
36 Lisa Larsen, "The Woman Behind the Camera," *Esquire*, May 1950, 50.
37 Gilbert Millstein, "The Modeling Business," *Life*, March 25, 1946, 113.
38 Sir Mix-A-Lot's preferred body part was the woman's backside ("You can do side bends or sit-ups/But please don't lose that butt), but both men—thirty-five years apart—were concerned that exercise might reduce the size of their favorite body part. "Slenderella," *Collier's*, December 1956, 46.
39 Louise Paine Benjamin, "The Girl I Would Like to Propose To," *Ladies Home Journal*, June 1946, 179.
40 J. B. Rice, "Do You Know Your Women?" *Esquire*, March 1948, 41.
41 Robert Franklyn and Marcia Borie, *A Doctor's Quick Way to Achieve Lasting Beauty and How to Play the Beauty Game* (New York: Information Incorporated, 1970), 178.
42 "Do Husbands Like Plump Wives?" *McCall's*, March 1951, 6–8.
43 Rice, "Do You Know Your Women?," *Esquire*, 41.
44 Herb Graffis, "The Weigh with Women," *Esquire*, September 1948, 76.
45 Harry Golden, "Diet Craze and Sugar," *Jet*, March 7, 1964, 8.
46 Marilyn Monroe, "How I Stay in Shape," *Pageant*, 1952, 126.
47 "A Nymph of El Escorial," *Esquire*, April 1957, 131.
48 "Rosemarie Hillcrest," *Playboy*, October 1964, 113.
49 "Will Success Spoil Jayne Mansfield?" *Playboy*, February 1956, 66.
50 "Feminine Fashions Through the Ages," *Beauty Parade*, March 1946, 22.
51 Herb Graffis, "For Whom the Belle Dresses," *Esquire*, March 1948, 69.
52 "Will This Be Next?" *Beauty Parade*, December 1948, 58–59.
53 "There Ought to Be a Law," *Beauty Parade*, July 1949, 21.
54 "The New, New, New, New Look!" *Flirt*, October 1948, 25; "Will This Be Next?" *Beauty Parade*, December 1948, 58–59.
55 "Feminine Fashions Through the Ages," *Beauty Parade*, March 1946, 22.
56 Walter Sorell, "Beauty Is Her Duty," *Esquire*, September 1947, 53.
57 Stuart Cloete, "The High Cost of Loving," *Esquire*, October 1957, 57, 149.
58 "Behold! The Perfect Lady!" *Flirt*, March 1948, 24.
59 Jay Smith, "The Big Bosom Battle," *Playboy*, September 1955, 26, 42.
60 "The Playboy Advisor," *Playboy*, March 1970, 47.
61 "The Playboy Advisor," *Playboy*, August 1970, 37.
62 "The Wimmin', God Bless 'Em," *Chicago Defender*, February 14, 1953, 10.
63 Betty South, "The Trouble with Women Is Men," *Esquire*, April 1952, 31, 128–9.
64 On average, Playmates between 1965 and 1970 had a 35.7 inch bust, a full inch smaller than the magazine's chestiest five-year period—1955 to 1959—when the average Playmate's bust was 36.8 inches. But women with the largest breasts during the late 1950s typically were actresses like Jayne Mansfield (40–21–32) or often-utilized pin-up models like Eve Meyer or Marguerite Empey instead of Hefner's girl-next-door types. Even if models had more modest measurements than in previous years, *Playboy* erased any evidence that their current models might not "measure-up" to centerfolds from the magazine's earliest years. The accompanying text with the Playmates fold-out picture did not mention a model's proportions in the late 1960s unless she had at least a thirty-six-inch bust. Data sheets reveal that those Playmates whose "vital statistics" were not documented in the magazine had breast measurements of thirty-four and thirty-five inches. So, even at these more moderate measurements, Playmate bust-size easily exceeded those of 1960s fashion models.
65 Harold Koda, *Extreme Beauty: The Body Transformed* (New Haven, CT: Yale University Press, 2001).
66 Ralph Lee Smith, "All the Twiggies Want to be Sophia," *True*, November 1967, 58.
67 Garry Valk, "Letter from the Publisher," *Sports Illustrated*, January 16, 1967, 4.

68 Sarah Ballard, "From Baja with Love," *Sports Illustrated*, February 7, 1989, http://sportsillustrated.cnn.com/vault/article/magazine/MAG1068176/2/index.htm.
69 *Sports Illustrated*, "The 19th Hole: Readers Take Over," January 28, 1969, 28.
70 *Life* photographer Philippe Halsman captured this image of Monroe in 1952 during an assignment early in her career. The photograph was not included in the article. Monroe appeared on the cover of *Life* magazine on April 7, 1952, just before the release of breakout rolls in *How to Marry a Millionaire* and *Gentlemen Prefer Blondes*. Halsman followed Hollywood's newest star, capturing shots of her daily exercise regime. Halsman recorded Monroe—barefoot and in blue jeans and a terry-cloth bikini top—doing military presses and lifting weight bars and dumbbells in her apartment. Despite one line in the article about Monroe using barbells to fight "gravity," Halsman's images of the actress lifting weights never made it into the magazine, opting instead for the editorial decision to print a side-by-side comparison with the late actress Jean Harlow, both photographed from behind. "Hollywood Topic A-Plus: Whole Town's Talking about Marilyn Monroe," *Life*, April 7, 1952, 101–104.
71 Whitney Darrow, Jr., "The Wasteful, Phony Crash Dieting Craze," *Life*, January 19, 1959, 114.

6

(BIG AND) BLACK IS BEAUTIFUL

Body Image and Expanded Beauty Ideals

> *I want a big fat mama*
> *I want a big fat mama*
> *I want a big fat mama*
> *With the meat shaking*
> *On her bones*
>
> —Lucky Millinder, "Big Fat Mama" (1941)

In a widely covered media event, advocates for women's liberation protested the Miss America pageant in Atlantic City on September 7, 1968. Demonstrators acted in guerilla theater skits, marched with protest placards, lobbied the pageant's contestants as they arrived at the event, and disposed of "oppressive" female accoutrements like bras, high heels, and women's magazines into a "Freedom Trash Can." A press release explaining the demonstration described how organizers chose the Miss America pageant as the site for the protest because the beauty contest created "an image that oppresses women in every area in which it purports to represent us."[1] At the end of the day-long rally, a sheep was crowned Miss America, symbolizing the protesters' belief that the antiquated pageant was little more than a cattle auction.[2]

At the same moment that white women decried Atlantic City's Miss America pageant, a few blocks away at the Ritz Carlton Hotel, Philadelphian Saundra Williams accepted the title of Miss Black America.[3] Williams, the contest's first winner, was from a middle-class family and had worked to integrate businesses in her college town of Princess Anne, Maryland. In front of an audience of around 300 people, Williams outperformed the seven other contestants. Her talent was an original African-inspired dance and she styled her hair in an Afro. "It was like an impossible dream coming true," she recalled. "For years I'd been brainwashed into thinking that beauty consisted of straight hair, a thin, straight nose and thin lips. The contest proved what I'd recently learned—black is beautiful."[4] At five feet, four inches and weighing 125 pounds, *Seventeen* magazine would have described the beauty queen's build as "stocky."[5]

The pageant's creator, J. Morris Anderson, produced the Miss Black America Pageant to protest the absence of African American women in Atlantic City's televised event. The contest did not start until midnight on September 8, in fact, because Anderson hoped media from the white pageant would stop by afterward. The alternative pageant capped what had become a growing rejection of white beauty standards. Two years earlier, in June of 1966, Diana Smith graced the cover of *Ebony* magazine. Her presence signaled the first appearance of an Afro on the cover of the middle-class African American publication. The cover story read, "The Natural Look: New Mode for Black Women." Smith was neither a celebrity nor a model, yet she held the coveted space where black entertainers like Lena Horne and Dorothy Dandridge had previously appeared. As a twenty-year-old civil rights worker, Smith symbolized not only 1960s political activism, but also an ideal where "natural" trumped white America's beauty standards.

Cosmetics industry giant Helena Rubenstein was quoted to have once famously said, "there are no ugly women, only lazy ones." According to this mantra, any woman could achieve beauty if she truly aspired to obtain it. But what Rubenstein ignored was whiteness. Black scholar Maxine Leeds Craig notes that not only did black women experience unequal access to education, housing, and job opportunities, they also "bore the shame of being women in unacceptable bodies."[6] In earlier periods, American beauty standards were set by Europeans, despite the diversity of the population. For instance, Havelock Ellis, an influential British sexologist at the turn of the nineteenth and twentieth century, argued that a scientifically objective chain of beauty ran parallel to Darwin's evolutionary chain of being. According to Ellis, white Anglo-Saxon women presented the mostly highly evolved end of the beauty scale while women of color occupied a space at the other end of the spectrum.[7]

While cosmetic surgery became more accessible to the average American, historian Elizabeth Haiken finds few instances of African Americans pursuing these corrective procedures. She argues that those who sought surgery did so to improve their economic situation.[8] In this way, black cosmetic surgery patients mirrored the desires of models and starlets who believed larger breasts would help them in a competitive job market. Although no mention of breast implants or surgical weight reductions entered the conversation in *Ebony* and other black periodicals, some black women sought plastic surgery to alter their faces to better resemble Anglo-Saxon features. In the 1950s and 1960s, rhinoplasty was also popular among women of Jewish or Middle Eastern descent. Two of the most popular "corrections" within the African American community were nose narrowing and lip thinning. One surgeon in Harlem claimed that ninety percent of his operations were those two procedures.[9] An advertisement in the *Chicago*

Defender proclaimed that the surgery was inexpensive, relatively painless, and with little chance of scarring.[10] One Chicago model, twenty-five-year-old Marjorie Zinn, boasted that after surgery, her new features made her face look leaner, her cheekbones higher, and a new dimple had even appeared in her smile.[11] However, as articles, photography, and letters to the editor in *Ebony* and other black magazines reveal, women like Zinn were in the minority.

Historians have articulated the impact of the Black Power movement on civil rights and America as a whole. Scholarship on the "Black is Beautiful" phenomenon describes this assertion of racial pride exhibited by African American men and women rejecting white ideals of style, beauty, and personal identity. However, historians have awarded the 1960s and the 1970s with the most scholarly attention. While this is important, the "Black is Beautiful" movement cannot be understood without first acknowledging the seeds of this discontent and alienation. In the twenty years separating World War II and the Miss Black America beauty pageant, the African American community did not passively accept white America's standards of beauty. Black mass media did not universally promote lightened skin, relaxed hair, and the body of Marilyn Monroe. Through black periodicals, movies, and other media, rather than yielding to narrow ideals of fashion, body, and cosmetic culture, African American women and men broadened their definition of beauty. Discontent found within the generally conservative middle-class readership of *Ebony* magazine, in addition to more liberal black periodicals, demonstrates that the black middle class rejected white beauty standards decades before "Black Power" of the mid-1960s.

Black Periodicals and Their Readers

The black middle class has long held a unique position in American society. Because of the economic uniformity of black society immediately after Emancipation, status groups based on community positions rather than wealth emerged. These status distinctions were based on characteristics such as manners, morals, and connections to white ancestry rather than socioeconomic class.[12] In the early 1900s, a new black middle class emerged due to white America's reluctance to provide basic services to its African American population. Occupations such as insurance providers, dentists, undertakers, realtors, and doctors formed the core of this growing minority class.[13] One scholar, denouncing E. Franklin Frazier's scathing attack on the black middle class, contends that because of this socioeconomic diversity, the importance of status factors such as skin color and social links with whites declined.[14] In the immediate postwar period, the black middle class expanded along with civil rights legislation that opened up additional occupations to black men and women as well as the new postwar affluence and consumption patterns. Indeed, this new black middle class doubled in size by the 1960s.[15]

Members of the growing black middle class, like their white counterparts, consulted cultural tools such as periodicals to guide them through their newly acquired social mobility. At the epicenter of the emergent black periodical industry was John H. Johnson. Originally from rural Arkansas, Johnson migrated to Chicago with his family in his early teens. After graduating from high school with high honors, he gained employment at the Supreme Liberty Life Insurance Company with the plan to attend college after saving enough money. Early in 1942, Johnson's employer and mentor, Harry H. Pace, asked his ambitious pupil to compile information about current events in the black world from various newspapers and other media sources. Pace and his family were passing for white in the Chicago suburbs, but the insurance company president wanted to keep abreast of the happenings in the black community. This experience inspired Johnson to create a magazine that would similarly enlighten the entire African American community. Later in the year, with a modest loan from Citizen's Loan Corporation, using his mother's new furniture as collateral, and the partnership of *Chicago Defender* editor Ben Burns, Johnson purchased $500 worth of stamps and sent a letter to twenty thousand African American households, inquiring if they would be interested in subscribing to a new black magazine. The resulting periodical, *Negro Digest*, consisted of a compilation of intellectual articles on race and black history.[16]

Recognizing that Henry Luce's *Life* magazine was the only other periodical selling as much as *Negro Digest* in the black community, Johnson soon entertained the idea of creating a "lighter" publication. By creating *Ebony*, a magazine similar to *Life*, Johnson acknowledged that America was a two-society nation—one white and one black.[17] The magazine's mission statement made no apologies for its purpose: "As you can gather, we're rather jolly folks, we *Ebony* editors. We like to look at the zesty side of life … not enough is said about all the swell things we Negroes can do and will accomplish. *Ebony* will try to mirror the happier side of Negro life."[18] The magazine's first issue in November of 1945 contained columns on race, youth, personalities, culture, entertainment, and humor.[19] Print advertisements for consumer products were visibly absent from this first issue. Early in the magazine's life, Johnson avoided printing small advertisements; he wanted to attract national companies who would buy four-color advertisements like those in *Life* or *Look* magazine. At least one *Ebony* reader, Beaulah Harris, appreciated the lack of hair-straightening and skin-lightening products in the first issue: "*Ebony* is a live, real life magazine that we need, want and have been longing for. Please keep it clean like it is. We do not want advertisements of how to get white. We are beautiful as a race as we are—we only need more intelligence and more race pride."[20] Johnson could hold out for only so long, however. Despite selling over one hundred thousand copies of each issue in the early months of *Ebony*, the success and cheap production costs of *Negro Digest* were the only things keeping the more expensive entertainment magazine afloat. In May 1946, *Ebony* printed its first advertisement (Figure 6.1). Pictured was an exotic-looking woman with a low-cut sarong, holding onto a bamboo curtain. Her dark, long, black hair hung loose and flowing and a fully bloomed flower was perched behind one ear.

112 (Big and) Black Is Beautiful

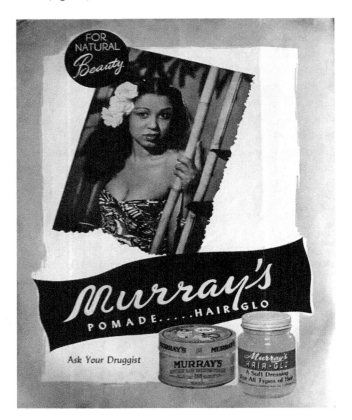

FIGURE 6.1 Murray's Pomade advertisement in the May 1946 issue of *Ebony Magazine*.

The advertisement enticed readers to purchase "Murray's Pomade and Murray's Hair Glo" for "Natural Beauty." The product promised "natural" hair that did not occur "naturally" for African American women.[21]

Almost universally, black women in America straightened their hair during the late 1940s through the early 1960s. At least one author has argued that hair straightening had become, not the "damaging influence of a white beauty standard," but rather a coming-of-age ritual for young girls.[22] Within the black community, straight hair was not only the preferred look but also a marker of one's position in society. Relaxed hair represented wealth, education, and access to society. But despite the association with middle-class mores, many readers acknowledged the hypocrisy of *Ebony*'s editorial policy to include articles on racial pride and yet sell advertising space to "whitening" products. One mother wrote in, "With a daughter approaching her teens, I've become very conscious of this especially when she asks, 'Is it true, blondes have more fun?'"[23] In addition to hair texture, the hue of one's skin could also be a factor in determining beauty for black females.

Dorothea Towles, one of the most successful African American models of the 1950s and 1960s, was light skinned and eventually dyed her hair blonde. Important black singer-actresses such as Lena Horne and Dorothy Dandridge were similarly light complexioned. Although John H. Johnson accepted advertisements for skin-bleaching products in *Ebony*, his editorial rant in May 1946 declared:

> Beauty is skin deep—and that goes for brown as well as white skin. You'd never think it though, to look at the billboards, magazines, and pinup posters of America. Cheesecake ... is all white. But the Petty girl notwithstanding, Negro girls are beautiful too. And despite the fact that Miss America contests hang out "for whites only" signs, there are thousands of Negro girls lovely enough to compete with the best of white America in pulchritude.[24]

While the editor admonished white beauty standards, the inclusion of advertisements for products like Nadinola Bleach Cream ("Give Romance a Chance! Don't let a dull, dark complexion deprive you of popularity!") negated the cohesion of the magazine's message.[25]

Ebony's readership was not blind to or accepting of these mixed messages. Multiple letters to the magazine throughout the postwar period mirrored the concerns of one reader: "How can you, *Ebony*, sacrifice our integrity and hypocritically continue to proudly devote pages to colored women ... and at the same time sell space to a product which forwards the opinion that success comes with fair skin?"[26] Although advertisements for skin bleachers and hair straighteners had appeared in black periodicals since the mid-nineteenth century, the readership of *Ebony* in the postwar period began to rebel and protest their inclusion.

Ebony magazine provides a window to black ideals and diversity because the periodical highlighted black women and their bodies. Despite the "lighter" tone of the magazine, many readers felt that the inclusion of "cheesecake" photography was unnecessary and improper. An early example of the complex issues regarding standards of beauty and morality came with coverage of the "Miss Fine Brown Frame" beauty pageant in 1947. In a win for race pride, Evelyn Sanders, the contestant with the darkest complexion, took the grand prize. Sanders had made her own revealing bikini for the contest, fearing that the pageant "would be won by some nearly-Caucasian face atop a light brown frame." Indeed, the judges started to crown a light-skinned girl, but the audience disagreed, and according to the *Ebony* article, let the judging panel know that "for once, white standards of beauty would not be forced upon them." The judges then compromised, giving Sanders the cash and the light-skinned girl the title. But when "[f]ists shot up threateningly from the audience," Sanders was crowned the queen.[27] On the one hand, this account reveals the rejection of white standards of beauty; instead of allowing a light-complexioned contestant to win the pageant, the audience demanded that Sanders, the beauty hopeful with the darkest skin, be awarded the title. Light-skinned African American women far outnumbered their darker-complexioned sisters in beauty contests. But with measurements of 35–23–36, Sanders fell well within the white body ideal. In the article's accompanying photo, Sander's measurements were printed next to each respective body part, just as in white publications, but with her head cropped out of the photograph. The resulting image is a scantily clad, headless figure. Mrs. Pauline Thomas of Detroit agreed with other readers, calling the image a "disgrace to the magazine" and insisting that Sanders could have put on a pair of shorts.[28] *Ebony* did not hide readers' dissatisfaction with the pictorial, and in later volumes cut back on cheesecake photography. Instead, Johnson launched a series of alternate periodicals such as *Jet* in 1951 and the short-lived *Tan Confessions* (1950–1952), where pin-up photography occupied a more prominent position, although neither magazine reached the commercial success of *Ebony*.

The presence of cheesecake photography in black periodicals was important despite the grumblings of *Ebony*'s conservative readership. Joanne Meyerowitz argues that rather than objectifying women for the sake of the male viewer, black models in mainstream magazines were ammunition against racist and classist beauty ideals.[29] Marjorie Byer agrees, noting that black "pin-up" girls and pageant winners demonstrated to white America that African American women were beautiful, too.[30] A number of African American co-eds found themselves celebrated in the pages of black magazines in the postwar years for winning multi-racial beauty pageants. Chicago's Clarice C. Davis at the University of Illinois reigned as the very first African American homecoming queen for a Big Ten Conference school in 1951. Davis was voted the winner by her classmates over eight other contestants, both white and black.[31] And in August 1964, Patricia Evans placed first at the Miss America Modeling Contest and became the first black model to appear in *Seventeen* magazine.[32]

Although women of color had made inroads into beauty contests, minority models were offered few opportunities in men's magazines. Black men wanted to see women of color celebrated on the glossy page, but most "girlie" magazines failed to hire women of color beyond a few, token "exotic" models who could pass for a number of races or ethnicities depending on the costume. In August 1964, a reader bemoaned this lack of diversity amongst *Playboy* Playmates with a poem:

> Hey great
> Forward looking
> *Playboy* magazine;
> Hey iconoclastic
> Philosopher of
> The modern age;
> Hey value examiner
> For the American
> People
> Why does foldout

Beauty come in
But one color? Eh?[33]

Women of color, coincidentally, began appearing in *Playboy* in that same issue, albeit a decade after the periodical's introductory issue. China Lee, a five-feet-four-inch "training Bunny" at the Chicago Playboy Club with 35–22–35 measurements, became the first woman of color to appear in the coveted Playmate section. The popularity of the Asian American bunny was made apparent when Lee was later voted a finalist in the Playmate of the Year competition.

A few months later, in March 1965, Hugh Hefner introduced his first African American Playmate, Jennifer Jackson of Chicago. Jackson's twin sister, Gloria Johnson, was the first African American "Bunny" at the Chicago Playboy Club. At five feet, eight and a half inches, 130 pounds, and with "vital statistics" of 36–23–36, Jackson was significantly taller and weighed more than previous Playmates. Not once did the accompanying article mention her race, although it was apparent from reader responses that they did not need to see the color of her skin labeled in order to recognize her "otherness." The response to Jackson's inclusion was mixed; many applauded Hefner and the magazine for being forward thinking, while others actually *mailed back* the centerfold from their copy of the March issue. One such reader who returned the pullout section noted, "we entreat you to return to your time-tested format of Playmate selection, which is more in line with the thinking of the vast majority of your readers."[34] The next African American centerfold would not appear until October 1969, over four years later. The failure of Hefner and other men's magazine editors to insert diversity into the pages of their magazines made it public that if men wanted to see women of color in print, they would have to publish their own magazines.

The attempt to sate black male readers' desire was *Duke* magazine. Published out of Chicago in 1957, the city that had given birth to *Playboy* magazine a few years earlier, *Duke* was the first and last attempt at a *Playboy/Esquire* periodical for and by African American men. The next mainstream magazine geared toward black men was *Players* in November 1973, although the periodical came from the white publishers of *Adam*. Ex-employees of the Johnson Publishing Company formed the core editorial staff of the new magazine, reflecting John H. Johnson's reluctance to follow the *Playboy* model. *Duke* reflected the desire rather than the reality of black men in the 1950s—flashy cars, expansive wardrobes, and "damn near white" girlfriends.[35] In its pilot issue in June 1957, *Duke* editor Dan Burley had this to say about the publication's mission:

> *Duke* will strive to cater to the sophisticated, urbane tastes of our Ivy-minded males who have advanced fully enough so that virility is more than a word and adult truly connotes manhood in all its glories. We have no causes and no axes to grind except to bring moments of pleasure to he-men and their female friends of like mind with an amusing, delightful package of

assorted goodies, ranging from top-notch fiction to the pinup ladies placed on display in our "Duchess of the Month" department each issue.[36]

Mirroring *Playboy*'s mission statement a few years earlier, *Duke* strove to appeal to an educated black readership with a balance of girl-next-door centerfolds, urbanity, sexuality, and humor.[37]

The flagship issue featured fiction from well-respected authors such as Chester Himes, Erskine Caldwell, and Langston Hughes, with humor from others like Geo S. Schuyler and Ray Bradbury. Sandwiched between works of fiction and cartoons was the centerfold pin-up girl—the only page of the magazine printed in color—which featured the "Duchess of the Month." If Playboys had Playmates, then Dukes had Duchesses. "Every Duke to the royal manor born most certainly deserves and delights in a duchess," the text that accompanied the first foldout announced. The original "Duchess" was Eleanor Crews of Chicago who, during the day, was employed as an insurance company underwriter, but had also appeared as a model on the pages of *Jet* magazine. Later Duchesses were mostly models and aspiring actresses. Crew and her other Duchess counterparts were generally very light skinned, not unusual for African American models at the time. Like the majority of *Playboy* centerfolds, Crews was not entirely nude, but instead wore a terrycloth towel draped over her lower torso, hiding her from the camera's view, and a strategically placed arm covered her bare breasts.

Black-and-white photos depicted everyday activities in the same format as *Playboy*'s centerfolds. But the descriptions that accompanied that month's "Duchess," and even the name itself, suggested an untouchableness. Unlike the Playmates, who appeared eager for "play," their African American doppelgangers posed more of a challenge. Crews enjoyed oil painting and "reading deep stuff like Edgar Allan Poe and Leo Tolstoy." Her profile portrayed a woman who did it all: not only did she have a steady job, but she was a talented enough dancer to have once been an instructor, and she reportedly took classes at the Art Institute of Chicago to learn more about painting with oils.[38]

Another Duchess, Dorothy Peterson, was a dancer and singer with plans to tour with Duke Ellington. A former model, Peterson also attended classes at the University of Southern California, where she studied psychology.[39] Maxine Chancellor, the July 1957 Duchess, was also a model and aspiring actress, but as the accompanying text noted, "she's no ordinary, humdrum girl, but a cultured charmer" who enjoyed spending time at art galleries and bookstores.[40] Although a number of *Playboy* Playmates were college students, and one was even working toward a master's degree, more typical were women like June 1956's Playmate, Gloria Walker, who loved puppies and pigeons and people.[41] While Hefner continued to portray his centerfolds as physically and intellectually accessible, *Duke* readers were hard-pressed to win the attention of this kind of royal woman. *Duke* folded after only a six-issue run. The black middle class remained a relatively small group in the 1950s and, despite the success of *Ebony*, the failure of *Duke* magazine demonstrated that a mass market of affluent, urbane African American male consumers was still in the future.[42]

Expanded Beauty Ideals

While Hollywood and women's magazines helped shape American ideals of bodily perfection, the movie-making industry had less of an influence on African American women's body image. Unlike their white counterparts, the most popular celebrities in the black community were largely singers rather than actresses. The most famous crossover stars, Lena Horne and Dorothy Dandridge, both curvy yet slender actresses, first gained fame as jazz singers. Black scholar Maxine Leeds Craig surveyed African American women who'd grown up in the postwar years and asked if they had identified with any celebrities; her interviewees noted they had not, but found Lena Horne, Dorothy Dandridge, and Diahann Carroll to be the most beautiful.[43] Hollywood at this time was not yet ready to embrace black actresses for parts beyond maids, jungle roles, or chorus-girl bit parts.[44] "I suppose everybody in America, especially girls, dreams about the movies and Hollywood," one hopeful black starlet told *Ebony*. "And the way the stars get discovered ... Lana Turner was sipping a malted on a high stool. Yes, it might even happen to you—except if you're colored!"[45]

Despite the lack of opportunities for African American starlets in the movies, however, black periodicals held an optimistic attitude about black women's chances as fashion models. In 1946, Ed Brandford and Barbara Watson founded the first black modeling agency, New York's Brandford Modeling School. Watson considered the "perfect figure model" to have a 34–36-inch bust and 34-inch hips, but noted that a few of the top fashion photographers were asking for taller models with wider hips and larger breasts. "Slowly, but surely," she declared, "the rounded figure is coming back into vogue."[46] Ophelia DeVore of New York's Del Marco Model Agency similarly looked for black models with pin-up- and cover girl-type measurements. She noted that while high-fashion magazines went for a more slender look, publications like *Seventeen* looked for models with "fuller figures." John Powers, who had a reputation in the white model industry for only employing willowy waifs, declared in an article published in *Ebony*, "There is no set formula for female beauty, no rigid rules to follow in determining who is beautiful and who is not."[47] Although a lean figure was still popular for white, high-fashion modeling, black models with more shapely silhouettes won beauty contests and pin-up prizes and earned employment as chorine girls. Cordie Smith, Chicago's most photographed black model, had measurements of 35.5–25–35.5, and she weighed 130 pounds in 1955.[48] African American magazines told their readers that the well-rounded and curved figure was regaining popularity, whereas white periodicals warned that fashion magazines only desired rail-thin beauties.

Mainstream (white) magazines were largely silent about celebrity exercise regimes, but black periodicals assured readers that their favorite stars' fitness was the product of rigorous effort. Even in the fantasy play-world of Hollywood, "alluring movie queens have to bend over backwards to maintain those out-of-the-world shapes." Dorothy Dandridge reported she maintained her 36–24–36.5, five feet, five-and-a-half-inch, 110–115-pound frame by going to the gym. She remarked it was a "sin" for a woman not to preserve her figure for as long as she could.[49] Black periodicals of the period also openly discussed reducing diets. Similar to white periodicals, magazines like *Jet* and *Ebony* reported on the eating regimes of celebrities. Lena Horne reportedly avoided foreign foods "because of tendency to be hippy."[50] A chorus girl in three Broadway shows, Carmen Alexander, also worried about her hips. When she worked in an office, a girdle could handle the problem areas, but as a chorus girl, hiding her hips was not an option.[51] But unlike white celebrity stories, not all stars' diets were regimented or successful. Internationally famous entertainer Josephine Baker told *Ebony* that she never monitored her food intake, but when she noticed her dresses getting too tight, she went on a diet of nothing but carrots. Dinah Washington, blues singer, reportedly lost thirty-five pounds in six weeks with pills and injections from her doctor; the rest of the time she ate whatever she wanted, including pig's feet. Gospel singer Mahalia Jackson gained 110 pounds because she could not resist her own cooking, and operatic singer Marian Anderson admitted she failed to follow her own diet prescription of avoiding bread, potatoes, and desserts.[52]

In addition to exercise and reducing diets, guarding one's femininity required a balance in the kind and intensity of athletic activities. Historian Susan K. Cahn has argued that black and white female athletes were celebrated for their athletic prowess, but only if they exuded traditional female beauty ideals.[53] Cahn focuses on track-and-field stars in her analysis of black athletes in the postwar period, but if one casts a wider scope, a more ambiguous interpretation exists. African American periodicals celebrated black women's achievements in masculine sports like roller derby and wrestling with far less discussion of femininity and beauty than their white media counterparts. Throughout the 1950s, African American women made up more than two-thirds of American women competing in track-and-field events.[54] More than any other sport, track garnered a "masculine" reputation; the 1950s Olympic committee even considered eliminating track events that were not considered "feminine." African American women's achievements in track reinforced the harmful stereotype that black women were less womanly than whites. As Cahn observes, athletics could "affirm the dignity and capabilities of African American womanhood," but it could also play into stereotypes of black women as animalistic, primal, and mannish.[55] *Ebony* attempted to counteract negative stereotypes about black female athletes. One 1955 article noted that track-and-field was slowly gaining more acceptance due to the international fame of many of the black female competitors. Moreover, fewer girls avoided the sport for fear of it making them "masculine freaks," and as the article boasted, boys learned that a girl track star "can be as feminine as the china-doll type." Frances Kaszubski, an Amateur Athletic Union official who supervised the American girls at the Pan-American games, additionally argued, "If more girls knew how to run … fewer of them would be so awkward."[56] In this way, *Ebony* advertised that participation in track-and-field would not threaten a woman's femininity, but rather could potentially add grace and poise. Most white media ignored female black track stars despite heralding their male counterparts as the answer to the Russians.[57] Cahn notes that athletes of all ages and races received the most media praise when they met popular beauty ideals.[58] Track speedster Wilma Rudolph appeared sporadically in *Life* magazine after her Olympic success in the 1960s. She was called "lissome" compared with her "hardy" Soviet competitors.[59] The only female African American athlete to appear regularly in the white press was tennis champion Althea Gibson, whom one magazine described as "lanky" and as playing "with the slam-bang determination she once used fighting kids in Harlem."[60] Althea Gibson became the most popular black female athlete in the white press, yet she was not heralded as a beauty queen.

Despite the black press's concerns regarding track-and-field participants, they did not appear dedicated to portraying other sports' athletes as overtly feminine. Periodicals highlighted the achievements of female athletes in high-contact activities as varied as judo, wrestling, high diving, and baseball. The mother of speed-skating star Gayle Ann Fannin told *Ebony*, "when I realized she was determined to race, I gave up my dream of dainty, pretty costumes, stuck her in dungarees and told her to forget how she looked."[61] Female wrestling was an odd voyeuristic phenomenon popular in both black and white magazines in the postwar period. Magazines noted that while the majority of women spent hours perfecting glamour "in an effort to land a husband," the wrestling rings around the country were filling with a new kind of woman who, forsaking femininity, spent her time building muscles instead.[62] Even roller derby garnered attention. Although one headline noted that derby star Quintina Cosby "add[ed] glamour to rough, grueling indoor sport," the accompanying photo essay pulled no punches, showing Cosby in various action poses, blocking, pushing, tripping, and tackling other players. The article described her as "[u]nusually strong and possess[ing] of real stamina" and that she had trained her body to take the "jolting body checks" common in the sport. Cosby's coaches ranked her higher than most of the boys skating in New York's Junior Roller Derby.[63] Gloria Jean Thompson, a twenty-five-year-old female boxer, appeared in a number of black periodicals. Purportedly she avoided marriage because it would not only interfere with her career, but she was afraid "if I was married and my husband fouled up, I would hit him just like I do another fighter."[64] However, to avoid rumors about her private life, Thompson never wore pants in public.[65] Baseball player Toni Stone became the first female to play on a professional baseball team in the Negro American League in 1953. She was effective at the plate, "swinging a man-sized bat," and her speed matched and surpassed many of her teammates, beating out many bunts. Her teammates, while acknowledging her gender, treated her no differently from the other players.[66] When Stone appeared at a public event wearing a pink flowered dress, one onlooker marveled "I thought she'd be chewing tobacco and swearing like a man."[67] Although black periodicals published articles reasserting the femininity of their track-and-field athletes, participants of other sports who appeared in those same magazines were celebrated for their physical prowess, with little concern about defending their femininity or physical beauty.

Just as the representation of female athletes differed in black periodicals, the same can also be said for dieting advice. In 1956, the *Chicago Defender* began posting the daily column "The Housewives Corner," featuring two women who planned on losing a pound a day through dieting. Mrs. Beatrice Mendenhall and her friend Mrs. Marian Mims, whose combined weight totaled over 600 pounds, posted their weekly diets and their progress in the column.[68] The friends began with a "conditioning" diet for two weeks to ready their bodies for the rigid daily diet of 750 calories that would follow. At the start of their third week, they began their goal of losing a pound of flesh a day. Cognizant that slender-seeking women reading the column would also have a family to feed, the *Defender* listed a meal for the family and one for the dieter in each article. Moreover, the *Chicago Defender* paid special attention to these diets being both economical and practical and listed different lunch options for both working women and for housewives. Details such as these could not be found in the typical high-fashion magazine. While dieting advice existed in black newspapers and magazines, these periodicals highlighted the dangers of reducing in ways that were largely ignored by white magazines until the diet pill scare of the late 1960s. Horror stories about fad diets instructed African American women to maintain balanced diets and to be realistic about monthly weight-loss goals. A once-beautiful model, readers were warned, had wasted away to a human skeleton of seventy-eight pounds after embarking on a fad diet of lemon juice, hot water, cola drinks, and an occasional hot dog.[69] Moreover, standardized height and weight tables were not always appropriate guides and black women were cautioned against a "mechanical approach" to dieting. Dr. Hilde Bruch, a weight management specialist, warned that some overweight people should avoid dieting altogether. "There are many people whose well-being is affected if they try to push their weight below a certain level which may be somewhat higher than that of the standard tables," she argued in *Jet* magazine.[70]

Similar to the re-appropriation of what was considered "bad" hair and the "wrong" skin color, could fat be beautiful, too? In 1962, 23.5 percent of white women were 20 percent or more over the ideal weight for their frame–height–age, compared with 41.7 percent of black women.[71] Longtime *Ebony* editor Era Bell Thompson pointed out that food was a status symbol for black America "after generations of living on crumbs from the Big Table." She created her own tongue-in-cheek "Soul Food Diet" in the pages of *Ebony* in the style of diets found in white women's magazines:

> Breakfast: 1/2 cup pot liquor concentrate. 1 toasted cornbread stick
> Lunch: dandelion green sandwich. 1 cup watermelon juice

Dinner: choice of 2 steamed chicken necks or 1 small pig's foot. 9 black-eyed peas cooked in clear water.
Dessert: 1 slice bread soaked in diet sorghum

Thompson, in an attempt to ascertain if she was overweight, also gave herself an "obesity test" similar to one that appeared in *Seventeen* magazine in May 1969. *Seventeen*'s self-examination encouraged young women to look in the mirror and discern which areas needed toning and to pinch their bodies. If more than an inch of flesh resulted between the forefinger and thumb, "you're probably too fat."[72] Performing this self-test, Thompson declared, "One look in the mirror … should have eliminated the other two tests." Thompson momentarily bemoaned that someone as industrious as herself, having worked her way through college cleaning houses, should certainly have had the stamina to rid herself of a bulbous middle. But the pursuit of a slender figure was not simply a matter of willpower. Economics and racial discrimination had a role to play as well. Referring to elitist "fat farms" like Elizabeth Arden's "Maine Chance" diet camp, Thompson observed, "Neither can I afford, nor would I likely be accepted by a 600-calorie, $100-a-day fat farm even if its gymnasium has wall-to-wall carpeting and a swimming pool filled with fat-free milk."[73] After dismissing exercise and diet drinks like Sego or Metrecal, Thompson decided to diet. She calculated that by cutting 500–1,000 calories from her daily food regime, she could slim down to an appropriate 120 pounds—appropriate for her height and build, according to insurance tables.

Thompson began her diet in earnest, counting her calories for each meal. By the time she finished her calculations, however, her meal was cold and unappetizing. When she was five pounds lighter, a neighbor brought over a chocolate cake and Thompson suddenly found herself six pounds heavier than her pre-diet weight. "[I]t will take 42 days of sheer torture and determination to undo the damage [of the cake]," she reported. "In the meantime, I will wear clothes two sizes too large, and friends will grudgingly say, 'My, how you've lost!'"[74] Letters to the magazine revealed the gratefulness of *Ebony*'s female readers for the change-of-pace story. Calling the story "marvelous," one reader noted the timeliness of the article and its subject material. Another joked, "I never realized anyone could draw such perfect pictures of me without seeing me … it is so nice to know we Big Fat Mamas are still being recognized."[75]

Black professionals mirrored their white counterparts in terms of mass consumption patterns and the Protestant work ethic, but they joined the black working class in a cross-socioeconomic appreciation for a wide array of body types. Beauty had little to do with size or weight. Instead, middle-class black women were encouraged to "exemplify domesticity," remain feminine, and present themselves as respectable.[76] *Ebony* annually published its "Best Dressed Women in America" list, which highlighted African American women of different ages and sizes. To be featured in this coveted column required only a generous and conservative wardrobe. This mindset and acceptance of many body types contrasts sharply, however, with middle-class attitudes about hair. Scholars of black history note the significance of straightened hair as a marker of one's position in society.[77] The flat-ironed look required frequent visits to beauty salons and dedicated upkeep. During the civil rights movement in the 1950s and 1960s, careful grooming was an important part of the middle-class strategy. Susannah Walker notes that photographs of African American protestors reveal carefully dressed and coifed women with straightened hair.[78] When Afros became popular among the youth and the working class in the late 1960s, this trend horrified middle-class blacks. Weight, by contrast, never evoked the class or generational divides as attitudes about black women's hair did.

Despite concerns about dieting, foundation garments, and exercise, black periodicals celebrated women who embraced their larger frames; not every woman had to be "the perfect 36" to be heralded as a success. In this way, postwar African American men and women broadened beauty ideals. One *Jet* article boldly declared that fat women were better lovers than their skinny sisters. Dr. Julian Lewis of Chicago proclaimed, "Fat women are fat because they do not restrain themselves in the things that give them pleasure. The overeating that fattens them," he continued, "shows a lack of inhibitions and above average sexual proclivities naturally follow."[79] The article noted that despite the popularity of "pocket-size[d]" women, larger women rarely had trouble finding husbands, reasoning that men preferred to come home from work and be "mothered" by a filled-out mate. "[S]lenderness in itself is no criterion for success in a woman's world," *Jet* magazine articulated, noting that this was particularly true for female musicians. Gospel singer Mahalia Jackson observed, "My work for the Lord is more important than reducing. I was born big and fat for a purpose and there is no need for me to try and look different now."[80] One blues singer, Big Maybell, noted, "I'm not worried about gaining weight—I don't want to lose a pound. I think I'm prettiest when I'm fat."[81] The Peters Sisters, a singing trio weighing in at over 800 pounds, joked in their act about riding in small elevators or tipping over small European taxis.[82] Supremes singer Mary Wilson did not shy away from publicizing her curves either. "Already considered quite voluptuous," *Ebony* reported, "she wants to add few pounds for insurance."[83] Another singer, Ruth Brown, described as "a visual as well as vocal delight" and who apparently had the best voice since Sarah Vaughan, used her size 16 figure to "put all the oomph" into her soulful ballads.[84] And swing singer June Richmond, at 270 pounds, noted that her weight was part of her "professional personality." Photos showed Richmond consuming a large breakfast in bed, but also discussed her success; the popular singer owned a $40,000 home in Hollywood where she lived with her two daughters.[85] Not only were these "plus-sized" women professionally successful, numerous articles charted their personal happiness with marriages and maintaining a family.

In addition to celebrating fat celebrities, fashion columns in black periodicals reflected more options for women than those presented in mainstream white magazines. "Styles for the Not-So-Thin" highlighted a new fashion line for women under five feet, five inches tall, with rounded hips and busts, and less visible waistlines. While Christian Dior's "New Look" made these women look "short, squat, and dumpy," his new line created a less exaggerated silhouette, both fashionable and flattering.[86] When the House of Dior introduced the "Flat Look" in the mid-1950s, *Jet* magazine declared that the fashion house had "uncorked what was perhaps the greatest controversy since the U.S. atom-bombed Nagasaki."[87] Although equally unpopular in the white and black community, the shapeless silhouette was once again introduced in 1960. Yves Saint-Laurent, top designer for Dior, called his design the "Silhouette of the Future." At least in the black community in the 1960s, the bust-flattening, knee-revealing fashion was considered unflattering. One Howard University student, Sheila Gregory, observed, "I should think that for slender women of slight build, Dior's new look would be very attractive. I don't think, however, that it would be becoming to me."[88] Black journalists predicted the style would "fall as flat as the fashions."[89]

Rather than looking to Paris for the newest fashions, more popular fashion trends in black women's magazines were those that could be flattering to a variety of body types. Moreover, *Ebony* employed "plus-size" models in their nationally touring fashion troupe. One of the touring models, Michelle Zeno, was 193 pounds and five feet ten inches tall, which was twenty pounds over MetLife's maximum weight range for a woman with a large frame. A *Jet* 1955 article about beachwear found styles that every woman could comfortably wear, whether very tall, very slender, or too fleshy. The article noted that suits could be found to "hide a multiple of faults" like flower-printed beachwear with small skirts or one-piece suits to hide "too much tummy." The author cautioned readers that scant bathing suits should only be worn by those with near-perfect figures, so "consider your assets before investing in an all-revealing bikini suit."[90] Another column highlighted a summer swimwear collection in which "even the less-than-Venus girl can arrange to exude boat-loads of beguilement by strolling surf-side." This "Covered Up" collection concealed a bit more skin, hid the midriff, and added an extra inch to pant legs.[91] White women's magazines exhibited minimal sympathy for heavier women when compared with the articles in the black press. *Life* highlighted a fashion-friendly clothing line, but only for adolescent girls. Designer Emily Wilkens used black fabric and stripes to "elongate chunky young figures" and created styles "designed to flatten-embarrassing adolescent curves." As the text indicates, however, this was not the ideal figure with which white teenage girls should be satisfied.[92]

Moreover, while the white fashion world became obsessed with the lanky model Twiggy in the mid-1960s, the black press found her laughable. The *Chicago Defender* joked that whenever Great Britain faced a financial crisis, they called an emergency meeting to create a scheme to siphon money from the former colonies. "All we have to do, gentlemen, is go into one of the Cockney districts and pick out a teenage girl who is flat-chested, bird-legged and looks undernourished. Then we tell the Ameddicans [*sic*] that this girl is the world's most sought after fashion model … I recommend calling her either 'The Splinter' or 'Twiggy.'"[93] Another columnist noted, "We'd hate to break anybody's baloon [*sic*], but British model Twiggy's appeal comes from the fact that she knows she's ugly. If a Soul Sister looked anything like Twiggy, she'd be in a whole world of trouble—and we mean trouble."[94] The urgency for extreme slenderness never resonated in the African American community. The ultra-thin fashion model of the 1960s was a white body issue.

Conclusions

In two separate health-screening projects in 1950, the general population between the ages of fifteen and fifty-nine in Richmond, Virginia and in Atlanta, Georgia was weighed, with some dramatic results. In Richmond, Virginia, over 30 percent of white men, black men, and black women were found to be 10 percent above average weight, or "overweight." Only 13.3 percent of white women were 10 percent above the average weight. Similar numbers were collected in Atlanta, with nearly 25 percent of the city's black and white men weighing in at 10 percent above average. And 15.7 percent of white women were considered "overweight" compared to 39.3 percent of black women. The numbers concerning "obesity" were even more remarkable. In the city of Richmond, 6.2 percent of white women and 12.9 percent of white men were 20 percent or more above "average" weight. This aligns with the 1959 Build and Blood Pressure study of 6 percent of women and 11 percent of American men considered "obese."[95] For black women, 29.9 percent of Richmond's and 26.2 percent of Atlanta's female black population was recorded as 20 percent or more above average weights.[96]

Moreover, in a 1966 study, researchers discovered that white teens wanted to lose more weight than African American girls, even though the black teens weighed more. In this longitudinal study, which followed one thousand students over their entire high-school career, black, white, and Asian girls were able to pinpoint their current weight with precise accuracy. All three groups' "desired" weight was significantly lower than how much they actually weighed, with white girls showing the greatest gap between actual weight and desired weight. Black girls on average weighed more than the other two groups, with a higher prevalence of "obesity." Their desired weight was also close to ten pounds more than the desired weight for white girls. One-fifth of black teens wanted *larger* hips and thighs and more black girls were concerned about *underweight* than white girls, which led researchers from the Nutrition Division of the School of Public Health at UC-Berkeley to conclude, "The ideal figure, it appears, is not the same for Negro and Caucasian girls."[97] One could argue that these figures are intrinsically tied to socioeconomics and regional differences. Similar studies also highlighted the prevalence of "obesity" in lower economic groups.[98] But what this data suggests overall is the impact of outside cultural forces beyond the pressure of medical and actuarial advice.

Social historian Peter Stearns argues that African Americans had a wider view of beautiful women because (1) God does not make mistakes and (2) priority was given to dealing with race issues over size. Stearns traces the roots of these beliefs to African matriarchies and attitudes about working women during Reconstruction. "Unlike their white counterparts," he argues, "most black women have always worked, even when married; and in some physical labor, size was a positive advantage, associated with strength, not fat."[99] Although convincing, Stearns cannot explain why "plus-size" women continued to be celebrated in the postwar years. The success ethic of the new black middle class, as promoted by John H. Johnson and *Ebony*, suggests that to be associated with this socioeconomic level, the (male) breadwinner needed an ample salary. Black men took pride in the fact that their wives need not financially contribute to maintaining their middle-class status. If body size was associated with strength and work, it would be more logical then that small, frail black women were seen as the ideal body type in the years after World War II.

Naomi Wolf's "Beauty Myth" similarly cannot explain this phenomenon.[100] Wolf argues that in eras when women realize more political and economic gains, beauty ideals become more rigid and unattainable. She observes that as women demand more public recognition, smaller body types become *en vogue* so women literally take up less space. While the beginning of the second wave of feminism coincides with the popularity of thin fashion models like Twiggy and Penelope Tree, the same does not apply to black women and the civil rights movement. Black America's newspapers and magazines, in fact, *discouraged* women from mimicking the hyper-thin look and warned readers about the dangers of excessive dieting and unhealthy food habits.

The study of black periodicals in the postwar era reveals beauty standards that were more realistic and attainable. Black women sought magazines like *Ebony*, *Jet*, and others that spoke to their lived experiences. Black beauty queens and magazine pin-up girls showed white America that black was beautiful, too. And because the average African American cover girl weighed more and had broader measurements than the typical white model, magazines fêted a more realistic body type. More importantly, unlike their white counterparts, black periodicals showed an open celebration of "plus-size" models, celebrities, and female athletes who did not conform to or fit white ideals of acceptable femininity. Without black, emaciated models staring back at them from the covers of their magazines, the charge that "overweight" and "obesity" was killing Americans and that "thin was in" did not have the same impact on black women as it did on their white counterparts.

Notes

1 "No More Miss America! Ten Points of Protest," in *Sisterhood is Powerful: An Anthology of Writings from the Women's Liberation Movement*, ed. Robin Morgan (New York: Random House, 1970), 521.

2 For more on the pageant and its protest, see Rosalyn Baxandall and Linda Gordon, *Dear Sisters: Dispatches from the Women's Liberation Movement* (New York: Basic Books, 2001), 184–187; Maxine Leeds Craig, *Ain't I a Beauty Queen?: Black Women, Beauty, and*

the Politics of Race (New York: Oxford University Press, 2002), 3–18; and Sara M. Evans, *Born for Liberty* (New York: Free Press, 1997), 173–179, 283.

3 This was not the first national African American beauty contest. Attempts at a national contest similar to the Miss America pageant format originated in 1944 with the Miss Sepia America pageant, held in Chicago, Illinois, in 1944. Other nationwide contests with regional and state representatives followed, such as the Miss Bronze America contest, held in Atlantic City, New Jersey, in 1945.
4 "Face to Face with Miss Black America," *Seventeen*, March 1969, 151.
5 "Size-Wise Diet," *Seventeen*, May 1969, 144.
6 Craig, *Ain't I a Beauty Queen?*, 24–25.
7 Havelock Ellis, *Studies in the Psychology of Sex, vol. 4: Sexual Selection in Man* (Philadelphia, PA: F. A. Davis, 1905), 158.
8 Elizabeth Haiken, *Venus Envy: A History of Cosmetic Surgery* (Baltimore, MD: The John Hopkins University Press, 1997), 213.
9 "Plastic Surgery: Many Negroes Narrow Noses, Thin Lips Through Operations," *Ebony*, May 1949, 19.
10 "Advertisement," *Chicago Defender*, February 11, 1956, 10.
11 "The Girl Who Changed Her Face," *Ebony*, March 1956, 77–79.
12 Bart Landry, *The New Black Middle Class* (Berkeley, CA: University of California Press, 1987), 22–29.
13 Ibid., 21.
14 Mary Pattillo-McCoy, *Black Picket Fences: Privilege and Peril among the Black Middle Class* (Chicago, IL: The University of Chicago Press, 1999), 17. Pattillo-McCoy challenges E. Franklin Frazier, *Black Bourgeoisie: The Rise of a New Middle Class* (New York: The Free Press, 1957). Frazier's hypothesis that the black middle class mirrors white middle class and has no cultural roots in either the black or white world has been widely contested in recent scholarship.
15 Ibid., 3.
16 John H. Johnson, *Surviving Against the Odds* (New York: Warner Books, 1989), 123.
17 Korey Bowers Brown, "Ideals, Images, Identity: *Ebony* Magazine in an Age of Black Power, 1965–1970." Master's thesis, Vanderbilt University, 2000, 3.
18 "Mission Statement," *Ebony*, November 1945, 1.
19 For more on the early years of *Ebony*, see Adam Green, *Selling the Race: Culture, Community, and Black Chicago, 1940–1955* (Chicago, IL: University of Chicago Press, 2007), 129–177.
20 "Letters and Pictures to the Editor," *Ebony*, January 1946, 51.
21 "Advertisement," *Ebony*, May 1946, 1.
22 Susanna Walker, *Style and Status: Selling Beauty to African American Women, 1920–1975* (Lexington, KY: The University Press of Kentucky, 2007), 129.
23 "Letters to the Editor," *Ebony*, January 1966, 4.
24 "Backstage," *Ebony*, May 1946, 4.
25 "Advertisement," *Ebony*, November 1959, 39.
26 "Letters to the Editor," *Ebony*, May 1948, 8.
27 "Miss Fine Brown Frame: Darkest Girl in Contest Wins First Prize," *Ebony*, May 1947, 47.
28 "Letters to the Editor," *Ebony*, August 1947, 4.
29 Joanne Meyerowitz, "Women, Cheesecake, and Borderline Material: Responses to Girlie Pictures in the Mid-Twentieth Century U.S.," *Journal of Women's History* 8 (1996): 20.
30 Marjorie Lee Bryer, "Pinups, *Playboy*, Pageants and Racial Politics, 1945–1966," PhD diss., University of Minnesota, 2003.
31 "Queen of Illini," *Jet*, November 22, 1951, 33.
32 "Teen-Age Beauty with Brains," *Ebony*, August 1964, 77–78.
33 "Dear Playboy," *Playboy*, August 1964, 9.

34 "Dear Playboy," *Playboy*, May 1964, 13.
35 Dian Hanson, *Dian Hanson's The History of Men's Magazines*, Volume II (Los Angeles, CA: Taschen, 2004), 388, 392.
36 "Duke Debut," *Duke*, June 1957, 2.
37 For more on *Duke* magazine, see Kinohi Nishikawa, "Race, Respectability, and the Short Life of *Duke* Magazine," *Book History* 15, no. 1 (2012): 152–182.
38 "Introducing the Duchess of the Month," *Duke*, June 1957, 34.
39 "Duchess of the Month," *Duke*, September 1957, 34.
40 "Duchess of the Month," *Duke*, July 1957, 32–33.
41 "Miss June," *Playboy*, June 1956.
42 Although many popular men's magazines such as *Playboy* purportedly featured the girl-next-door in their centerfolds, African American models better bodily matched the realities of the average American woman. Typical *Playboy* centerfolds had larger breasts, thinner waists, and more slender hips than the black models featured in African American periodicals. Compared with other men's magazines primarily aimed at a white audience, the Duchesses in *Duke* measured up more modestly at 34.5–22.5–35. The average measurements for women in white men's pin-up magazines between 1955 and 1959 were 37.5–24–36, and in *Playboy* specifically, statistics for centerfold Playmates averaged 36.78–23–35.2 in those same years. Duchesses were even less chesty than the models who appeared in Johnson's *Jet* magazine, at 35–23–35.7 during that five-year span (based on the average of every measurement mentioned in the magazines between 1945 and 1970).
43 Craig, *Ain't I a Beauty Queen?*, 30.
44 "Hollywood's Unknown Negro Beauties," *Jet*, November 22, 1951, 59.
45 "I Tried to Crash the Movies," *Ebony*, August 1946, 6.
46 "What Is the Perfect Figure?" *Jet*, June 26, 1952, 33–34.
47 John Powers, "The Most Beautiful Negro Women in America," *Ebony*, November 1949, 44.
48 "What Is the Perfect Figure?" *Jet*, June 26, 1952, 33–34.
49 "Film Formula for Glamour," *Ebony*, June 1948, 32.
50 "Meet the Real Lena Horne," *Ebony*, November 1947, 11.
51 "I Tried Crashing the Movies," *Ebony*, February 1946, 22.
52 "Diets of the Stars: Wealthy or Poor, Famous or Unknown, Everybody Is Trying to Lose Weight," *Ebony*, May 1960, 106–110.
53 Susan, K. Cahn, *Coming on Strong: Gender and Sexuality in Twentieth-Century Women's Sports* (Cambridge, MA: Harvard University Press, 1998).
54 Ibid., 120.
55 Ibid., 121.
56 "Fastest Women in the World: Fleet Track Lassies Win Fame at Mexico's Pan-American Games," *Ebony*, May 1955, 27.
57 "The U.S. Picks a Strong Olympic Team," *Life*, July 19, 1948, 17–25.
58 Cahn, *Coming on Strong*, 136–137.
59 "Olympian Quintessence," *Life*, September 19, 1960, 115.
60 "New Tennis Threat," *Life*, April 3, 1950, 32.
61 "Speed Skater: St. John's University Co-ed Seeks Olympic Fame in 1964," *Ebony*, December 1962, 119.
62 "Lady Wrestlers," *Jet*, February 21, 1952, 57–58.
63 "Roller Derby Star," *Ebony*, May 1954, 56–57.
64 "Lady Boxer: Husky Gloria Thompson," *Ebony*, March 1949, 32.
65 "The Truth About Women Athletes," *Jet*, August 5, 1954, 58.
66 "Lady Ball Player," *Ebony*, July 1953, 48.
67 "The Truth About Women Athletes," *Jet*, August 5, 1954, 56.
68 "Get on the Mark! Diet with a Fat Girl and Lose Pound a Day!" *Chicago Defender*, June 12, 1956, 14.

69 "Is Dieting Dangerous?" *Jet*, March 11, 1954, 30.
70 Ibid., 29–30.
71 Peter N. Stearns, *Fat History: Bodies and Beauty in the Modern West* (New York: New York University Press, 1997), 133.
72 Alice Lake, "Obesity: Rate Your Weight," *Seventeen*, May 1969, 187.
73 Ibid.
74 Ibid., 124–130.
75 "Letters to the Editor," *Ebony*, October 1968, 24–25.
76 Monika N. Gosin, "The Politics of African-American Women's Beauty in Ebony Magazine: The 1960's and 1970's." MA essay, University of California, San Diego, 2004, 125.
77 Ayana D. Byrd and Loris L. Tharps, *Hair Story: Untangling the Roots of Black Hair in America* (New York: St. Martin's Press, 2001), 47.
78 Walker, 145.
79 "Why Fat Women are Better Lovers," *Jet*, December 23, 1953, 20–22.
80 "Famous Fat Women," *Jet*, May 8, 1952, 56–63.
81 "Big Maybell: Three Hundred Pounds of Rhythm and Blues," *Ebony*, February 1955, 104.
82 "The Biggest Act in Show Business," *Ebony*, February 1951, 87–90.
83 "The Supremes Make It Big," *Ebony*, June 1965, 87.
84 "Ruth Brown: Best Voice Since Vaughan," *Jet*, January 31, 1952, 64.
85 "June is Busting Out All Over," *Ebony*, September 1946, 46–47.
86 "Styles for the Not-So-Thin," *Ebony*, September 1948, 52.
87 "Will Dior's Bustline Be a Bust?" *Jet*, October 14, 1954, 38.
88 William Boone, "Will New 'Flat Look' Last Long?" *Jet*, April 7, 1960, 42.
89 Ibid., 43.
90 "Bathing Suits Every Woman Can Wear," *Jet*, July 7, 1955, 38–41.
91 "Covered Up," February 1964, *Ebony*, 107.
92 "New Young Styles: Emily Wilkens' Spring Designs are Kind to Plump Teen-agers," *Life*, March 18, 1946, 87.
93 Dick West, "England Extracts Colonial Money," *Chicago Defender*, April 5, 1967, 14.
94 Ole Nosey, "Everybody Goes When the Wagon Comes," *Chicago Defender*, April 3, 1967, 14.
95 Society of Actuaries, Build and Blood Pressure Study 1959, 18.
96 "Estimated Prevalence of Overweight in the United States," *Public Health Reports* (1896–1970) 69, no. 11 (November 1954): 1084–1086.
97 Ruth Huenemann, Mary C. Hampton, Leona R. Shaprio, and Albert R. Behnke, "Adolescent Food Practices Associated with Obesity," *Federation Proceedings* 25, no. 1 (1966): 4–10; Ruth L. Huenemann, Leona R. Shapiro, Mary C. Hampton, and Barbara W. Mitchell, "A Longitudinal Study of Gross Body Composition and Body Conformation and Their Association with Food and Activity in a Teen-Age Population," *American Journal of Clinical Nutrition* 18 (May 1966): 325–335.
98 Johanna T. Dwyer, Jacob T. Feldman, and Jean Mayer, "The Social Psychology of Dieting," *Journal of Health and Social Behavior* 11, no. 4 (December 1970): 269–287; Ruth Huenemann, Mary C. Hampton, Leona R. Shaprio, and Albert R. Behnke, "Adolescent Food Practices Associated with Obesity," *Federation Proceedings* 25, no. 1 (1966): 4–10.
99 Stearns, *Fat History*, 90–92.
100 Naomi Wolf, *The Beauty Myth: How Images of Beauty Are Used Against Women* (New York: Bantham Doubleday Dell Publishing, 1991), 272.

7

NOT OVER 'TIL THE FAT LADY SINGS

Fighting Fat Stigma

> *We will feel better when we are not fat, they say. We will be happier. We can buy pretty clothes, and people will think we are beautiful. All true of course. And all false.*
> —Aljean Harmetz[1]

Throughout the 1950s and into the early part of the 1960s, the *Ladies Home Journal* featured weight loss "success" stories. The women introduced in the monthly column represented a broad range of motivations, weight-loss methods, and results. But universally, starting with Helen Fraley's original success story in August 1952, all wanted to be significantly thinner than their present figure. On average, the highlighted women originally weighed 203.5 pounds with measurements of 42.25–34–50. After dieting and exercising for several months, they reduced their figures to obtain a 35.5–25.5–37 silhouette and weighed on average 133 pounds. Most women lost over seventy pounds on a daily diet averaging just over 1,000 calories. It is important to note that "obesity-related" health issues did not cause apprehension or inspire these women to lose weight. Worry over diabetes, hypertension, and other alleged symptoms of overfat did not appear in the monthly feature. Only when "overweight" complicated pregnancies and thus strained otherwise stable marriages were medical concerns expressed. Instead, women wrote in to the magazine recalling the shame and humiliation they had once endured for being fat.

Nicknames like "baby blimp" or "fatty-fatty two-by-four" plagued their childhood experiences. They felt unpopular, uncomfortable in their own skin, and ashamed that they could not fit into the latest, youthful fashions. Two of the most salient motivations for reducing teens were dating and clothes. The majority of the young women writing to the *Ladies Home Journal* lamented that boys they had crushes on would not date them because of their size. Overweight teens could not fit into age-appropriate clothing; the size of their bodies required that they shop in the "chubby section" or wear matronly fashions. As teenager Connie Calabro lamented, "Girls felt sorry for me. Boys didn't like me. In fact, I didn't even like myself. I wanted so desperately to be able to dress like the other girls. But I looked like a tub in sweaters and skirts." Calabro claimed that the only party she ever got invited to was the first skating outing of the season—if the ice withstood her weight, all the other teens knew it was safe for them to skate.[2]

Studies at the time discovered a similarity between psychological traits of obese adolescent girls and those of ethnic and racial minorities. As victims of prejudice, both groups exhibited characteristics such as passivity, obsessive concern with self-image, the expectation of rejection, and progressive withdrawal.[3] But unlike fixed race or ethnicity, Americans held that the fat person herself was personally responsible. If she simply stopped overeating, this belief contended, she would be "cured." Anxiety over what number glared back at them on the scale impacted not only fat teenagers. In a 1969 study of high school students, 78 percent of obese girls self-reported weights lower than they actually were. But 42 percent of the "lean" girls did the same. Regardless of where on the weight spectrum a young woman's body fell, a tendency to underreport weight existed. Researchers also found no difference in the frequency of weighing according to weight. In other words, fat teens did not weigh themselves more or less than other girls.[4]

Not only was it shameful to *be* fat, but young women also experienced stigmatization while dieting. Lynn Mabel-Lois, an early fat activist, described the humiliation of taking rainbow-colored diet pills in middle school. "To be fat and taking pills makes you twice removed from the world," she recalled. She trained herself to take her pills without water at school because she was too embarrassed to ask permission to go to the drinking fountain.[5] Another woman remembered the shame of taking her Metrocal can to lunch for school, humiliated that her stepmother would not disguise the diet drink in a thermos for her.[6] Dieting was a personal, private act that occurred in public spaces, yet mass media advised teens to keep their diets hidden. Magazines like *Seventeen* published a "Secret Summer Diet" in 1968 that promised teenagers they could "shed an inch or two of hips or midriff strictly on the sly."[7] A fifteen-year-old who weighed 160 pounds at five feet two inches wanted to lose weight, but her parents would not allow her to diet. *'Teen*'s beauty editor suggested she diet "quietly since no one in your family seems to have your best figure interests at heart."[8] This secrecy was suggested to older women as well. "I have known too many women who have made themselves obnoxious bores by pivoting eternally on the subject of their reducing programs," cautioned one woman.[9] Milwaukee pharmacist Hugo Hoffman noted that women were embarrassed to purchase diet pills, candies, and other slimming products. He observed that in his own store, only "strangers" purchased such items; women went out of their way to buy diet products in stores where they would not be recognized.[10]

Although women's magazines instructed their readers to not talk about their diets, the multitude of published "success" stories indicated that once off the diet, bragging about the self-control and hard work put into one's new figure was permissible. Moreover, support groups like TOPS and Weight Watchers broke through the silence and private shame of "plus-sized" Americans. But the contrast between dieting groups, where members talked about their struggles and triumphs over eating, and women's magazines, which instructed dieting secrecy, no doubt created a mixed message for those wishing to reduce. Should one diet in private and keep her efforts a secret from others? Or should she join a weight-loss group and publicly share her failures and successes? Women's magazines seemed to say to their readers that being overweight was an affliction to keep private. Although columns stressed that *everyone* was on a diet, they also warned readers not to concern others with their personal weight issues.

The burden of being fat and female went beyond private and public shame. It went beyond adolescent teasing, limiting one's wardrobe, or the ability to get a date. It also impacted access to a college education and securing employment. One of the first-account storylines in the *Ladies Home Journal* proclaimed, "I had to lose 60 pounds to go to college." The accompanying article described how a young woman was denied admission to Edinboro State College in Pennsylvania because she weighed 197 pounds. A letter from the director of admissions told the eighteen-year-old college applicant that her weight "would be a detriment to your being enrolled as a student at this college."[11] Edinboro State College, which focused on educating and training future teachers, accepted and denied applicants based on whether the applicant was a "good prospective teacher candidate." Admission was based upon a number of criteria, including "general scholarship, character and personality, health and physical vigor, and command of English." Among the numerous reasons an applicant could be denied admission included "marked obesity."[12] Being "overweight" was considered detrimental, unhealthy, and unwanted for potential teachers. The rejection letter was a horrible blow. She told her mother, "I don't care!" But she did:

> Having lived a long time with the "stigma" of being "FAT," I had no self-esteem. I was a chubby child and grew into a very overweight young lady. And trust me, I was reminded of that by everyone—my parents, friends of the family, my brother, and classmates at every grade level ... I was pretty much reduced to a pathetic person. I felt sorry for myself, was angry at myself, I WISHED to be thin a lot, I wanted to go to sleep and wake up "normal" and sometimes I wished I wouldn't wake up, but, of course, wishes don't just happen.[13]

Because she had always dreamed of being a teacher, she had only applied to Edinboro. She had a choice—give up on her dreams or lose the weight. She chose the latter. In order to convince the university that she would lose the required weight, she agreed to an appointment with the college physician, Dr. Miller, a man whom she recalled as weighing an unsettling 130 pounds. Dr. Miller had a brief conversation with her and she convinced him that she would lose the weight. In retrospect, she was grateful for the rejection; however, she later noted, "when I think about it now, it's very scary to think what that could have done to me and may have done to any other young person who may have received that [rejection] letter, too."[14] Karen Jones, chairman of the Connecticut chapter of the National Association to Aid Fat Americans (now the National Association to Advance Fat Acceptance), experienced similar academic discrimination based on her weight. She recalled that even though she graduated in the top 5 percent of her high school class, she was denied admission to the college of her choice, while a thin classmate with the same credentials was admitted. When Jones was finally admitted to Syracuse University, she was still rejected by its School of Education because of her weight.[15] A 1966 study by the Harvard School of Public Health highlighted that this was not just an issue isolated to teachers. Fat women overall had a one-third less chance of getting into college than their thin classmates. Research exposed that fat men, however, had a slightly better chance of being admitted into college than fat women.[16]

Similarly, fat women faced more serious economic repercussions than fat men. According to fat historian Anne Scott Beller, "[B]y limiting her choice of college in late adolescence and thus significantly restricting her subsequent marital options in her early twenties, a woman's tendency to gain weight may have a substantial, if not a major, effect on her social and socioeconomic status as a married adult."[17] A team of contemporary medical experts agreed, noting, "If their weights are excessive, females are at a greater social disadvantage both in their relationships with other females and in their relationship with males. Their social mobility is also inhibited to a greater extent. Successful men are often overweight or obese; successful career women and the wives of famous men rarely are."[18] For fat women, more so than for men, academic exclusion and discrimination in the workplace were commonplace.

Fat women faced three obstacles in hiring practices. Most tangible, health and life insurance once again negatively impacted employment opportunities. Because of the belief that "obese" people were a higher health risk than those of "average" weight, employers could deny employment if one's company required all workers to be covered under their life insurance policy. If a fat person was not denied coverage outright, they at least had to pay a higher premium for a Substandard policy. A second myth that complicated employment was equating fat with personal characteristics incompatible in a work environment. Stereotypes such as that fat people were lazy, were not hard workers, or were slow and incapable of performing a job with any physical requirements persisted. One woman, Rita Hornak, was denied employment because her potential employers believed, based on her size, that she would be a lazy and indifferent worker.[19] Even without the health risks associated with "obesity," the association of fatness with self-indulgence and lack of control made fat an unhireable trait. Finally, fat women faced sexism in employment. Noting that thin bodies were considered "fashionable," members of the fat activist group, the Fat Underground, wrote, "In our sexist society we must use our bodies to sell ourselves to employers and our employers in turn sell us to anyone coming in contact with their firm."[20] Considered unattractive, fat women would not serve as effective representatives of a company.

Fat Power

The decades of the 1960s and 1970s have been associated with the fight for civil rights for several minority and underrepresented groups—African Americans, women, American Indians, Mexican Americans, and gays and lesbians. It produced rally cries such as "Black Power" and "Red Power." The decades also provoked "Fat Power," an explicit effort to eradicate fat shame as well as discriminatory practices against fat Americans. The history of the Fat Acceptance movement is the story of two organizations, divided by gender, goals, and geography. The seeds of the Fat Acceptance movement first bloomed in June 1967 with the first recorded fat activist demonstration, a "Fat-In" in the Sheep Meadow of New York City's Central Park. Five hundred demonstrators swarmed the park grounds, carrying banners proclaiming "Fat Power" and "Buddha Was Fat," while others wore buttons that read "Take a Fat Girl to Dinner" and "Help Cure Emaciation." The demonstrators picnicked on calorific food throughout the day, and instead of burning carbohydrates, they burned diet books and a life-sized poster of the British model, Twiggy. New York's local WBAI radio personality, Steve Post, a 210-pound, five-foot-eleven-inch man, organized the event. He told reporters that the Fat-In's purpose was to "protest discrimination against the fat."[21] A few months later, Lew Louderback, a fat man married to a fat woman, published an essay in the *Saturday Evening Post*, entitled "More People Should Be Fat." Louderback's article and subsequent book, *Fat Power: Whatever You Weigh Is Right* (1970), called for the American Civil Liberties Union (ACLU) to recognize the fat community as a persecuted minority. In his writings, Louderback dismissed the pressures of the fashion and reducing industry, and he astutely identified a very real socioeconomic connection to one's waistline.[22]

William Fabrey, a New York City architect and self-identified "fat admirer," contacted Louderback after reading his article. Fabrey was not fat himself, but he was tired of the repeated discrimination his wife Joyce faced. Fabrey met his wife when he was a student at Cornell and she a student at Ithaca. He wanted to meet fat women, whose body type he preferred, but supposedly could not find any because of Cornell's policy against admitting fat students. He claimed that one of the reasons for this was the belief that overweight or obese students would not be able to climb the steep hills of Ithaca, New York.[23] With Louderback's assistance, Fabrey went on to create the National Association to Aid Fat Americans (now the National Association to Advance Fat Acceptance). Founded on June 13, 1969,

NAAFA was a civil rights organization oriented to demonstrate against fat discrimination. In its early years, NAAFA limited its political activity to writing corporations and protesting commercial advertisements they found repugnant. The group's primary objective was to change the low self-esteem of the average fat person. Fabrey, the organization's founder and its first president, recalled, "our main opposition was not intellectual truth, but the emotional reactions of people who had invested a lifetime in believing themselves and others inferior because of weight."[24] The organization had its own constitution and bylaws, but it existed more as a consciousness-raising group, limited to New York City, where fat men and women could meet other fat people as well as those attracted to fat people. The group had no agenda against its members losing weight and was welcoming of individuals of every size, fat or not. In fact, one member likened the organization to the National Association for the Advancement of Colored People because of its mixed membership.[25] When NAAFA continued to focus on fat acceptance at social events like dances and mixers, key members left the organization, Lew Louderback included, to pursue more politically charged activities.

On the West Coast, two women, Sara Golda Bracha Fishman and Judy Freespirit, were reading Louderback's *Fat Power* and, inspired by his book, created their own NAAFA branch.[26] The Los Angeles chapter, first founded in 1973, was confrontational from the start. Part of this can be attributed to Fishman and Freespirit's professional training as radical therapists. Radical therapy, according to Fishman, developed in the 1970s as "an in-your-face rebuke to the mainstream mental health profession." Conventional therapy placed the onus of change on the treated individual; radical therapy sought to change society itself, not the victim. Within a radical feminist context, they opposed the mixed nature of NAAFA, whose membership included both men and women and individuals of all sizes. When the New York chapter asked them to moderate their activist approach, the California group separated from NAAFA and created a separate organization, the Fat Underground.[27]

In the organization's manifesto, penned by Freespirit and Fishman, they espoused full equality for fat people, named the reducing industry as an enemy, and demanded that diet foods, surgical procedures, fat farms, diet doctors, and others acknowledge the health dangers of their products and procedures. They rejected the belief that fat people were unfit, pointing to the reducing industry and medical community as responsible for the creation of a harmful myth, while also critiquing the fashion industry, insurance companies, and psychiatry. "Fat people of the world unite!" they urged. "You have nothing to lose."[28] By rejecting the membership of fat men, the Fat Underground aimed to confront the double oppression of being a woman and being fat. They served as a support group for fat women who, unlike the New York membership of NAAFA, did not intend to diet. They held weekly consciousness-raising sessions at Westside Women's Center in Los Angeles, and soon expanded their activities to public protests and rallies.

The Fat Underground constructed its mission around seven facts pertaining to health and weight to combat stereotypes about fat people and to do battle with the reducing industry and medical community. "Doctors are the enemy," Fishman proclaimed. "Weight loss is genocide."[29] They noted the ineffective, long-term effects of a reducing diet, claiming that 99 percent of dieters gained the weight back within five years or less. Moreover, 90 percent of those who regained the weight, they claimed, added *more* weight than they had lost. "Reducing is a $10 billion industry annually. Someone is making a lot of money off the public's fear of fat," they reasoned. "Your (temporary) loss is their gain, and they want to keep it that way."[30] They argued that most fat people did not eat more than thin people. They noted the health dangers of "yo-yo" dieting and argued that fat people were "health risks" only because excessive and extreme diets weakened their bodies. In response to correlations between high blood pressure, diabetes, and other chronic diseases, they disagreed, noting that these were caused by stress, not "overweight" as the insurance statisticians and medical advisers suggested. They maintained that because of America's "thin society," fat people were over-stressed and self-loathing. Fat people who lived in areas of the country where their weight was not a problem, they contended, were in fact as healthy as slender people.[31]

Despite being a significantly smaller organization than NAAFA, which by then had several chapters, mostly on the East Coast, the Fat Underground became the face and voice of the Fat Acceptance movement in the 1970s. Similar to other militant, civil rights separatist groups like the Black Panthers or the American Indian Movement (AIM), the Fat Underground's confrontational style garnered more mass media attention than the more conservative agenda of NAAFA. Like other integrationist civil rights organizations, NAAFA wanted to carve out space for fat people within the existing system; the Fat Underground strove to change the system itself. Freespirit commented, "Their [NAAFA]'s idea of activism was to go to the Cerebral Palsy Foundation and do volunteer work so that people would say that fat people are nice. Ours was to demonstrate—break into a university lecture hall at UCLA during a class on behavior modification (for weight loss) and take over the classroom."[32]

The Fat Underground was the first to theorize fat oppression and used the model of feminism as a way to organize. Lesbian feminists played a prominent role in radical women's groups like the Fat Underground. However, early in the gay rights movement, lesbians in postwar America were not blind or impervious to mainstream feminine body ideals. Some, in fact, took offense at the suggestion that they or their partner's figures might not "stack up." In a description of North Beach, the Greenwich Village of San Francisco, *Pageant* magazine contributor Daniel Dixon described Phyllis Lyon, editor of the Daughters of Bilitis' (DOB) literary magazine, *The Ladder*, as being "burly." Coming to her partner's rescue, Del Martin responded, "WE DO HEARTILY DENY THAT PHYLLIS LYON IS BURLY." Referring to Funk & Wagnall's College Standard Dictionary, Martin noted that "burly" is defined as "Large of body; bulky; stout;

lusty." The president of the DOB continued, "Those who have made the personal acquaintance of Phyllis Lyon would hardly call her large of body, bulky or stout. She has a trim figure—34 bust, 24 waist (may be slightly larger after recent Holiday parties) and 36 hips—considered by many as 'very nice.' Is our editor burly? We think not!"[33] Integration was key for the early homophile movement. This was mirrored in the organization's early appeals to its members to adhere to traditional femininity.

The DOB, the first lesbian-rights organization in the country, frequently argued that femininity was a lesbian's best weapon against discrimination. In the introductory years of the *Ladder*, the DOB's literary magazine, butch culture came under attack. One woman wrote to the magazine's editors, saying, "the kids in fly-front pants and with the butch haircuts and mannish manner are the worst publicity we can get." Del Martin, the president of the DOB, replied, "Very true. Our organization has already touched on that matter and has converted a few to remembering that they are women first ... so their attire should be that which society will accept."[34] Another early publication that took offense to lesbians being less than feminine was Lisa Ben's *Vice Versa*, the very first lesbian publication, written and edited entirely by Ben (pseudonym of Edith Eyde) in the late 1940s. The modest publication mirrored the DOB's attitude shunning masculine-appearing lesbians. In a poem, Ben writes, "How willingly we go with tresses shorn/ And beauty masked in graceless, drab attire/ A roses' loveliness is to admire;/ Who'd cut the bloom and thus expose the thorn?"[35] Rather than celebrating butch culture for rejecting heteronormativity, the middle-class sensibilities of *The Ladder* and *Vice Versa* urged readers to behave and fashion themselves in a feminine manner. In their view, femininity not only served to "disguise" lesbianism, but it also made nontraditional sexuality more palatable. But by the 1970s, in the wake of the Stonewall Rebellion and the creation of the Gay Liberation Front, lesbian feminists began to rebel against not only femininity but thinness at all costs as well. Organizations such as the Fat Underground represented a blending of radical feminism, gay rights, and body acceptance.

A (Limited) Backlash?

A groundswell of support for Fat Acceptance increased toward the latter half of the 1960s and into the 1970s. In 1975, Lane Bryant, a specialty department store that catered to "stout" women, gathered prominent customers for four days to ask them for advice. The assembled panel varied from well-known women like Dorothy Shula, wife of the Miami Dolphin's head football coach, Don Shula, to Lynn Tate, a Philadelphia housewife. The panel's purpose was to end discrimination against fat women and to prove that larger bodies did not make women any less attractive or intelligent. One of the panelists was Martha Jean "The Queen" Steinberg, a size-18 disc jockey from Detroit. "Because of women's lib, we're going to have a lot more big women," she predicted. "Woman are tired of the façade and the false eyelashes, and finally we're saying, 'We're just going to be ourselves.'" However, the biggest complaint of the panel was that even the models in the Lane Bryant catalog were not "plus-sized." "We're told it's not a sin to be fat," noted Broadway actress Grace Keagy, "but even in the Lane Bryant catalogue, you can't find a heavy model."[36] Totie Fields, a fat singer and comedian, even considered starting her own clothing line for fat women, but intended on labeling the clothes as size 3, 5, and 7, noting, "[m]entally, it will make us feel better."[37] To some, the tides seemed to be turning.

Growing support for Fat Liberation was the result of not only the growing women's and gay rights movements; it also appeared as a backlash to the monopoly Twiggy and her androgynous, skinny facsimiles held in the world of high fashion. Actress Lynn Redgrave observed the power of women's magazines and their take on fashion: "Everybody aspires to look the way the magazines tell us to ... If we all lived in the times of Rembrandt and Rubens, Twiggy would have to go to a fat farm to get fat."[38] Twiggy, Penelope Tree, and others like them shaped the popular body type of the late 1960s, characterized by an adolescent androgyny and angularity. Twiggy, however, did not experience the same popularity outside of teen culture. In fact, non-fashion and non-teen magazines like *Life* and *Look* marveled and poked fun at the tiny teen, describing her as a "boy-girl" model with the figure of a five-year-old child.[39] "I hope she doesn't feel too guilty about the large number of 'sway-backs' she will undoubtedly inspire in the present generation of sheep," wrote one reader. Another did not directly attack thin models, but marveled at how Twiggy was more popular than her British counterpart, Jean "the Shrimp" Shrimpton, calling the former "sexless" while Shrimpton was "a girl-woman-goddess type."[40] Shrimpton, another popular British model, was seven years older than Twiggy with more traditional high-fashion measurements of 34–24.5–34 at five feet nine inches tall.

The influence of the Twiggy body type was not inevitable, even with Hollywood's eminence fading. In November 1967, *Vogue* featured the mannequin models for André Courrèges, the French designer responsible for pulling the miniskirt into *haute couture*. Of his models, Courrèges claimed, "I don't care about their measurements or their weight ... it is much more important that she be feminine and vigorous." *Vogue* printed the measurements of three Courrèges models. The women, on average, stood five feet eight inches, were 24.5 years old, weighed 126 pounds with bust measurements of 34.75, and had uncommon hip proportions for a high-fashion model at nearly 37 inches. When asked about the curvaceousness of his models, Courrèges replied, "Hips are feminine. A woman needs hips to be a woman."[41] Although tiny-bodied teens did not monopolize high-fashion magazines, the impact of Courrèges' curvy models was minimal. Twiggy was featured on the cover of the November *Vogue* issue and nearly every other cover for the rest of the decade. In the 1970s, fashion mannequins began to display a wider range of physical types, but the impact of the Twiggy-couture silhouette persisted. "Beauty" continued to be personified by youthfulness and extreme slenderness.

The belief that the scale should reflect a certain number or that one should possess a certain bust-to-waist-to-hip measurement impacted not only individual self-esteem and body cathexis. It also had a dramatic and negative impact on relationships throughout one's adolescence and one's ability to get into college or secure employment, along with the stability of one's marital life. Despite the criticism and counterattack against the extreme slenderization of American culture, it existed as a limited backlash. Not even white female celebrities were immune from this constant surveillance, celebrated when they lost weight and repulsive when they gained it back. Black periodicals heralded fat female celebrities as successful and lovely, but this positive reporting contrasted sharply with coverage in mainstream (white) media. The careers and media portrayal of "Mama" Cass Elliot of the singing group the Mamas and the Papas and of British actress Lynn Redgrave are illustrative of this discord.

Born Ellen Naomi Cohen on February 19, 1941, "Mama" Cass Elliot is best known for her tenure with the popular pop-folk singing group, the Mamas and the Papas (Figure 7.1). American media from Los Angeles to New York found it difficult to not discuss Elliot's weight, similar to fan magazines of the 1950s that continually referenced the bust-waist-hip measurements of the most buxom Hollywood starlets. Elliot was referred to as a "Hearty Performer" and was called the "large, homey

FIGURE 7.1 The Mamas and the Papas, 1967. Cass Elliot stands at the back; Denny Doherty, Michelle Phillips, and John Phillips are at the front.

foil" to the "ethereal beauty" of bandmate Michelle Phillips.[42] Despite contributing Elliot's powerful contralto to her extra-large frame, *Life* magazine described the singer as "hefty" with a "full-moon face" while identifying her co-"Mama," Michelle Phillips, as "model-looking."[43] Phillips was a litmus test to which Elliot was constantly compared. In a story introducing the band in 1966, Phillips was described as having "long blonde hair, a memorably pretty face and the willowy figure of a model, which she once was." Elliot, pictured in the background, a tiny figure compared with the group's other three members who appeared in the foreground, "plumply peer[ed] from behind purple Ben Franklin specs."[44] If Elliot's numerical weight (which at various times fluctuated between 220 and 294 pounds) was not directly cited, reporters used the fat thesaurus and other mean-spirited puns in their coverage of the singer-actress. In discussing an upcoming television appearance, one columnist noted: "you're going to be seeing a lot of her (all 238 pounds) with increasing regularity."[45] Even stories celebrating her thirtieth birthday party could not resist a reference to her weight. When Al Ruddy, a TV producer, gave Elliot a Cartier bracelet for her birthday, one newspaper reported, "Cass was touched (thru [*sic*] all that flesh) to the heart."[46] Revealed posthumously, band members Denny Doherty and Michelle Phillips's brother, Russell Gilliam, claimed that John Phillips had originally kept Elliot out of the band for being "too fat."[47]

After the Mamas and the Papas disbanded in 1968, Elliot continued to work; she released five solo albums and appeared on a number of variety television programs like *The Carol Burnett Show*, the *Julie Andrews Show*, *Johnny Carson*, and *Hollywood Squares*. She also acted in straight dramas with appearances on *Young Dr. Kildare* and *Marcus Welby, M.D*, and she had her own TV series in the works about a "large woman" who owned a restaurant.[48] Even though she reportedly rejected acting offers because she "[didn't] want to play the girl with the glandular problem in the corner," she was continually cast in these roles.[49] On *Marcus Welby, M.D.*, she portrayed a fat girl with a weight problem. The *Young Dr. Kildare* episode was entitled, "Charlotte Wage Makes Lots of Shade," where she played a woman whose life was jeopardized by her "obesity."[50] In the post–Mamas and the Papas years, Elliot made clear she wanted to shed her image as "Mama" Cass, but denied concerns about shedding weight. "Professionally, my weight has never been any problem," she told Norma Lee Browning of the *Chicago Tribune*. In her private life, she called visible hipbones "highly overrated" and boasted that she had never had problems in the "romance department" because of her weight.[51] Her public persona, celebrity, and success were supposedly redefining the concept of beauty. She was compared to Barbra Streisand, with one magazine writer claiming, "What Streisand did for Jewish girls in Brooklyn, Cass Elliot was doing for fat girls everywhere. The diet food people must have hated her the way nose surgeons are said to hate Streisand."[52] Contemporaries Elliot and Streisand had become international celebrities despite their nontraditional appearances. But while Streisand flatly refused rhinoplasty, the same cannot be said for Elliot and weight loss. Descriptions of Elliot's relationship with her body fluctuated as much as her actual reported weight. In some interviews, the singer declared satisfaction with her body and in others, she celebrated recent weight loss or discussed whatever latest fad diet she was following.

After the Mamas and the Papas disbanded, Elliot dieted for six months to prepare for a much-hyped solo performance at Caesar's Palace in Las Vegas. It was to be her first performance as Cass Elliot and not "Mama" Cass. "When I say I dieted," she later recalled, "I mean I almost didn't eat and I ended up with a bleeding ulcer." The performance was widely panned as a disaster. "I opened up my mouth to sing and ruptured my vocal chords."[53] In the wake of the Vegas catastrophe, Elliot vowed she had given up on weight loss.[54] She was not happy with her weight, but she was "resigned" to it. But history repeated itself when Elliot booked a two-week engagement at the Palladium in London in 1974. The tour was practically sold out, and she had lost seventy pounds in preparation. Her agent, Allan Carr, testified that "she always seemed to be on a diet of some kind or another, always losing and gaining weight."[55] After the success of the Palladium performances, she had been taking a break before embarking on a three-week tour of England—also sold out—at the time of her death.[56]

The initial report about Elliot's death on July 29, 1974, alleged that she had choked on a ham sandwich while eating in bed. The first doctor on the scene noted the sandwich and soda on a bedside table and originally believed asphyxiation had been the cause of death.[57] Other rumors indicated a heroin overdose, that the FBI had assassinated her, and that she had been pregnant with John Denver's baby. But days after her death, when the coroner's report was released, the world found out what had killed Cass Elliot—fat. Reports made it clear that Elliot's death was the result of "obesity." The attending doctor, Dr. Gavin Thurston, ruled out the initial theory that she had choked on food. Instead, Thurston believed Elliot had suffered a heart attack brought on by "overweight." In the absence of drugs or alcohol found in her body, the doctor reported that part of her heart had turned to fat "due to obesity." At the time of Elliot's death, the pop star weighed 220 pounds. Dr. Thurston erroneously called her "twice the proper weight" for a woman of her height and build.[58] At five feet and five inches, the average "large framed" American woman weighed 142 pounds with an "ideal" weight between 133 and 150 pounds. Even though she had reportedly lost seventy pounds in the last few months of her life, the coroner's report said the effort was "too little, too late."[59] She had done this to herself, the reports concurred—suicide through food.

Lynn Redgrave—Once a Fatty, Always a Fatty

In 1966, the year the Mamas and the Papas released their debut album, a "fat" Lynn Redgrave received an Oscar nod for Best Actress for her title role in the movie *Georgy Girl*. Redgrave, unlike the media's tragic portrayal of Cass Elliot, was considered a fat-to-riches success story. Her five-feet-ten-inch frame kept her 180 pounds from "resembling a complete butterball," and from being enlisted in what one *New York Times* reporter described as "the sorority of Fat Female Performers," of which Cass Elliot was a member.[60] According to MetLife's standardized tables, Redgrave was only seven pounds above the "desired" weight for her height and frame. And despite the success of *Georgy Girl*, which earned her both a Golden Globe and an Academy Award nomination, Redgrave was continually described in unflattering terms—"The Toadstool Turned into a Truffle," one headline read, calling her a "pudgy Cinderella" who suddenly found her "big square foot" fitting into the glass slipper. She was described as having "a little round mouth invented for devouring hot-fudge sundaes" and claimed that her weight fluctuated "according to her mood."[61] After the success of *Georgy Girl*, Redgrave persisted in being remembered as "the fat girl" and continually received offers to play fat-girl parts. Not wanting to be limited professionally because of her size, she vowed to lose the weight. She tried, by her own accounts, everything from health farms, to hormone injections, to fad diets like only eating bananas and milk, to fasting. But the weight continued to come back time and again. "People with excess pounds are well aware of it," Redgrave told the *Los Angeles Times* in 1972. "They don't need anyone to tell them that they are fat." She noted that the only solution was to develop eating habits to maintain a "normal weight."[62] "[T]hat thin person inside of her screaming to get out" finally clawed its way out when Redgrave successfully kept the weight off through a "diet" of eating just one meal a day.[63] Even after the weight loss, however, she was still best remembered as the "fat girl" from *Georgy Girl* and did herself no favors when she took on the principal role in the Broadway play *My Fat Friend*, about a "fat duckling" who, through weight loss, becomes a "svelte swan." To prepare for the role, Redgrave wore foam fat pads under her costume until the end of the performance when her character, Vicky, goes through a transformation to lose the weight, and in her new body, she is ready to take on a new life.[64]

Redgrave, unlike Elliot, was a lauded as a success story, similar to the women whose testimonials appeared in the *Ladies Home Journal*. She had been "fat," lost weight through self-denial, and succeeded in keeping the pounds off. Elliot, despite her numerous attempts to lose weight, always gained it back, sometimes in excess of her original, pre-dieting weight. Professionally and personally, Redgrave was considered stable, like the number that showed up on her bathroom scale. She married fellow English actor John Clark in 1967 and with him had three children. Elliot's life and weight were in constant flux, bouncing from one partner to the next, one professional endeavor to another. In the obituaries that followed Elliot's death, every attempt was made to assert how she had *tried* to change. She had *tried* to lose the weight. But perhaps her obituary in the *New York Times* best epitomized the attitude toward Elliot's weight when they wrote that she singularly proved "that one didn't have to be beautiful or thin to be successful."[65]

Conclusions

On August 26, 1974, President Gerald Ford proclaimed a "Women's Equality Day" to celebrate the fifty-fourth anniversary of women's suffrage. At the time, thirty-three of the thirty-eight required states had already ratified the ill-fated Equal Rights Amendment. Across the country, feminist organizations celebrated in their own ways. In Chicago, members of the local National Organization for Women (NOW) chapter put on an original play entitled, "A Funny Thing Happened on the Way to Equality" and picketed at the Sears Tower to protest sex discrimination in the hiring and promotion practices at Sears, Roebuck & Company. In Boston, feminists raised money to fight anti-abortion efforts; in Philadelphia, women demonstrated at the US Department of Labor offices to protest the agency's Manpower Administration; and in New York City, the Victoria Woodhull Marching Band played at a rally in front of Federal Hall.[66] In Los Angeles, members of the Fat Underground and the Fat Women's Problem-Solving Group—another fat acceptance organization that found its origins in the Radical Feminist Therapy Center—took to the stage wearing black armbands and carrying candles as if in a funeral procession. Cass Elliot had died in her bed just one month prior. Lynn Mabel-Lois (now Lynn McAfee) spoke to the assembled crowds on behalf of the collective about Elliot's recent death. She praised all that Elliot had represented and ended her speech by accusing the medical profession of murdering her. "Naomi Cohen [Cass Elliot] choked on the culture, on the stale empty air and worthless standards of our conditioning," Sharon Bas Hanna of the Fat Underground later wrote.[67]

Cass Elliot was an unlikely martyr for the Fat Acceptance movement because of her complicated relationship with her body, her numerous failed attempts to lose weight, the resulting fluctuating weight, and her seeming inability to be comfortable in her own skin. But even so, her death was a missed opportunity for the cause. While the controversy around Elliot's death did not silence the Fat Libbers, it certainly complicated the Fat Underground's denial that fat was a killer when every major newspaper around the country repeated the same story—"Mama" Cass Elliot had died because she was too fat. The Fat Acceptance movement posted modest victories in the years after Women's Equality Day. In 1980, the first national feminist conference of fat activists and Bostonian Judith Stein successfully lobbied the publishers of *Our Bodies, Ourselves* to revise its anti-fat and pro-diet stance. The Fat Underground lost momentum by the early 1980s with the death of a key member, Reanne Fagan, and the relocation of founding members Sharon Bas Hannah and Sara Fishman (a.k.a. Vivian F. Mayer, a.k.a. Aldebaran) to the East Coast. Too many once-active members of the organization became discouraged with the group's inability to effect real change and diverted their attentions elsewhere to topics where they believed they could witness real change within their lifetime.[68] Fat liberation never entirely disappeared, however, morphing into fat feminism and the discipline of fat studies. The National Association to Aid Fat Americans, now renamed the National Association to Advance Fat Acceptance, reclaimed its position as the voice of Fat Liberation.

Notes

1. Aljean Harmetz, "Oh How We're Punished for the Crime of Being Fat," *Today's Health*, January 1974, 22.
2. Dawn Crowell Norman, "I Hated My Looks Until I Lost 40 Pounds," *Ladies Home Journal*, August 1956, 56.
3. Lenore F. Monello and Jean Mayer, "Obese Adolescent Girls: An Unrecognized 'Minority' Group?" *American Journal of Clinical Nutrition* 13 (1963): 35–39; Helen Channing and Jean Mayer, "Obesity—Its Possible Effect on College Acceptance," *The New England Journal of Medicine* 275 (1966): 1172–1174.
4. Johanna T. Dwyer, Jacob J. Feldman, C. C. Seltzer, and Jean Mayer, "Body Image in Adolescents: Attitudes Toward Weight and Perceptions of Appearance," *Journal of Nutrition Education* 1, no. 2 (Fall 1969): 15–16.
5. Lynn Mabel-Lois, "We'll Worry About That When You're Thin," in *Shadow on a Tightrope: Writings by Women on Fat Oppression*, eds. Lisa Schoenfielder and Barb Wieser (San Francisco, CA: Aunt Lute Books, 1983), 62.
6. Terre Poppe, "Fat Memories From My Life," in *Shadow on a Tightrope: Writings by Women on Fat Oppression*, eds. Lisa Schoenfielder and Barb Wieser (San Francisco, CA: Aunt Lute Books, 1983), 68.
7. "Secret Summer Diet," *Seventeen*, July 1968, 98.
8. "Dear Beauty Editor," *'Teen*, March 1968, 34.
9. Jean Z. Owen, "I Lost 100 Pounds," *Ladies Home Journal*, February 1951, 155.
10. "The Big Bulge in Profits," *Newsweek*, July 23, 1956, 62.
11. Dawn Crowell Ney, "I Had to Lose 60 Pounds to Go to College," *Ladies Home Journal*, May 1961, 33.
12. Admission guidelines for Edinboro State College, 1961. These guidelines remained in the admission catalog until the 1970–1971 school year.
13. Anonymous, email message to author, March 31, 2010.
14. Ibid.
15. Nancy Pappas, "Group Contends 'Fat is Beautiful,'" *Hartford Courant*, November 18, 1973, n.p.
16. "College Admission Hint: Lose Weight," *New York Times*, November 24, 1966, 45; Helen Channing and Jean Mayer, "Obesity—Its Possible Effect on College Acceptance," *The New England Journal of Medicine* 275 (1966): 1172–1174.
17. Anne Scott Beller, *Fat and Thin: A Natural History of Obesity* (New York: Farrar, Straus, and Giroux, 1977), 11–12.
18. Jean Mayer, Johanna Dwyer, and Jacob Feldman, "The Social Psychology of Dieting," *Journal of Health and Social Behavior* 11, no. 4 (1970): 279.
19. Dawn Crowell Ney, "Too Pretty to Be Fat," *Ladies Home Journal*, January 1962, 10, 82.
20. Fat Underground, "Job Discrimination" (Los Angeles, CA, 1974).
21. "Food for Thought," *Sports Illustrated*, June 19, 1967, 12.
22. Lew Louderback, "More People Should Be Fat," *Saturday Evening Post*, November 4, 1967, 10–12; Louderback, *Fat Power: Whatever You Weigh Is Right* (New York: Hawthorn Books, 1970).
23. Judy Klemesrud, "There Are a Lot of People Willing to Believe Fat Is Beautiful," *New York Times*, August 18, 1970, 38.
24. William Fabrey, "Thirty-Three Years of Size Acceptance in Perspective—How Has It Affected the Lives of Real People?" Keynote Address, Big as Texas Conference, March 16, 2001. http://bigastexas.tripod.com/~bigastexas/2001event/bat2001.html.
25. Judy Klemesrud, "There Are a Lot of People Willing to Believe Fat Is Beautiful," *New York Times*, August 18, 1970, 38.
26. Both Fishman and Freespirit have gone by several names over the years, including the aliases Sara Aldebaran and Vivian F. Mayer for Fishman and Judith Louise Berkowitz for Freespirit. For continuity and clarity, I will refer to them as Fishman and Freespirit throughout.

27 Sara Golda Bracha Fishman, "Life in the Fat Underground," *Radiance*, Winter 1998, http://www.radiancemagazine.com/issues/1998/winter_98/fat_underground.html.
28 Judy Freespirit and Aldebaran, "Fat Liberation Manifesto," in *Shadow on a Tightrope: Writings by Women on Fat Oppression*, eds. Lisa Schoenfielder and Barb Wieser (San Francisco, CA: Aunt Lute Books, 1983), 52–53.
29 Sara Golda Bracha, "Life in the Fat Underground," *Radiance*, January 31, 1998, 32.
30 Fat Underground, "Before You Go on a Diet, Read This" (Los Angeles, CA, 1974).
31 Ibid.
32 J. E. Relly, "The Big Issue: A Fat–Acceptance Movement Welcomes America's New Majority," *Tucson Weekly*, October 5, 1998, http://www.weeklywire.com/ww/10-05-98/tw_feat.html.
33 Del Martin, "Is Our Editor Burly?" *The Ladder* 2, no. 4 (January 1958), 16–17. Capitalization and underlining original.
34 *The Ladder* 1, no. 2 (November 1956), 3.
35 Lisa Ben, quoted in Rodger Streitmatter, *Unspeakable: The Rise of the Gay and Lesbian Press in America* (Boston, MA: Faber and Faber, 1995), 10.
36 Judy Klemesrud, "In a Society That Worships Slimness and Stalklike Size 5 Fashion Models, the Fat Woman Often Is America's Forgotten Person," *New York Times*, April 28, 1975, C9.
37 Klemesrud, "The Forgotten Woman in the 'Skinny Revolution,'" *New York Times*, December 1, 1969, 58.
38 Klemesrud, "Lynn Redgrave Fat? Only with Pads Now: Still 'Georgy Girl,'" *New York Times*, April 13, 1974, 14.
39 "Is It a Girl? Is It a Boy? No, It's Twiggy," *Look*, April 4, 1967, 84–90.
40 "Letters to the Editor," *Look*, May 16, 1967, 4.
41 "Beauty Bulletin: New Body—More Woman Than You'd Think," *Vogue*, November 1967, 136–138.
42 "Cass Elliot, Pop Singer, Dies; Star of the Mamas and the Papas: A Hearty Performer," *New York Times*, July 29, 1974, 36.
43 "These Are the Mamas," *Life*, September 30, 1966, 77.
44 Pete Johnson, "Mamas, Papas Gave Birth to a Trend," *Los Angeles Times*, September 1, 1966, D14.
45 Norma Lee Browning, "No More 'Mama' for Cass Elliot," *Chicago Tribune*, November 12, 1972, NW 1.
46 "Icing on the Cake," *Chicago Tribune*, September 24, 1972, E4.
47 Eddie Fiegal, *Dream a Little Dream of Me: The Life of Cass Elliot* (Chicago, IL: Chicago Review Press, 2007), 147; Matthew Greenwald, *Go Where You Wanna Go: The Oral History of The Mamas and The Papas* (New York: Cooper Square Press, 2002), 59.
48 Browning, "No More 'Mama' for Cass Elliot," *Chicago Tribune*, November 12, 1972, NW 1–2.
49 "Singer Mama Cass Elliot Dead," *Chicago Tribune*, July 30, 1974, 12.
50 "Cass Elliot in a Dramatic Debut," *Los Angeles Times*, November 2, 1972, R3.
51 Browning, "No More 'Mama' for Cass Elliot," *Chicago Tribune*, November 12, 1972, NW 1–2.
52 William Kloman, "Sink Along with Mama Cass," *Esquire*, June 1969.
53 "Mama Cass in Training for Night Club Re-Entry," *Ocala Star Banner*, December 15, 1972, 9A.
54 "Cass Elliot, Pop Singer, Dies; Star of the Mamas and the Papas: A Hearty Performer," *New York Times*, July 29, 1974, 36; Norma Lee Browning, "No More 'Mama' for Cass Elliot," *Chicago Tribune*, November 12, 1972, NW1-2.
55 "Cass Elliot's Death Laid to Heart Attack," *Los Angeles Times*, August 6, 1974, B2.
56 Browning, "Tragedy Follows Joy for Cass in London," *Chicago Tribune*, August 1, 1974, A11.

57 "Cass Elliot, Pop Singer, Dies; Star of the Mamas and the Papas: A Hearty Performer," *New York Times*, July 29, 1974, 36; "Singer Mama Cass Elliot Dead," *Chicago Tribune*, July 30, 1974, 12.
58 "Cass Elliot's Death Linked to Heart Attack: Notes on People," *New York Times*, August 6, 1974, 39.
59 "Cass Elliot's Death Laid to Heart Attack," *Los Angeles Times*, August 6, 1974, B2.
60 Klemesrud, "Lynn Redgrave Fat? Only with Pads Now," *New York Times*, April 13, 1974, 14.
61 Red Reed, "Lynn Redgrave: The Toadstool Turned into a Truffle," *New York Times*, October 1966, 113.
62 Lydia Lane, "Lynn Makes Diet Decision," *Los Angeles Times*, April 7, 1972, G9.
63 Klemesrud, "Lynn Redgrave Fat? Only with Pads Now," *New York Times*, April 13, 1974, 14.
64 Clive Barnes, "Stage: 'My Fat Friend' from Britain: Comedy by Lawrence," *New York Times*, April 1, 1974, 41.
65 "Cass Elliot, Pop Singer, Dies; Star of the Mamas and the Papas: A Hearty Performer," *New York Times*, July 29, 1974, 36.
66 Carol Kleiman, "Chicagoans Join Equality Fete," *Chicago Tribune*, August 24, 1974; "Women Celebrate Equality by Taking Issues Into Streets," *Los Angeles Times*, August 26, 1974, 2; Laurie Johnston, "Women's Equality Day Marked Here By Bus Route and Rally at Federal Hall," *New York Times*, August 27, 1974.
67 Sharon Bas Hannah, "Naomi Cohen Choked on the Culture," *Sister*, September 1974, n.p.
68 Sara Golda Bracha Fishman, "Life in the Fat Underground," *Radiance*, Winter 1998, http://www.radiancemagazine.com/issues/1998/winter_98/fat_underground.html.

8

BARBIE GETS A NEW BODY

> *Nothing tastes as good as being skinny feels.*
> —Kate Moss

In September 2010, CBS broadcasting premiered the pilot episode of their new Monday night sitcom, *Mike & Molly*. The program's premise revolves around Mike Briggs, a Chicago police officer, and Molly Flynn, a fourth-grade teacher. The two characters become acquainted at an Overeaters Anonymous meeting, begin to date, and get married in the following season. The sitcom was picked up by CBS for a full season run after it averaged 12.27 million viewers in its first few weeks, heralding it as the season's top new comedy on network television.[1] Praise and criticism for the prime-time program surfaced nearly as soon as the show premiered. While many applauded CBS for featuring two fat actors, criticism centered on the show's writing, namely that the writers relied on an alarming number of fat jokes.[2] Despite this, viewership continues to be high, and Melissa McCarthy, the lead actress, won an Emmy for "Best Actress in a Comedy Series" in 2011 and has become a crossover movie star, with Oscar and Golden Globe nominations.

A different kind of criticism for *Mike & Molly* came from Maura Kelly, a blogger for *Marie Claire* magazine. Responding to a CNN article that questioned if the intimacy between Mike and Molly made watchers uncomfortable, Kelly responded affirmatively:

> I think I'd be grossed out if I had to watch two characters with rolls and rolls of fat kissing each other ... because I'd be grossed out if I had to watch them doing anything. To be brutally honest, even in real life, I find it aesthetically displeasing to watch a very, very fat person simply walk across a

room—just like I'd find it distressing if I saw a very drunk person stumbling across a bar or a heroine [sic] addict slumping in a chair.[3]

Kelly further asserted that, since *Mike & Molly* features two fat actors, the show promotes "obesity." To add insult to injury, she ended the piece with basic diet and exercise suggestions to those reading her blog. The response to the article was immediate, resulting in a subsequent blog post in which Kelly apologized for her "insensitivity" to the issue. She justified her explicit bias as being negatively influenced by her own struggles with anorexia and the desire to be thin. Kelly's original blog is hardly surprising considering the history of American women's body ideals and America's aversion to fat. What was alarming was that *Marie Claire*, a women's magazine that describes itself as progressive (its motto is "More Than a Pretty Face"), allowed the author to post an op-ed piece filled with such blatantly discriminatory and insulting rhetoric. CeCe Olisa, author of "The Big Girl Blog," tweeted that reading the article made her feel like she had caught her best friend talking about her behind her back.[4] In a whirlwind of damage control, *Marie Claire* countered the Kelly blog with a number of "love your body" opinion pieces. However, Joanna Coles, editor-in-chief for the magazine, continued to defend Kelly as a "provocative" writer and noted she was "excited and moved" by the over twenty-eight thousand emails the magazine received in the span of a few days regarding the Kelly post.[5] It is not a stretch to conclude that if this discriminatory op-ed story had been written about any other underrepresented group, Maura Kelly would have been fired. The fat community, however, is not recognized as a minority group, and Kelly was not dismissed from the *Marie Claire* staff.

Title VII of the Civil Rights Act of 1964 bans discrimination on the basis of a number of factors such as gender, race, and religion, but it does not protect those considered "overweight" or "obese." Instead, our mass media portrays fat as *ugly* and *unhealthy*. The myths and stereotypes are numerous and damaging. Fat people are lazy. Fat people are stupid. But perhaps the most dangerous myth is that fat *kills*. Weight is a number on a scale—a number, we are told, that is tied to our self-worth and our health. In 2004, the Centers for Disease Control and Prevention (CDC) reported that more than 400,000 Americans die of "overweight" and "obesity" every year. The number was so alarmingly large that the CDC estimated it would soon surpass smoking as the leading cause of "preventable deaths."[6] America was in the midst of an "obesity epidemic." Pundits, borrowing language from the September 11, 2001 terrorist attacks, called fatness the "terrorism from within" and declared a "war on fat." A year later, a federal report announced that the original CDC findings were inflated and their methodology was flawed. The updated report adjusted the 400,000 reported fat deaths to 26,000.[7] Few took note of the retracted federal report, however, and continued to cling to the original 400,000 deaths figure.

Americans do not suffer from an "obesity epidemic." They suffer from a weight-loss crisis. Americans spend over $40 billion on dieting and diet-related products each year. Food products are not priced per calorie, but instead take advantage of the pocketbooks of those desiring to cut back and slim down. Healthy food is more expensive than food high in sugars and fats and producers charge more for the low-calorie/low-fat product than for "regular" manufactured goods. The assault against fat has less to do with concerns about health and more to do with greed and consumerism. The two major organizations for "obesity" research, the North American Association for the Study of Obesity and the American Obesity Association, both have financial connections to pharmaceutical or weight-loss companies.[8] As "Health at Every Size" activist Dr. Linda Bacon observes, studies such as the CDC's "obesity" death report "gives us permission to call our fear of fat a health concern, rather than naming it as the cultural oppression it is."[9] It's not fat that's killing people; it's discrimination. Today, body mass index (BMI) has replaced the MetLife tables as the most reliable indicator of "health." But just as Dublin's population was largely white, affluent, urban, and of Northern European ancestry, so too was the population from which "average" BMI was configured.[10] Independently funded studies show that 91 percent of what accounts for "health" has nothing to do with BMI, yet "overweight" and "obese" individuals are routinely denied insurance coverage based on their BMI instead of more telling factors such as tobacco and alcohol use or blood pressure, cholesterol, and blood sugar levels.[11] A new policy proposed by the Equal Employment Opportunity Commission (EEOC) would allow US employers to penalize their employees up to 30 percent of healthcare costs if they fail to have a BMI within the "normal" range. A 2016 study suggests, however, that BMI misclassifies nearly seventy-five million Americans as healthy or unhealthy; researchers found no correlation between one's BMI and health. Rates of BMI-defined obesity are higher within the African American community as well as for those with lower incomes. If the EEOC's proposal passes, this would disproportionately penalize those groups of people.[12]

Government agencies like the CDC regularly publish reports on how Americans are significantly fatter today than they were in decades past. Statistics released in 2016 announced that over 70 percent of Americans are "overweight" or "obese."[13] While data such as this is used to convince us to stop eating fast food and to exercise more regularly, what is more significant is that while the average American becomes fatter, the average fashion model becomes skinnier. In 1947, the average clothing model stood five feet four inches tall and weighed 125 pounds. In 1975, she had grown to five feet seven inches and weighed 118 pounds. Today, the typical fashion model weighs 117 pounds and stands five feet eleven inches. Most models are skinnier than 98 percent of American women.[14] Not only is the average woman becoming fatter, but the gap between ideals and reality is also widening. This does little to motivate the typical woman to cut back on calories and take the stairs instead of the elevator. Instead, these weight discrepancies create negative body esteem and urge women to crash diet, to starve themselves. Although the average American has changed in size since the 1960s, we have not changed in one aspect—we want results quickly and with little effort.

The desire to be "ten pounds thinner" is unlikely to vanish anytime soon, but Americans, especially women, need to understand their impulse to follow fad diets and exercise regimes. Why do women aspire to look like the celebrities on the covers of glossy magazines? Why are twig-thin fashion models more popular and better paid than "plus-size" models? Over half of teenage girls use unhealthy weight control behaviors such as skipping meals, fasting, smoking cigarettes, taking laxatives, or vomiting. Among first- to third-grade girls, 42 percent reportedly wish they were thinner and 81 percent of ten-year-old girls fear becoming fat.[15] More than two-thirds of women between the ages of eighteen and twenty-five would rather be mean or stupid than fat, and over 50 percent claim they would rather be hit by a truck than be fat.[16] Statistics such as these are altogether horrifying. Celebrating good health and longevity should become our priority rather than mimicking the too-thin woman on the cover of a magazine to fit a socially constructed and pseudo-medically approved aesthetic.

The Minority Body

Women of every age, race, class, and sexual orientation are bombarded with messages about obtaining the perfect body and that one can never be too thin. Today, however, African American women are fatter than European American women and lesbians weigh more than heterosexual women.[17] Straight women statistically outnumber lesbians amongst those diagnosed with eating disorders and lesbians disproportionately support fat activism. A study of twenty-four lesbians and twenty bisexual women revealed that the lesbians had higher self-esteem, less inclination to binge eat, and were more confident in their body appearance than the bisexual women.[18] This suggests that lesbians have a more positive relationship with food and their bodies. But, as Becky Thompson discovered, lesbians are not immune to binge eating and fasting strategies. Their purpose for doing so, however, differs from that of heterosexual women.[19] Laura S. Brown notes that fat oppression and homophobia are often linked. Lesbians have been taught that their gayness is wrong in the same way that fatness is wrong. Women who struggle with their sexuality, those who suffer from internalized homophobia, begin to oppress themselves with unhealthy diet strategies and negative body image.[20]

Some studies, similar to this project, suggest that the black mass media has historically celebrated a variety of body types, more so than white popular culture.[21] In present times, however, this may reflect economic rather than cultural differences. *Essence*, a magazine that, like *Ebony* during the postwar years, caters to a middle-class reading audience, regularly prints stories on body anxiety and the prevalence of eating disorders among black women. Moreover, contemporary studies of black women in college sororities reveal that this population is not "culturally protected" from negative body esteem.[22] As the economic gap between white and black America narrows, so has white beauty culture become more present among women of color. This is not to argue that being "overweight" or "obese" is desirable or even culturally accepted in the black community. Rather, a delicate balance exists between having curves and being "matronly," as the film *Precious* or the stereotype of "the Mammy"—the desexualized black woman—indicates. Contemporary research indicates that women of color and queer women have a more positive relationship with their bodies and with food. But cultural stigmas associated with fatness continue to seep into these minority populations.

The Solution?

Her name is Barbara Millicent Roberts, but you might know her simply as Barbie. And like the all-American woman she purports to represent, she has gone through a variety of changes in her fifty-seven years of existence. Barbie's genesis story tells that the plastic doll's creator, Ruth Handler, observed her daughter at play and noticed she often gave her dolls adult roles. Most dolls at the time were modeled after children themselves, and Handler believed designing a doll to look like an adult woman would sell. Competitors at the 1959 New York Toy Fair laughed at Handler, insisting that no child would play with a doll with breasts; yet, stores sold more than 300,000 Barbie dolls within the year. Today, the Mattel Toy Company sells a Barbie somewhere in the world every three seconds. Barbie has had over 150 professions since 1959. She's been a paleontologist, an astronaut, a computer programmer, and even the President of the United States; but it is her body and not the complexity of her résumé that has received the lion's share of criticism.[23] Numerous studies have identified a link between doll play and body image and suggest that girls who play with Barbie grow up having skewed ideas of what their own bodies should look like. According to these reports, by the time they are five years old, American girls have already been indoctrinated with beauty ideals.[24] Responding to downward sales trends and continued pressure for a "realistic" Barbie, Mattel dramatically redesigned the Barbie brand in January 2016. Referred to as "Project Dawn" by designers for Mattel, Barbie is now available in seven different skin tones and twenty-four hairstyles. And in the most radical departure from the improbably proportioned doll that first appeared in 1959, Barbie now comes in three different body shapes—petite, tall, and curvy.[25]

In recognizing their influence on vulnerable and impressionable populations, the mass media and other disseminators of popular imagery have a responsibility to promote healthy body ideals and to celebrate more realistic body types. Other countries have led the way in shedding fat bias and promoting more realistic body types. Banning airbrushed advertisements, particularly in magazines aimed at women sixteen and younger, has become a focus for the British Liberal Democratic party.[26] A similar reaction has yet to hit political consciousness in the United States. Some countries (although not the United States) now require a minimum BMI for fashion models, a hopeful step in the right direction but clearly not the solitary solution to our cultural obsession with slenderness. However, this growing trend to celebrate body diversity reached *Sports Illustrated*'s swimsuit edition in early 2016. For the first time in the magazine's history, the publication selected three separate cover models instead of one, producing three alternative covers that featured the straight-size model Hailey Clauson; size-16 model Ashley Graham; and mixed-martial artist and Ultimate Fighting Championship (UFC) fighter Ronda Rousey. Barbie's new body may not single-handedly solve the crisis of American women's body consciousness, but it's a start.

Notes

1. Robert Seidman, "CBS Gives Full Season Pickups to All New Series," *TV By the Numbers*, October 21, 2010, http://tvbythenumbers.com/2010/10/21/cbs-gives-full-season-pickups-to-all-new-series-hawaii-five-0-defenders-blue-bloods-mike-molly-my-dad-says/69152.
2. Cynthia Nichols, Babbi Kay Lewis, and M. K. Shreves, "'Fatties Get a Room!': An Examination of Humor and Stereotyping in *Mike and Molly*," *Journal of Entertainment and Media Studies* 1, no. 1 (2015): 99–126.
3. Maura Kelly, "Should Fatties Get a Room? (Even On TV?)," *Marie Claire*, October 25, 2010, http://www.marieclaire.com/sex-love/dating-blog/overweight-couples-on-television.
4. CeCe Olisa, "The Big Girl Blog on *Marie Claire*," The Big Girl Blog, October 29, 2010, http://www.thebiggirlblog.com/2010/10/thebiggirlblog-marie-claire/.
5. Leah Chernikoff, "*Marie Claire* EIC Joanna Coles Responds to Controversial Fatist Blog Post," *Fashionista*, October 26, 2010, http://fashionista.com/2010/10/exclusive-marie-claire-eic-joanna-coles-responds-to-controversial-fatist-blog-post/.
6. Ali H. Mokdad et al., "Actual Cases of Death in the United States, 2000," *Journal of the American Medical Association* 291 (2004): 1238–45.
7. Katherine M. Flegal et al., "Excess Deaths Associated with Underweight, Overweight, and Obesity," *Journal of the American Medical Association* 293, no. 15 (2005): 1861–67.
8. Linda Bacon, *Health at Every Size: The Surprising Truth About Your Weight* (Dallas, TX: BenBella Books, 2008), 148.
9. Ibid., 121.
10. Sander Gilman, *Obesity: The Biography* (New York: Oxford University Press, 2010), xi.
11. Deb Burgard, "What is 'Health at Every Size'?" in *The Fat Studies Reader*, eds. Ester Rothblum and Sondra Solovay (New York: New York University Press, 2009), 43.
12. A. Janet Tomiyama, J. M. Hunger, J. Nguyen-Cuu, and C. Wells, "Misclassification of Cardiometabolic Health When Using Body Mass Index Categories in NHANES 2005–2012," *International Journal of Obesity* 40, February 2016, http://www.nature.com/ijo/journal/vaop/naam/abs/ijo201617a.html.
13. National Center for Health Statistics, *Health, United States, 2015: With Special Feature on Racial and Ethnic Health Disparities* (Hyattsville, MD: 2016), http://www.cdc.gov/nchs/data/hus/hus15.pdf#053. Accessed November 10, 2016.
14. National Eating Disorders Association, "The War on Women's Bodies," https://www.nationaleatingdisorders.org/war-womens-bodies. Accessed March 14, 2011.
15. Statistics according to studies cited by the National Eating Disorders Association, http://www.nationaleatingdisorders.org/index.php. Accessed March 14, 2011.
16. Deborah L. Rhode, "The Injustice of Appearance," *Stanford Law Review* 61, no. 5 (March 2009), 1040.
17. Bianca D. M. Wilson, "Widening the Dialogue to Narrow the Gap in Health Disparities: Approaches to Fat Black Lesbian and Bisexual Women's Health Promotion," in *The Fat Studies Reader*, eds. Ester Rothblum and Sondra Solovay (New York: New York University Press, 2009), 55.

18 Allison M. Kase, "Lesbian and Bisexual Women: Attitudes, Behaviors, and Self-Esteem Related to Self-Image, Weight, and Eating," MA thesis, Loyola University Chicago, 1996.
19 Becky W. Thompson, *A Hunger So Wide and So Deep*. Minneapolis, MN: University of Minnesota Press, 1995.
20 Laura S. Brown, "Lesbians, Weight, and Eating. New Analysis and Perspectives," in *Lesbian Psychologies: Explorations and Challenges*, ed. The Boston Lesbian Psychologies Collective (Chicago, IL: University of Illinois Press, 1987), 294–296.
21 Joan Jacobs Brumberg, *The Body Project: An Intimate History of American Girls* (New York: Random House, 1997), 119.
22 Robin A. Selzer, "The Experience and Meaning of Body Image: Hearing the Voices of African American Sorority Women," PhD diss., Loyola University Chicago, 2006.
23 Charlotte Alter, "In Defense of Barbie: Why She Might Be the Most Feminist Doll Around," *Time*, February 6, 2014, http://time.com/4597/in-defense-of-barbie-why-she-might-be-a-feminist-doll-after-all/.
24 Doeschka Anschutz and Rutger Engels. "The Effects of Playing with Thin Dolls on Body Image and Food Intake in Young Girls." *Sex Roles* 63, no. 10 (2010): 621–630; Helga Ditmar, Emma Halliwell, and Suzanne Ive. "Does Barbie Make Girls Want to Be Thin? The Effect of Experimental Exposure to Images of Dolls on the Body Image of 5- to 8-Year-Old Girls," *Developmental Psychology* 42, no. 2 (2006): 283–292.
25 Michael Pearson, "Barbie's New Body: Curvy, Tall and Petite," *CNN*, January 28, 2016, http://www.cnn.com/2016/01/28/living/barbie-new-body-feat; Eliana Dockterman, "A Barbie for Every Body" *Time*, February 8, 2016: 44–50; Anna Hart, "Introducing the New, Realistic Barbie: 'The Thigh Gap Has Officially Gone,'" *The Telegraph*, January 28, 2016.
26 "Airbrushed Twiggy Photo 'Misleading,'" *BBC News*, December 16, 2009, http://news.bbc.co.uk/2/hi/uk_news/8415176.stm.

BIBLIOGRAPHY

Primary Sources

Manuscript Collections and Ephemera

Ben Burns Collection 1939–1999. Vivian Harsh Research Collection of Afro-American History and Literature, Chicago Public Library, Chicago, Illinois.

Louis Israel Dublin papers. 1906–1968. Modern Manuscripts Collection, History of Medicine Division, National Library of Medicine, Bethesda, Maryland.

GLBT Collection. Special Collections, Michigan State University, East Lansing, Michigan.

Historical Health Fraud Collection. American Medical Association Archives, Chicago, Illinois.

Russel B. Nye Popular Culture Collection. Michigan State University, Special Collections, East Lansing, Michigan.

Special Collections. Northwestern University, Evanston, Illinois.

Special Collections. University of Wisconsin-Milwaukee, Milwaukee, Wisconsin.

Gallup Polls

1949 Poll #450
Summer 1950 Poll #1950-0457: Life
June 1955 Poll #1955-0549
June 1959—Roper Commercial #111: Food and Eating Habits
Attitudes of American Women Poll, June–July 1962

Periodicals

Beauty Parade (1946–1949)
Calling All Girls (1963)

Chicago Defender (1945–1970)
Collier's (1945–1957)
Confidential (1954–1957)
Cosmopolitan (1945–1970)
Duke (1957)
Ebony (1945–1970)
Elle (1945–1970)
Esquire (1945–1972)
Flirt (1948–1953)
Glamour (1945–1970)
Jet (1951–1970)
The Ladder (1956–1970)
Ladies Home Journal (1945–1970)
Life (1945–1970)
Look (1945–1970)
Modern Screen
Motion Picture (1948–1963)
Movie Life
Movie Stars Parade
ONE Magazine (1953–1967)
Pageant (1953)
Photoplay (1954)
Photoplay Annual (1961)
Playboy (1953–1970)
Polly Pigtails (1953)
Reader's Digest (1954)
Screenland plus TV-Land (1965)
Screen Stars (1946–1963)
Screen Stories (1953)
Sepia (1952–1970)
Seventeen (1944–1970)
Sports Illustrated (1954–1970, 1989)
Tan Confessions (1950–1952)
'Teen (1957–1970)
Vice Versa (1947–1948)
Vogue (1945–1970)

Movies

How to Marry a Millionaire. Jean Negulesco. 1953.
Hugh Hefner: American Playboy. Kevin Burns. 1996.
Moon Over Miami. Walter Lang. 1941.
"Strictly Personal," United States Army Pictorial Service, 1945. US National Library of Medicine. Digital Collections: http://collections.nlm.nih.gov/muradora/objectView.action?pid=nlm:nlmuid-9422795-vid. Accessed January 26, 2017.
Will Success Ruin Rock Hunter? Frank Tashlin. 1957.

Academic and Professional Journals

Armstrong, Donald B., Louis Dublin, George M. Wheatley, and Herbert H. Marks. "Obesity and Its Relation to Health." *Journal of the American Medical Association* 147, no. 11 (1951): 1007–1014.

Aufricht, Gustave. "The Development of Plastic Surgery in the United States." *Plastic and Reconstructive Surgery* 1, no. 1 (1946): 3–22.

Barnes, H. O. "Reduction of Massive Breast Hypertrophy." *Plastic and Reconstructive Surgery* 3, no. 5 (1948): 560–569.

Barnes, H. O. "Breast Malformations and a New Approach to the Problem of the Small Breast." *Plastic and Reconstructive Surgery* 5, no. 6 (1950): 499–506.

Breslow, Lester. "Public Health Aspects of Weight Control." *American Journal of Public Health* 42 (1952): 1116–1121.

Channing, Helen, and Jean Mayer. "Obesity—Its Possible Effect on College Acceptance." *The New England Journal of Medicine* 275 (1966): 1172–1174.

Conway, Herbert. "Mammaplasty: Analysis of 110 Consecutive Cases with End-Results." *Plastic and Reconstructive Surgery* 10, no. 5 (1952): 303–315.

Conway, Herbert, and James Smith. "Breast Plastic Surgery: Reduction Mammaplasty, Mastopexy, Augmentation Mammaplasty, and Mammary Construction: Analysis of Two Hundred and Forty-Five Cases." *Plastic and Reconstructive Surgery* 21, no. 1 (1958): 8–19.

Dublin, Louis. "Fat People Who Lose Weight Live Longer." *Nutritional Symposium Series* 6 (1953): 106–122.

Dublin, Louis, and Herbert H. Marks. "Mortality Among Insured Overweights in Recent Years." *Transactions of the Association of Life Insurance Medical Directors of America* 35 (1951): 235–265.

Dwyer, Johanna T., Jacob T. Feldman, and Jean Mayer. "Adolescent Dieters: Who Are They? Physical Characteristics, Attitudes, and Dieting Practices of Adolescent Girls." *American Journal of Clinical Nutrition* 20, no. 10 (1967): 1045–1056.

—. "The Social Psychology of Dieting." *Journal of Health and Social Behavior* 11, no. 4 (1970): 269–287.

Dwyer, Johanna, Jacob T. Feldman, Carl C. Seltzer, and Jean Mayer. "Body Image in Adolescents: Attitudes Toward Weight and Perception of Appearance." *Journal of Nutrition Education* 1, no. 2 (1969): 14–19.

Dwyer, Johanna, and Jean Mayer. "Variations in Physical Appearance During Adolescence: Part 1: Boys." *Postgraduate Medicine* 41 (1967): 99–107.

—. "Variations in Physical Appearance During Adolescence: Part 2: Girls." *Postgraduate Medicine* 41 (1967): 91–97.

Edgerton, M. T., and A. R. McClary. "Augmentation Mammaplasty: Psychiatric Implications and Surgical Indications." *Plastic and Reconstructive Surgery* 21, no. 4 (1958): 279–305.

Edgerton, M. T., E. Meyer, and W. E. Jacobson. "Augmentation Mammaplasty II: Further Surgical and Psychiatric Evaluation." *Plastic and Reconstructive Surgery* 27, no. 3 (1961): 279–302.

Edwards, Benjamin F. "Teflon-Silicone Breast Implants." *Plastic and Reconstructive Surgery* 32, no. 4 (1963): 519–526.

Goldman, R. F., B. Bullen, C. Seltzer. "Changes in Specific Gravity and Body Fat in Overweight Female Adolescents as a Result of Weight Reduction." *Annals of the New York Academy of Sciences* 110 (1963): 913–917.

Gurdin, Michael, and Gene A. Carlin, "Complications of Breast Implantations." *Plastic and Reconstructive Surgery* 40, no. 6 (1967): 530–533.

Harris, Harold I. "Survey of Breast Implants from the Point of View of Carcinogenesis." *Plastic and Reconstructive Surgery* 28, no. 1 (1961): 81–83.

Huenemann, Ruth, Mary C. Hampton, Leona R. Shapiro, and Albert R. Behnke. "Adolescent Food Practices Associated with Obesity." *Federation Proceedings* 25, no. 1 (1966): 4–10.

Huenemann, Ruth L., Leona R. Shapiro, Mary C. Hampton, and Barbara W. Mitchell. "A Longitudinal Study of Gross Body Composition and Body Conformation and Their Association with Food and Activity in a Teen-age Population." *American Journal of Clinical Nutrition* 18 (1966): 325–335.

Johnson, Hugh A. "Silastic Breast Implants: Coping with Complications." *Plastic and Reconstructive Surgery* 44, no. 6 (1969): 588–591.

Jourard, Sidney M., and Paul F. Secord. "Body Cathexis and the Ideal Female Figure." *Journal of Abnormal and Social Psychology* 50 (1955): 243–246.

Keys, Ancel. "Obesity and Heart Disease: Editorial." *Journal of Chronic Diseases* 1 (1955): 456–461.

Keys, Ancel, Flaminio Fidanza, Martti J. Karvonen, Noboru Kimura, and Henry L. Tayler, "Indices of Relative Weight and Obesity." *Journal of Chronic Disease* 25 (1972): 329–343.

Knorr, Norman J., J. E. Hoopes, and Milton T. Edgerton. "Psychiatric-Surgical Approach to Adolescent Disturbance in Self Image." *Plastic and Reconstructive Surgery* 41, no. 3 (1968): 248–253.

Maddox, George, Kurt W. Back, and Veronica R. Liederman. "Overweight as Social Deviance and Disability." *Journal of Health and Social Behavior* 9, no. 4 (1968): 287–298.

Maddox, George, and Veronica Liederman. "Overweight as a Social Disability with Medical Implications." *Journal of Medical Education* 44 (1969): 214–220.

Maliniac, Jacques W. "Evaluation of Principal Mammaplastic Procedures." *Plastic and Reconstructive Surgery* 4, no. 4 (1949): 359–373.

Mayer, Jean. "Obesity: Causes and Treatment." *The American Journal of Nursing* 59, no. 12 (1959): 1732–1736.

—. "Obesity Control." *The American Journal of Nursing* 65, no. 6 (1965): 112–113.

Mayer, Jean, Joanna T. Dwyer, and Jacob T. Feldman. "The Social Psychology of Dieting." *Journal of Health and Social Behavior* 11, no. 4 (1970): 269–287.

Miner, Horace. "Body Ritual among the Nacirema." *American Anthropologist* 58, no. 3 (1956): 503–507.

Monello, Lenore F., and Jean Mayer. "Obese Adolescent Girls: An Unrecognized 'Minority' Group?" *American Journal of Clinical Nutrition* 13 (1963): 35–39.

National Center for Health Statistics. "Weight by Height and Age of Adults, United States, 1960–1962. *Vital Health Statistics*. Public Health Service Pub. No. 1000—Series 11, No. 14. Washington, DC: United States Government Printing Office, May 1966.

"New Build and Blood Pressure Study—A Preview." *Record of Society of Actuaries* 4, no. 4 (1978): 847–866.

Pangman, W. John. *Southern General Practitioner of Medicine and Surgery* 115, no. 12 (1953), n.p.

Peckos, Penelope S., John A. Spargo, and Felix P. Heald. "Program and Results of a Camp for Obese Adolescent Girls." *Postgraduate Medicine* 27 (1960): 527–533.

Regnault, Paule C. "Indications for Breast Augmentation." *Plastic and Reconstructive Surgery* 40, no. 6 (1967): 524–529.

Rees, Thomas D., and Christian C. Dupuis. "Unilateral Mammary Hypoplasia." *Plastic and Reconstructive Surgery* 41, no. 4 (1968): 307–310.

Seltzer, Carl C. "Limitations of Height-Weight Standards." *New England Journal of Medicine* 272 (1965): 1132.
—. "Some Reevaluations of the Build and Blood Pressure Study, 1959, as Related to Ponderal Index, Somatotype, and Mortality." *New England Journal of Medicine* 274 (1966): 254–259.
Snyderman, Reuven K., and Jesus G. Lizardo. "Statistical Study of Malignancies Found Before, During, or After Routine Breast Plastic Operations." *Plastic and Reconstructive Surgery* 25, no. 3 (1960): 253–256.
"The Build and Blood Pressure Study." *Transactions of Society of Actuaries* 11, no. 31 (1959): 987–997.

Court Cases

Ablard, Charles D., "In the Matter of the Complaint Against Tyler Pharmacal Distributors, Inc." H.E. Docket No. 4/232, July 14, 1958. http://www.usps.com/judicial/1958deci/4-232.htm.
"Misbranding of Formalon Cream." United States v. Daniel Platt (Formalon Company) F.D.C. No. 21466. January, 23, 1948. United States National Library of Medicine. http://archive.nlm.nih.gov/fdanj/handle/123456789/11293.
Tyler Pharmacal Distributors, Inc., Plaintiff-Appellant v. U.S. Department of Health, Education and Welfare, Defendant-Appellee. Docket No.16637, United States Court of Appeals Seventh Circuit, March 5, 1969. http://ftp.resource.org/courts.gov/c/F2/408/408.F2d.95.16637.16643.html.

Articles from the Popular Press, Periodicals

Barnes, Clive. "Stage: 'My Fat Friend' From Britain: Comedy by Lawrence." *New York Times*, April 1, 1974, 41.
Boyle, Hal. "Dagmar Trims Off 20 Pounds: Claims She Can Think Faster with Less Poundage." *The Spokesman-Review*, January 22, 1953, 16.
"Breast Surgery Suit Costs Doctor $13,000," *San Antonio Express*, December 1, 1967, 12.
Browning, Norma Lee. "No More 'Mama' for Cass Elliot." *Chicago Tribune*, November 12, 1972, NW 1–2.
—. "Sammy, Cass Triumph in London." *Chicago Tribune*, July 26, 1974, A2.
—. "Tragedy Follows Joy for Cass in London." *Chicago Tribune*, August 1, 1974, A11.
"Cass Elliot's Death Laid to Heart Attack." *Los Angeles Times*, August 6, 1974, B2.
"Cass Elliot's Death Linked to Heart Attack: Notes on People." *New York Times*, August 6, 1974, 39.
"Cass Elliot, Pop Singer, Dies; Star of the Mamas and the Papas: A Hearty Performer." *New York Times*, July 29, 1974, 36.
"College Admission Hint: Lose Weight." *New York Times*, November 24, 1966, 45.
"Crazy About Reducing." *Time*, August 6, 1956, 32.
"Danger of Being Too Fat." *U.S. News and World Report*, November 2, 1951, 19–21.
"Do Husbands Like Plump Wives?" *McCall's*, March 1951, 6–8.
Dublin, Louis. "Huge Tasks Lie Ahead." *Bismark Tribute*, September 19, 1944, n.p.
—. "Women are Different." *Your Life*, December 1950, 23–27.
—. "Stop Killing Your Husband!" *Reader's Digest*, July 1952, 107.
—. "Overweight, America's No. 1 Health Problem." *Today's Health*, September 1952, 18–21.

"Fashion: Up, Up, and Away." *Time*, December 1, 1967, 70–80.
"Fat and Unhappy." *Time*, October 20, 1947, 61–62,
Fat Underground. "Before You Go on a Diet, Read This." Los Angeles, CA, 1974.
——. "Job Discrimination." Los Angeles, CA, 1974.
Hannah, Sharon Bas. "Naomi Cohen Choked on the Culture." *Sister*, September 1974, n.p.
Harmetz, Aljean. "Oh How We're Punished for the Crime of Being Fat." *Today's Health*, January 1974, 21–24.
Hutchinson, Woods. "Fat and Fashion." *The Saturday Evening Post*, August 21, 1926, 60.
"Icing on the Cake." *Chicago Tribune*, September 24, 1972, E4.
"Insurance Ads Pave the Way for Dietary and 'Health' Foods." *Business Week*, December 6, 1952, 46–50.
Johnson, Pete. "Mamas, Papas Give Birth to a Trend." *Los Angeles Times*, September 1, 1966, D14.
Jones, Karen W. "Fat and Female—One Woman's View." *NAAFA Newsletter*, September–October 1974.
Klemesrud, Judy. "The Forgotten Woman in the 'Skinny Revolution.'" *New York Times*, December 1, 1969, 58.
——. "There Are a Lot of People Willing to Believe Fat Is Beautiful." *New York Times*. August 18, 1970, 38.
——. "The Fat Farms—Or, How to Come Home a Real Loser." *New York Times*, January 23, 1972, XX1.
——. "Now It's Skinny Lib with Loud Protest." *New York Times*, August 4, 1972, 36.
——. "From New York to the Bahamas on the Low-Calorie Cruise." *New York Times*, October 18, 1972, 52.
——. "Lynn Redgrave Fat? Only with Pads Now: Still 'Georgy Girl.'" *New York Times*, April 13, 1974, 14.
——. "A Week at a Health Manor on the Last Resort Diet: Fasting." *New York Times*, October 29, 1974, 42.
——. "In a Society That Worships Slimness and Stalklike Size 5 Fashion Models, the Fat Woman Often Is America's Forgotten Person." *New York Times*, April 28, 1975, C9.
——. "Don't Call It a Fat Camp." *New York Times*, August 4, 1975, 34.
Lane, Lydia. "Lynn Makes Diet Decision." *Los Angeles Times*, April 7, 1972, G9.
Louderback, Lew. "More People Should Be Fat." *Saturday Evening Post*, November 4, 1967, 10–12.
Mayer, Jean. "Overweight and Obesity." *The Atlantic*, August 1955, 69–72.
——. "It's Not Just Overeating That's Killing Us. It's Underexercising, Too." *Forbes*, October 1, 1969, 64.
McFarlane, Heather. "To My Sister Who Is Fat." *The Other Woman* 1, no. 6 (1973): 3–4, 19.
Mitchell, Pam, and Robin Newmark. "The Political History of Fat Liberation: An Interview." *The Second Wave*, Summer 1981, 32–37.
Nathan, Simon. "About the Nudes in *Playboy*." *U.S. Camera*, April 1962, 68–71.
"Obesity Blamed on Overbuying of Food." *Science Digest*, January 1956, 52.
"Obesity Called Waste of Manpower and Food." *Science News Letter*, June 16, 1951, 377.
"Obesity Is Not No. 1 U.S. Nutritional Problem." *Science News Letters*, December 27, 1952, 408.
Palmer, Karen. "War on Weight Begins: Digging in for Battle of the Bulge." *Oxnard Press Courier*, January 15, 1976.
Pappas, Nancy. "Group Contends 'Fat Is Beautiful.'" *Hartford Courant*, November 18, 1973.
Reed, Red. "Lynn Redgrave: The Toadstool Turned into a Truffle." *New York Times*, October 1966, 133.

"Revolution." *Time*, August 18, 1947, 22.
Riker, Barbara. "Winner in Weight Battle? Fat Chance." *Los Angeles Times*, November 17, 1974, WS1, 16.
"Shed Guilt, Not Pounds, Doctor Advises Fatties." *Los Angeles Times*. August 6, 1973, 3.
"Singer Mama Cass Elliot Dead." *Chicago Tribune*, July 30, 1974, 12.
Singer, Steve. "When They Start Telling You It's Easy to Lose Weight." *Today's Health*, November 1972, 47–49, 62.
Smith, Ralph Lee. "All the Twiggies Want to be Sophia." *True*, November 1967, 81–82.
Snider, Arthur J. "Overweight? Blame Our Soft, Lazy Way of Life." *Science Digest*, October 1958, 49–50.
"Study Challenges Obesity-Mortality Link." *Science Digest*, November 1957, 16.
"The Big Bulge in Profits." *Newsweek*, July 23, 1956, 61–63.
"The Pink Jungle." *Time*, June 16, 1958, 86–90.
Thomas, Bob. "Censor Trouble Seen in These Low Necklines." *Tri-City Herald*, June 11, 1951, 2.
"Trial Opened in Surgery Suit." *Bridgeport Post*, February 8, 1963, 52.
Walker, Gerald. "The Great American Dieting Neurosis." *New York Times Magazine*, August 23, 1959, 12.
"Why Are They Running, Stretching, Starving?" *Fortune*, August 1970, 133–135, 160–162.
Wyatt, Hugh. "Girls Can Put on Teflon Front Now." *Daily News*, June 27, 1970.

Books

American Medical Association. *Sports and Physical Fitness: JAMA Questions and Answers from 1965–1969*. Chicago, IL: Journal of the American Medical Association, 1970.
Aldrich, Ann. *We Walk Alone*. Greenwich, CT: Fawcett Publications, 1956.
—. *We, Too, Must Love*. Greenwich, CT: Fawcett Publications, 1958.
—. ed. *Carol in a Thousand Cities*. Greenwich, CT: Fawcett Publications, 1960.
—. *We Two Won't Last*. Greenwich, CT: Fawcett Publications, 1963.
Anonymous, *Go Ask Alice*. New York: Simon and Schuster, 1971.
Apton, Adolph Abraham. *Your Mind and Appearance: A Psychological Approach to Plastic Surgery*. New York, Citadel Press, 1951.
Association of Life Insurance Medical Directors and the Actuarial Society of America. *Medico-Actuarial Mortality Investigation, Volume I*. New York: Association of Life Insurance Medical Directors and the Actuarial Society of America, 1912.
Bannon, Ann. *Odd Girl Out*. New York: Gold Medal, 1957.
—. *I Am a Woman*. New York: Gold Medal, 1959.
—. *Women in the Shadows*. New York: Gold Medal, 1959.
—. *Beebo Brinker*. New York: Gold Medal, 1962.
—. *Journey to a Woman*. New York: Gold Medal, 1960.
Beller, Anne Scott. *Fat and Thin: A Natural History of Obesity*. New York: Farrar, Straus, and Giroux, 1977.
Blume, Judy. *Are You There God? It's Me, Margaret*. New York: Dell Publishing, 1970.
Borie, Franklyn, and Marcia Borie. *A Doctor's Quick Way to Achieve Lasting Beauty and How to Play the Beauty Game*. New York: Information Incorporated, 1970.
Brown, Rita Mae. *Rubyfruit Jungle*. New York: Bantam Books, 1973.
Bruch, Hilde. *The Importance of Overweight*. New York, W.W. Norton & Company, 1957.
Dade County Public Schools. *Secondary Physical Education: Body Mechanics for Girls: Grades 7–12*. Miami, FL: Dade County Board of Instruction, 1967.

Daye, Zenda. *How to Develop the Bust*. Sydney: World Wide Mail Order, 1952.
Drake, Debbie. *Dancerize*. Englewood Cliffs, NJ: Prentice-Hall, 1967.
Dublin, Louis I. *The Facts of Life: From Birth to Death*. New York: The Macmillian Company, 1951.
—. *Factbook on Man: From Birth to Death*. New York: The Macmillan Company, 1965.
Ellis, Havelock. *Studies in the Psychology of Sex, vol. 4: Sexual Selection in Man*. Philadelphia, PA: F. A. Davis, 1905.
Fogarty, J. Paul. *Your Figure, Ladies*. New York: Barnes, 1955.
Franklyn, Robert Alan. *On Developing Bosom Beauty*. New York: Fell, 1959.
—. *Beauty Surgeon*. Long Beach, CA: Whitehorn, 1960.
—. *The Art of Staying Young*. New York: Fell, 1964.
—. *Augmentation Mammaplasty*. Rome: International Academy of Cosmetic Surgery, 1976.
—. *The Clinical Atlas of Cosmetic Plastic Surgery: A Teaching Manual*. Geneva: International Academy of Cosmetic Surgery, 1976.
Friedan, Betty. *The Feminine Mystique*. New York: W.W. Norton and Company, 2001.
Gibb, Sara Lee. *Slim, Trim, Fun for Life*. Salt Lake City, UT: Bookcraft, 1968.
Heidenstam, Oscar. *Modern Health and Figure Culture*. London: Faber, 1960.
Kain, Ida Jean. *Get in Shape*. Philadelphia, PA: David McKay Company, 1944.
Kaufman, Harry. *Younger by the Year: An Illustrated Guide to Permanent Figure Control*. Barre, MA: Barre Publishers, 1968.
Kinsey, Alfred C. *Sexual Behavior in the Human Female*. Bloomington, IN: Indiana University Press, 1953.
Klaich, Dolores. *Woman + Woman: Attitudes Toward Lesbianism*. New York: Simon and Schuster, 1974.
La Barre, Harriet. *Plastic Surgery: Beauty You Can Buy*. New York: Holt, Rinehart and Wilson, 1970.
Lee, Terri. *Aquacises: Water Exercises for Fitness and Figure Beauty*. Falls Church, VA: 1969.
Louderback, Lew. *Fat Power: Whatever You Weigh Is Right*. New York: Hawthorn Books, 1970.
Martin, Della. *Twilight Girl*. San Francisco, CA: Cleis Press, 1961.
Metropolitan Life Insurance Company. *Metropolitan Life's Exercise Guide for Men and Women*. New York: Metropolitan Life Insurance Co., 1966.
Michaels, Rea. *Two-Way Street*. New York: Domino Books, 1964.
Milo, Mary and Manya Kahn. *6 Minutes to Figure Beauty: Words and Music to Grow Slim By*. New York: Everywoman's Family Circle, 1960.
National Center for Health Statistics, *Health, United States, 2015: With Special Feature on Racial and Ethnic Health Disparities*. Hyattsville, MD: 2016. http://www.cdc.gov/nchs/data/hus/hus15.pdf#053. Accessed November 10, 2016.
Nye, Dorothy. *Lady be Fit!: Exercises for Energy, Efficiency, and Lasting Health*. New York: Harper & Bros., 1942.
Obeck, Victor F. and Isadore Rossman. *Isometrics: The Static Way to Physical Fitness*. New York: Stavon, 1966.
Park, Reg. *Free Exercises and Weight Training for Women: A Course for Women Who Want a Beautiful Body*. Rochelle, NY: Sportshelf, 1963.
President's Council on Physical Fitness. *The U.S. Government Family Fitness Book: A Complete Program*. New York: Universal Pub & Distributing Corp., 1969.
Sears Roebuck Catalogue. Chicago, IL: Sears, Roebuck and Co., 1961.
—. Chicago, IL: Sears, Roebuck and Co., 1966.
Society of Actuaries. *Build and Blood Pressure Study*. Chicago, IL: Society of Actuaries, 1959.

Stewart, Anita L., Robert H. Brook, Robert L. Kane. *Conceptualization and Measurement of Health Habits for Adults in the Health Insurance Study: Prepared Under a Grant from the U.S. Department of Health, Education, and Welfare, Volume II: Overweight*. Santa Monica, CA: Rand, 1980.

Taylor, Valerie. *The Girls in 3-B*. New York: Gold Medal, 1959.

—. *Journey to Fulfillment*. New York: Midwood Tower, 1964.

Thorek, Max. *Plastic Surgery of the Breast and Abdominal Wall*. Springfield, IL: C.C. Thomas, 1942.

US Bureau of the Census. "Income Growth Rates in 1939 to 1968 for Persons by Occupation and Industry Groups, for the United States." *Current Population Reports* Series P-60, No. 69. Washington, DC: US Government Printing Office, 1970.

US Department of Health, Education, and Welfare. "Obesity and Health: A Source Book of Current Information for Professional Health Personnel." Washington, DC: US Government Printing Office, 1966.

Van de Velde, Theodore H. *Sex Efficiency Exercise for Women*. London: W. Heinemann, Ltd., 1955.

Van Doren, Mamie. *I Swing*. Chicago, IL: Novel Books, 1965.

Volin, Michael and Nancy Phelan. *Yoga for Beauty*. New York: Arc Books, 1966.

Waddy, Stacy Lett. *Posture and Poise*. Sydney: Dymock's Book Arcade, 1944.

Wallis, Earl L. *Figure Improvement Exercises for Women*. Englewood Cliffs, NJ: Prentice-Hall, 1965.

Whitcomb, Helen, and Rosalind Lang. *Charm for the Modern Woman*. New York: Gregg Division, McGraw-Hill, 1967.

Wyden, Peter. *The Overweight Society*. New York: Willow Marrow, 1965.

Young, Agnes Brooks. *Recurring Cycles of Fashion, 1760–1937*. New York: Cooper Square Publishers, Inc., 1966.

Secondary Sources

Theses and Dissertations

Baker, Nancy L. "A Study of the Effects of Exercise and Diet on Weight Loss of Gustavus Adolphus College Girls." MS thesis, Mankato State College, 1963.

Brown, Korey Bowers. "Ideals, Images, Identity: *Ebony* Magazine in an Age of Black Power, 1965–1970." MA thesis, Vanderbilt University, 2000.

Bryer, Marjorie Lee. "Representing the Nation: Pinups, *Playboy*, Pageants and Racial Politics, 1945–1966." PhD diss., University of Minnesota, 2003.

Chrietzberg, Agnes L. "The Effects of Mechanical Vibration on Spot Reduction of College Women." MS thesis, Florida State University, 1963.

Day, June I. "A Study of the Reduction of the Waistline of Women by Maximum Isometric Contraction of the Abdominal Wall." M.S. thesis, Louisiana State University and Agricultural and Mechanical College, 1957.

Fields, Jill Susan. "The Production of Glamour: A Social History of Intimate Apparel, 1909–1952." PhD diss., University of Southern California, 1997.

Fraterrigo, Elizabeth. "'Entertainment for Men': *Playboy*, Masculinity, and Postwar American Culture." PhD diss., Loyola University Chicago, 2004.

Frobish, Dennis Lee. "The Family and Ideology: Cultural Constraints on Women, 1940–1960." PhD diss., University of North Carolina at Chapel Hill, 1983.

Gosin, Monika N. "The Politics of African-American Women's Beauty in *Ebony* Magazine: The 1960s and 1970s." MA thesis, University of California-San Diego, 2004.
Kase, Allison M. "Lesbian and Bisexual Women: Attitudes, Behaviors, and Self-Esteem Related to Self-Image, Weight, and Eating." MA thesis, Loyola University Chicago, 1996.
Latteier, Carolyn. "Cosmetic Breast Surgery: The Origins, 1945–1968." MA thesis, Washington State University, 1997.
Oluwatosin, Abegbola. "Black Students' Reception of Black Female Images in Women's Fashion/Lifestyle Magazines." PhD diss., Howard University, 2002.
Regenhardt, Christy Erin. "Marilyn Monroe and American Masculinity, 1949–1962." MA thesis. University of Maryland at College Park, 1997.
Selzer, Robin A. "The Experience and Meaning of Body Image: Hearing the Voices of African American Sorority Women," PhD diss., Loyola University Chicago, 2006.
Waldfogel, Sabra. "The Body Beautiful, the Body Hateful: Feminine Body Image and the Culture of Consumption in 20th-Century America." PhD diss., University of Minnesota, 1986.

Articles and Essays

Alter, Charlotte. "In Defense of Barbie: Why She Might Be the Most Feminist Doll Around." *Time*. February 6, 2014. http://time.com/4597/in-defense-of-barbie-why-she-might-be-a-feminist-doll-after-all/.
American Society for Aesthetic Plastic Surgery. "11.5 Million Cosmetic Procedures in 2006." March 9, 2007. http://www.surgery.org/media/news-releases/115-million-cosmetic-procedures-in-2006.
—. "Breast Augmentation." http://www.surgery.org/consumers/procedures/breast/breast-augmentation. Accessed July 10, 2010.
Anschutz, Doeschka and Rutger Engels. "The Effects of Playing with Thin Dolls on Body Image and Food Intake in Young Girls." *Sex Roles* 63, no. 10 (2010): 621–630.
Atwater, Tony, and Kwadwo Anokwa. "Race Relations in *Ebony*: An Analysis of Interracial Statements in Selected Feature Stories." *Journal of Black Studies* 21 (1991): 268–278.
BBC News. "Airbrushed Twiggy photo 'misleading.'" December 16, 2009. http://news.bbc.co.uk/2/hi/uk_news/8415176.stm.
Berkman, Dave. "Advertising in *Ebony* and *Life*: Negro Aspirations vs. Reality." *Journalism Quarterly* 40 (1963): 53–64.
Berney, Adrienne. "Streamlining Breasts: The Exaltation of Form and Disguise of Function in the 1930s Ideals." *Journal of Design History* 14, no. 4 (2001): 327–342.
Brown, Laura S. "Lesbians, Weight, and Eating. New Analysis and Perspectives." In *Lesbian Psychologies: Explorations and Challenges*, edited by The Boston Lesbian Psychologies Collective, 294–310. Chicago, IL: University of Illinois Press, 1987.
Chambers, Jason. "Presenting the Black Middle Class: John H. Johnson and *Ebony Magazine*, 1945–1974." In *Historicizing Lifestyle: Mediating Taste, Consumption, and Identity from the 1900s to 1970s*, edited by David Bell and Joanne Hollows, 54–69. Burlington, VT: Ashgate Publishing Co., 2006.
Chernikoff, Leah. "*Marie Claire* EIC Joanna Coles Responds to Controversial Fatist Blog Post." *Fashionista*. October 26, 2010. http://fashionista.com/2010/10/exclusive-marie-claire-eic-joanna-coles-responds-to-controversial-fatist-blog-post/.
CNN Health, "FDA Allows Silicone Breast Implants Back on the Market," November 17, 2006. http://articles.cnn.com/2006-11-17/health/implants_1_implants-rupture-inamed-and-mentor-silicone?_s=PM:HEALTH.

Coleman, Barbara J. "Maidenform(ed): Images of American Women in the 1950s." In *Forming and Reforming Identity*, edited by Carol Siegel and Ann Kibbey, 3–29. New York: New York University Press, 1995.

Cosmeticsurg: The Science of Beauty. "Breast Augmentation Procedure." http://www.cosmeticsurg.net/procedures/Breast-Augmentation.php. Accessed July 10, 2010.

Costello, Brid. "Kate Moss: The Waif That Roared." *WWD*. November 13, 2009. http://www.wwd.com/beauty-industry-news/kate-moss-the-waif-that-roared 2367932?src=bblast/111309/a.

Czerniawski, Amanda M. "From Average to Ideal: The Evolution of the Height and Weight Table in the United States, 1836–1943." *Social Science History* 31, no. 2 (2007): 273–290.

Davis, Madeline, and Elizabeth Lapovsky Kennedy. "Oral History and the Study of Sexuality in the Lesbian Community." In *Hidden from History: Reclaiming the Gay & Lesbian Past*, edited by Martin Duberman, Martha Vicinus, and George Chauncey, 426–440. New York: Meridian, New American Library, Penguin Books, 1990.

Ditmar, Helga, Emma Halliwell, Suzanne Ive. "Does Barbie Make Girls Want to Be Thin? The Effect of Experimental Exposure to Images of Dolls on the Body Image of 5- to 8-Year-Old Girls," *Developmental Psychology* 42, no. 2 (2006): 283–292

Dockterman, Eliana. "A Barbie for Every Body." *Time*. February 8, 2016: 44–50.

Dworkin, Sari H. "Not in Man's Image: Lesbians and the Cultural Oppression of Body Image." *Women and Therapy* 8 (1989): 27–39.

Fabrey, William. "Thirty-Three Years of Size Acceptance in Perspective—How Has It Affected the Lives of Real People?" Keynote Address, Big as Texas Conference, March 16, 2001. http://bigastexas.tripod.com/~bigastexas/2001event/bat2001.html.

Fishman, Sara Golda Bracha. "Life in the Fat Underground." *Radiance*, Winter 1998.

France, Louise. "A Rare Interview with Penelope Tree, the Ultimate Sixties It Girl." *The Guardian*, August 3, 2008. http://www.guardian.co.uk/lifeandstyle/2008/aug/03/celebrity.women. Accessed April 2, 2010.

Haidarali, Laila. "Polishing Brown Diamonds: African American Women, Popular Magazines, and the Advent of Modeling in Early Postwar America." *Journal of Women's History* 17 (2005): 10–37.

Hamer, Diane. "'I Am a Woman': Ann Bannon and the Writing of Lesbian Identity in the 1950s." In *Lesbian and Gay Writing: An Anthology of Critical Essays*, edited by Mark Lilly, 47–75. Philadelphia, PA: Temple University Press, 1990.

Hart, Anna. "Introducing the New, Realistic Barbie: 'The Thigh Gap Has Officially Gone.'" *The Telegraph*, January 28, 2016.

Higginbotham, Evelyn Brooks. "Beyond the Sound of Silence: Afro-American Women's History." *Gender and History* 1 (1989): 50–67.

Hilts, Philip J., "Strange History of Silicone Held Many Warning Signs." *New York Times*, January 18, 1992, 1.

Hirsch, Paul. "An Analysis of *Ebony*: The Magazine and Its Readers." *Journalism Quarterly* 45 (1968): 261–270.

Horowitz, Daniel. "Rethinking Betty Friedan and The Feminine Mystique: Labor Union Radicalism and Feminism in Cold War America." *American Quarterly* 48, no. 1 (1996): 1–42.

Italie, Leanne. "Twiggy: 'It Could Have Gone Terribly Wrong,'" *Associated Press*, March 29, 2010. http://www.timesfreepress.com/news/local/story/2010/mar/30/twiggy-it-could-have-gone-terribly-wrong/11319/. Accessed January 26, 2017.

Jancovich, Mark. "The Politics of *Playboy*: Lifestyle, Sexuality and Non-Conformity in American Cold War Culture." In *Historicizing Lifestyle: Mediating Taste, Consumption and*

Identity from the 1900s to 1970s, edited by David Bell and Joanne Hollows, 70–87. Burlington, VT: Ashgate Publishing, 2006.

Jun, Catherine. "Roseville Woman Says Hooters Put Her on Probation for Weight Gain." *The Detroit News*, May 19, 2010, http://detnews.com/article/20100519/METRO03/5190346/1014/rss03.

———. "Hooters Official Disputes Two Suits Claiming Weight Discrimination." *Detroit News*, June 2, 2010, http://www.callsam.com/bernstein-media-center/richard-bernstein-news-fighting-for-justice/victim-of-weight-discrimination-sues-hooters-restaurants/hooters-official-disputes-two-suits-claiming-weight-discrimination.

Keller, Yvonne. "'Was It Right to Love Her Brother's Wife So Passionately?' Lesbian Pulp Novels and U.S. Lesbian Identity, 1950." *American Quarterly* 57, no. 2 (2005): 385–410.

Kelly, Maura. "Should Fatties Get a Room? (Even On TV?)" *Marie Claire*, October 25, 2010. http://www.marieclaire.com/sex-love/dating-blog/overweight-couples-on-television.

Khailova, Ladislava. "The Mid-Century Pulp Novel and the Imagining of Lesbian Community." In *Invisible Suburbs: Recovering Protest Fiction in the 1950s United States*, edited by Josh Lukin. Jackson, MS: University Press of Mississippi, 2008.

Krebs, Albin. "Rita Hayworth, Movie Legend, Dies." *New York Times*, May 16, 1987. http://www.nytimes.com/learning/general/onthisday/bday/1017.html.

Kron, Joan. "Nipping and Tucking in Tinseltown." *Allure*, May 1995. http://www.facelift.com/1995_niptucktinseltown_home.html.

May, Elaine Tyler. "Explosive Issues: Sex, Women, and the Bomb." In *Recasting America: Culture and Politics in the Age of Cold War*, edited by Lary May, 154–170. Chicago, IL: The University of Chicago Press, 1989.

Meyerowitz, Joanne. "Beyond the Feminine Mystique: A Reassessment of Postwar Mass Culture, 1946–1958." *Journal of American History* 79, no. 4 (1993): 1455–1482.

———. "Women, Cheesecake, and Borderline Material: Responses to Girlie Pictures in the Mid-Twentieth Century U.S." *Journal of Women's History* 8 (1996): 9–35.

Myers, Anna, Jennifer Taub, Jessica F. Morris, and Esther D. Rothblum. "Beauty Mandates and the Appearance Obsession: Are Lesbians Any Better Off?" In *Looking Queer: Body Image and Identity in Lesbian, Bisexual, Gay, and Transgender Communities*, edited by Dawn Atkins, 17–26. New York: Haworth, 1998.

National Eating Disorders Association, "The War on Women's Bodies." https://www.nationaleatingdisorders.org/war-womens-bodies. Accessed March 14, 2011.

Nestle, Joan. "Butch-Femme Relationships: Sexual Courage in the 1950s." In *A Restricted Country*, edited by Joan Nestle, 100–109. Ithaca, NY: Firebrand, 1987.

———. "The Femme Question." In *The Persistent Desire: A Femme-Butch Reader*, edited by Joan Nestle, 140–142. Boston, MA: Alyson Publications, Inc., 1992.

Nishikawa, Kinohi. "Race, Respectability, and the Short Life of Duke Magazine." *Book History* 15, no. 1 (2012): 152–182.

Ogden, Cynthia, Cheryl D. Fryar, Margaret D. Carroll, and Katherine M. Flegal. "Mean Body Weight, Height, and Body Mass Index, United States 1960–2002." Centers for Disease Control and Prevention. *Vital and Health Statistics* No. 347 (October 27, 2004), 1–18.

Olisa, CeCe. "The Big Girl Blog on Marie Claire." *The Big Girl Blog*, October 29, 2010. http://www.thebiggirlblog.com/2010/10/thebiggirlblog-marie-claire/.

Pearson, Michael. "Barbie's New Body: Curvy, Tall and Petite." *CNN*, January 28, 2016. http://www.cnn.com/2016/01/28/living/barbie-new-body-feat.

Peiss, Kathy. "On Beauty—and the History of Business." In *Beauty and Business Commerce, Gender, and Culture in Modern America*, edited by Philip Scranton, 7–23. London: Routledge, 2001.

Relly, J. E. "The Big Issue: A Fat-Acceptance Movement Welcomes America's New Majority." *Tucson Weekly*, October 5, 1998. http://www.weeklywire.com/ww/10-05-98/tw_feat.html.

Rensenbrink, Greta. "Fat's No Four-Letter Word: Fat Feminism and Identity Politics in the 1970s and 1980s." In *Historicizing Fat in Anglo-American Culture*, edited by Elena Levy-Navarro, 213–244. Columbus, OH: The Ohio State University Press, 2010.

Rhode, Deborah L., "The Injustice of Appearance," *Stanford Law Review* 61, no. 5 (2009), 1034–1090.

Rich, Adrienne. "Compulsory Heterosexuality and Lesbian Existence." *Journal of Women's History* 15, no. 3 (2003): 11–48.

Rossi, Lee D. "The Whore vs. the Girl-Next-Door: Stereotypes of Woman in *Playboy*, *Penthouse*, and *Oui*." *Journal of Popular Culture* 9 (1975): 90–94.

Sargent, Lesli W., Wiley Carr, and Elizabeth McDonald. "The Significant Coverage of Integration by Minority Group Magazines." *Journal of Human Relations* 13 (1965): 484–491.

Schoenfielder, Lisa, and Barb Wieser, eds. *Shadow on a Tightrope: Writings by Women on Fat Oppression*. San Fransisco, CA: Aunt Lute Books, 1983.

Seidman, Robert. "CBS Gives Full Season Pickups to All New Series." *TV By the Numbers*, October 21, 2010. http://tvbythenumbers.com/2010/10/21/cbs-gives-full-season-pickups-to-all-new-series-hawaii-five-0-defenders-blue-bloods-mike-molly-my-dad-says/69152.

Swartz, Mimi. "Silicone City: The Rise and Fall of the Implant—Or How Houston Went from an Oil-Based Economy to a Breast-Based Economy. *Texas Monthly* 23, no. 8 (1995), 64–79.

Take Off Pounds Sensibly (TOPS). "History of TOPS." http://www.tops.org/tops/TOPS/History2.aspx?WebsiteKey=a56ba4c3-a91c-4d57-b04a-b38d910feec5. Accessed January 26, 2017.

US Department of Health and Human Services. "Medical Devices." http://www.fda.gov/medicaldevices/. Accessed July 24, 2010.

Williams, Megan E. "The Crisis Cover Girl: Lena Horne, The NAACP, and Representations of African American Femininity, 1941–1945." *American Periodicals* 16 (2006): 200–218.

Welsch, Janice. "Actress Archetypes in the 1950s: Doris Day, Marilyn Monroe, Elizabeth Taylor, Audrey Hepburn." In *Women and the Cinema: A Critical Anthology*, edited by Karyn Kay and Gerald Peary, 99–111. New York: E. P. Dutton, 1977.

Welter, Barbara. "The Cult of True Womanhood." *American Quarterly* 18 (1966): 151–174.

Westbrook, Robert. "'Want a Girl, Just Like the Girl That Married Harry James': American Women and the Problem of Political Obligation in World War II." *American Quarterly* 42 (1990): 587–614.

Books

Ainley, Rosa. *What Is She Like?: Lesbian Identities from the 1950s to the 1990s*. London: Cassell, 1995.

Allen, Robert C. *Horrible Prettiness: Burlesque and American Culture*. Chapel Hill, NC: The University of North Carolina Press, 1991.

Anderson, Karen. *Wartime Women: Sex Roles, Family Relations, and the Status of Women during World War II*. Westport, CT: Greenwood Press, 1981.

Bacon, Linda. *Health at Every Size: The Surprising Truth About Your Weight*. Dallas, TX: BenBella Books, 2008.

Bailey, Beth. *From Front Porch to Back Seat: Courtship in Twentieth-Century America*. Baltimore, MD: The Johns Hopkins University Press, 1989.

Banet-Weiser, Sarah. *The Most Beautiful Girl in the World: Beauty Pageants and National Identity*. Berkeley, CA: University of California Press, 1999.

Banner, Lois. *American Beauty*. New York: Knopf, 1983.

Banta, Martha. *Imaging American Women: Idea and Ideals in Cultural History*. New York: Columbia University Press, 1987.

Baxandall, Rosalyn and Linda Gordon. *Dear Sisters: Dispatches from the Women's Liberation Movement*. New York: Basic Books, 2001.

Benwell, Bethan, ed. *Masculinity and Men's Lifestyle Magazines*. Malden, MA: Blackwell Publishing, 2003.

Bérubé, Allan. *Coming Out Under Fire: Gays and Lesbians in World War II*. New York: Free Press, 1990.

Betrock, Alan. *Pin-up Mania!: The Golden Age of Men's Magazines, 1950–1967*. Brooklyn, NY: Shake Books, 1993.

Blackwelder, Julia Kirk. *Styling Jim Crow: African American Beauty Training During Segregation*. College Station: Texas A & M University Press, 2003.

Blum, Virginia L. *Flesh Wounds: The Culture of Cosmetic Surgery*. Berkley, CA: University of California Press, 2005.

Boero, Natalie. *Killer Fat: Media, Medicine, and Morals in the American "Obesity Epidemic."* New Brunswick, New Jersey: Rutgers University Press, 2012.

Bogle, Tom. *Toms, Coons, Mulattoes, Mammies & Bucks: An Interpretive History of Blacks in American Films*. New York: Continuum International Publishing Group, 2001.

Bordo, Susan. *Unbearable Weight: Feminism, Western Culture, and the Body*. Berkeley, CA: University of California Press, 2004.

Boyd, Nan Alamilla. *Wide-Open Town: A History of Queer San Francisco to 1965*. Berkeley, CA: University of California Press, 2005.

Breines, Wini. *Young, White, and Miserable: Growing Up Female in the Fifties*. Boston, MA: Beacon Press, 1992.

Brumberg, Joan Jacobs. *Fasting Girls: The Emergence of Anorexia Nervosa as a Modern Disease*. Cambridge, MA: Harvard University Press, 1988.

—. *The Body Project: An Intimate History of American Girls*. New York: Random House, 1997.

Bullough, Vern. *Before Stonewall: Activists in Lesbian and Gay Rights in Historical Context*. New York: Harrington Park Press, 2002.

Butler, Judith. *Gender Trouble*. New York: Routledge, 1990.

Byrd, Ayana. *Hair Story: Untangling the Roots of Black Hair in America*. New York: St. Martin's Press, 2001.

Cahn, Susan K. *Coming on Strong: Gender and Sexuality in Twentieth-Century Women's Sports*. Cambridge, MA: Harvard University Press, 1998.

Chafe, William. *The Paradox of Change: American Women in the 20th Century*. New York: Oxford University Press, 1991.

Collins, Max Allan. *Men's Adventure Magazines in Postwar America: The Rich Oberg Collection*. Los Angeles, CA: Taschen, 2004.

Cogan, Frances B. *All-American Girl: The Ideal of Real Womanhood in Mid-Nineteenth-Century America*. Athens: University of Georgia Press, 1989.

Cohen, Lizabeth. *A Consumer's Republic: The Politics of Mass Consumption in Postwar America*. New York: Alfred A. Knopf, 2003.

Cooper, Charlotte. *Fat Activism: A Radical Social Movement*. Bristol, England: HammerOn Press, 2016.

Corber, Robert J. *Homosexuality in Cold War America: Resistance and the Crisis in Masculinity*. Chapel Hill, NC: Duke University Press, 1997.

Costello, John. *Virtue Under Fire: How World War II Changed Our Social and Sexual Attitudes.* Boston, MA: Little Brown, 1985.
Craig, Maxine Leeds. *Ain't I a Beauty Queen?: Black Women, Beauty, and the Politics of Race.* New York: Oxford University Press, 2002.
Currie, Dawn. *Girl Talk: Adolescent Magazines and Their Readers.* Buffalo, NY: University of Toronto Press, 1999.
Davis, Kathy. *Reshaping the Female Body: The Dilemma of Cosmetic Surgery.* New York: Routledge, 1995.
De Beauvoir, Simone. *The Second Sex*, trans. H. M. Parshley. New York: Vintage Books, 1989.
Deford, Frank. *There She Is: The Life and Times of Miss America.* New York: Viking Press, 1971.
D'Emilio, John. *Sexual Politics, Sexual Communities.* Chicago, IL: University of Chicago Press, 1998.
D'Emilio, John and Estelle B. Freedman, *Intimate Matters: A History of Sexuality in America.* Chicago, IL: University of Chicago Press, 1988.
Douglas, Susan J. *Where the Girls Are: Growing Up Female with the Mass Media.* New York: Times Books, 1994.
Eisler, Benita. *Private Lives: Men and Women of the Fifties.* New York: Franklin Watts, 1986.
Ehrenreich, Barbara. *The Hearts of Men: American Dreams and the Flight from Commitment.* Garden City, NY: Anchor Press/Doubleday, 1983.
Endres, Kathleen L. and Terese L. Lueck, eds. *Women's Periodicals in the US: Consumer Magazines.* Westport, CT: Greenwood Press, 1995.
Etcoff, Nancy D. *Survival of the Prettiest: The Science of Beauty.* Anchor, 2000.
Evans, Harold, Gail Buckland, and David Lefer. *They Made America: From the Steam Engine to the Search Engine: Two Centuries of Innovators.* New York: Little, Brown and Co., 2004.
Evans, Sara M. *Born for Liberty.* New York: Free Press, 1997.
Faderman, Lillian. *Surpassing the Love of Men: Romantic Friendships Between Women from the Renaissance to the Present.* New York: Harper Collins, 1981.
—. *Odd Girls and Twilight Lovers: A History of Lesbian Life in Twentieth-Century America.* New York: Penguin, 1992.
Farrell, Amy. *Fat Shame: Stigma and the Fat Body in American Culture.* New York: New York University Press, 2011.
Farrell-Beck, Jane and Colleen Gau. *Uplift: The Bra in America.* Philadelphia, PA: University of Pennsylvania Press, 2002.
Ferguson, Marjorie. *Forever Feminine: Women's Magazine's and the Cult of Femininity.* Exeter, NH: Heinemann, 1983.
Fontanel, Beatrice. *Support and Seduction: A History of Corsets and Bras.* New York: Henry N. Abrams, 2001.
Forrest, Katherine V. *Lesbian Pulp Fiction: The Sexually Intrepid World of Lesbian Paperback Novels, 1950–1965.* San Francisco, CA: Cleis Press, 2005.
Fraterrigo, Elizabeth. *Playboy and the Making of the Good Life in Modern America.* New York: Oxford University Press, 2009.
Gavenas, E. Mary Lisa. *Color Stories: Behind the Scenes of America's Billion-Dollar Beauty Industry.* New York: Simon & Schuster, 2007.
Gilbert, James A. *Men in the Middle: Searching for Masculinity in the 1950s.* Chicago, IL: University of Chicago Press, 2005.
Gilman, Sander. *Making the Body Beautiful.* Princeton, NJ: Princeton University Press, 2001.
—. *Obesity: The Biography.* New York: Oxford University Press, 2010.

Gimlin, Debra. *Body Work: Beauty and Self-Image in American Culture.* Berkeley, CA: University of California Press, 2002.

Green, Adam. *Selling the Race: Culture, Community, and Black Chicago, 1940–1955.* Chicago, IL: University of Chicago Press, 2007.

Griffin, Gabriele. *Heavenly Love?: Lesbian Images in Twentieth-Century Women's Writing.* New York: Manchester University Press, 1993.

Griggs, Claudine. *S/he: Changing Sex and Changing Clothes.* New York: Berg, 1998.

Haiken, Elizabeth. *Venus Envy: A History of Cosmetic Surgery.* The Johns Hopkins University Press, 1999.

Halberstam, David. *The Fifties.* New York: Villard Books, 1993.

Halberstam, Judith. *Female Masculinity.* Durham, NC: Duke University Press, 1998.

Hanson, Dian. *Dian Hanson's The History of Men's Magazines,* Volume I. Los Angeles, CA: Taschen, 2004.

—. *Dian Hanson's The History of Men's Magazines,* Volume II. Los Angeles, CA: Taschen, 2004.

Hartmann, Susan M. *The Home Front and Beyond: American Women in the 1940s.* Boston: Twayne Publishers, 1982.

Harvey, Brett. *The Fifties: A Women's Oral History.* New York: Harper Collins Publishers, 1993.

Haskell, Molly. *From Reverence to Rape: The Treatment of Women in the Movies.* Chicago, IL: University of Chicago Press, 1987.

—. *Holding My Own in No Man's Land: Women and Men and Film and Feminists.* New York: Oxford University Press, 1997.

Head, Edith and Paddy Calistro. *Edith Head's Hollywood.* New York: E. P. Dutton, Inc., 1983.

Hine, Thomas. *Populuxe.* New York: Alfred A. Knopf, 1986.

Honey, Maureen. *Creating Rosie the Riveter: Class, Gender, and Propaganda during World War II.* Amherst, MA: University of Massachusetts Press, 1984.

Hoobler, Dorothy and Thomas Hoobler. *Vanity Rules: A History of American Fashion and Beauty.* Brookfield, CT: Twenty-First Century Books, 2000.

Horowitz, Robert and Arwen Mohun, eds. *His and Hers: Gender, Consumption, and Technology.* Charlottesville, VA: University of Virginia Press, 1998.

Jacobson, Matthew Frye. *Whiteness of a Different Color: European Immigrants and the Alchemy of Race.* Cambridge, MA: Harvard University Press, 1998.

Jeffries, Lesley. *Textual Construction of the Female Body: A Critical Discourse Approach.* New York: Macmillan, 2007.

Jewell, Sue K., *From Mammy to Miss America and Beyond: Cultural Images and the Shaping of US Social Policy.* New York: Routledge, 1993.

Jezer, Marty. *The Dark Ages: Life in the United States, 1945–1960.* Boston, MA: South End Press, 1982.

Johnson, John H. *Succeeding Against the Odds.* New York: Warner Books, 1989.

Kaplan, E. Ann, ed. *Women in Film Noir.* London: British Film Institute, 1999.

Kennedy, Elizabeth Lapovsky and Madeline D. Davis. *Boots of Leather, Slippers of Gold: The History of a Lesbian Community.* New York: Penguin, 1994.

Kirshner, Jonathan. *Hollywood's Last Golden Age: Politics, Society, and the Seventies Film in America.* Ithaca, NY: Cornell University Press, 2012.

Kitch, Carolyn. *The Girl on the Magazine Cover: The Origins of Visual Stereotypes in American Mass Media.* Chapel Hill, NC: The University of North Carolina Press, 2001.

Koda, Harold. *Extreme Beauty: The Body Transformed.* New Haven, CT: Yale University Press, 2001.

Landry, Bart. *The New Black Middle Class*. Berkeley, CA: University of California Press, 1987.
Latteier, Carolyn. *Breasts: The Women's Perspective on an American Obsession*. New York: The Haworth Press, 1998.
LaVine, W. Robert. *In a Glamorous Fashion: The Fabulous Years of Hollywood Costume Design*. New York: Charles Scribner's Sons, 1980.
Levy-Navarro, Elena, ed. *Historicizing Fat in Anglo-American Culture*. Columbus, OH: The Ohio State University Press, 2010.
Lhamon, W. T., Jr., *Deliberate Speed: The Origins of a Cultural Style in the American 1950s*. Washington, DC, Smithsonian Institution Press, 1990.
Lohof, Bruce. *American Commonplace: Essays on the Popular Culture of the United States*. Bowling Green, OH: Bowling Green University Popular Press, 1982.
Lowe, Margaret A. *Looking Good: College Women and Body Image, 1875–1930*. Baltimore, MD: Johns Hopkins University Press, 2003.
Luciano, Lynne. *Looking Good: Male Body Image in Modern America*. New York: Hill and Wang, 2001.
Marlin, Karal Ann. *As Seen on TV: The Visual Culture of Everyday Life in the 1950s*. Cambridge, MA: Harvard University Press, 1994.
May, Elaine Tyler. *Homeward Bound: Families in the Cold War Era*. New York: Basic Books, 1988.
—. *Pushing the Limits: American Women, 1940–1961*. New York: Oxford University Press, 1994.
May, Lary. *Screening Out the Past: The Birth of Mass Culture and the Motion Picture Industry*. Chicago, IL: University of Chicago Press, 1983.
Meyerowitz, Joanne, ed. *Not June Cleaver: Women and Gender in Postwar* America, *1945–1960*. Philadelphia, PA: Temple University Press, 1994.
Miller, Douglas T. and Marion Nowak. *The Fifties: The Way We Really Were*. Garden City, NY: Doubleday & Company, Inc., 1975.
Miller, Russell. *Bunny: The Real Story of* Playboy. New York: Holt, Rinehart, and Winston, 1984.
Morgan, Robin, ed. *Sisterhood Is Powerful: An Anthology of Writings from the Women's Liberation Movement*. New York: Random House, 1970.
National Eating Disorders Association. http://www.nationaleatingdisorders.org/information-resources/general-information.php#facts-statistics. Accessed March 14, 2011.
Nidetch, Jean and Joan Rattner Heilman. *The Story of Weight Watchers*. New York: W/W Twenty-First Corp., 1970.
Oakley, Ronald J. *God's Country: America in the Fifties*. New York: Dembner Books, 1986.
Oliver, J. Eric. *Fat Politics: The Real Story behind America's Obesity Epidemic*. New York: Oxford University Press, 2006.
O'Neill, William L. *American High: The Years of Confidence, 1945–1960*. New York: The Free Press, 1986.
Parfrey, Adam. *It's a Man's World: Men's Adventure Magazines: The Postwar Pulps*. Los Angeles, CA: Feral House, 2003.
Pattillo-McCoy, Mary. *Black Picket Fences: Privilege and Peril among the Black Middle Class*. Chicago, IL: University of Chicago Press, 1999.
Peiss, Kathy. *Cheap Amusements: Working Women and Leisure in Turn-of-the-Century New York*. Philadelphia, PA: Temple University Press, 1986.
—. *Hope in a Jar: The Making of American's Beauty Culture*. New York: Metropolitan Books, 1998.

Pendergrast, Mark. *Mirror Mirror: A History of the Human Love Affair with Reflection.* New York: Basic Books, 2003.

Pendergast, Tom. *Creating the Modern Man: American Magazines and Consumer Culture, 1900–1950.* Columbia, MO: University of Missouri Press, 2000.

Piepmeier, Alison. *Out in Public: Configurations of Women's Bodies in Nineteenth-Century America.* Chapel Hill: University of North Carolina Press, 2004.

Pipher, Mary. *Reviving Ophelia: Saving the Selves of Adolescent Girls.* New York: G.P. Putnam's Sons, 1994.

Pitman, Joanna. *On Blondes.* New York: Bloomsbury, 2003.

Polykoff, Shirley. *Does She … Or Doesn't She? And How She Did It.* Garden City, NY: Doubleday, 1975.

Radway, Janice. *Reading the Romance: Women, Patriarchy, and Popular Literature.* Chapel Hill, NC: University of North Carolina Press, 1984.

Riordan, Teresa. *Inventing Beauty: A History of the Innovations That Have Made Us Beautiful.* New York: Broadway, 2004.

Rooks, Noliwe M. *Hair Raising: Beauty, Culture, and African American Women.* New Brunswick, NJ: Rutgers University Press, 1996.

—. *Ladies' Pages: African American Women's Magazines and the Culture That Made Them.* New Brunswick, NJ: Rutgers University Press, 2004.

Rothblum, Esther and Sondra Solovay. *The Fat Studies Reader.* New York: New York University Press, 2009.

Schwartz, Hillel. *Never Satisfied: A Cultural History of Diets, Fantasies, and Fat.* New York: The Free Press, 1986.

Scranton, Philip. *Beauty and Business: Commerce, Gender, and Culture in Modern America.* New York: Routledge, 2000.

Segrave, Kerry. *Suntanning in 20th Century America.* Jefferson, NC: McFarland Company, Inc., 2005.

Seid, Roberta Pollack. *Never Too Thin: Why Women Are at War with Their Bodies.* New York: Prentice Hall Press, 1989.

Simic, Zora. "Fat as a Feminist Issue." In *Fat Sex: New Directions in Theory and Activism,* edited by Helen Hester and Caroline Walters, 15–35. New York: Routledge, 2015.

Smith, Patricia Juliana. *The Queer Sixties.* New York: Routledge, 1999.

Smith, E. O. *When Culture and Biology Collide.* New Brunswick, NJ: Rutgers University Press, 2002.

Solinger, Rickie. *Wake Up Little Susie: Single Pregnancy and Race before Roe v. Wade.* New York: Routledge, 1992.

Spigel, Lynn. *Make Room for TV: Television and the Family Ideal in Postwar America.* Chicago, IL: University of Chicago Press, 1992.

—. *Welcome to the Dreamhouse: Popular Media and Postwar Suburbs.* Durham, NC: Duke University Press, 2001.

Stearns, Peter N. *Fat History: Bodies and Beauty in the Modern West.* New York: New York University Press, 2002.

Steele, Valerie. *Fashion and Eroticism: Ideals of Feminine Beauty from the Victorian Era to the Jazz Age.* New York: Oxford University Press, 1985.

Streitmatter, Roger. *Unspeakable: The Rise of the Gay and Lesbian Press in America.* Boston, MA: Faber and Faber, 1995.

Stryker, Susan. *Queer Pulp: Perverted Passions from the Golden Age of the Paperbacks.* San Francisco, CA: Chronicle Books, 2001.

Tenner, Edward. *Our Own Devices: The Past and Future of Body Technology.* New York: Knopf, 2003.
Theriot, Nancy M. *Mothers and Daughters in Nineteenth-Century America: The Biosocial Construction of Femininity.* Lexington, KY: The University Press of Kentucky, 1996.
Thompson, Becky W. *A Hunger So Wide and So Deep.* Minneapolis, MN: University of Minnesota Press, 1995.
Todd, Jan. *Physical Culture and the Body Beautiful: Purposive Exercise in the Lives of American Women, 1800–1870.* Macon, GA: Mercer University Press, 1998.
Van Doren, Mamie. *Playing the Field: My Story.* New York: G. P. Putnam's Sons, 1987.
Walker, Nancy A. *Shaping Our Mothers' World: American Women's Magazines.* Jackson, MS: University Press of Mississippi, 2000.
—. *Women's Magazines, 1940–1960: Gender Roles and the Popular Press.* Boston, MA: Bedford/St. Martin's, 1998.
Walker, Susannah. *Style and Status: Selling Beauty to African American Women, 1920–1975.* Lexington, KY: The University Press of Kentucky, 2007.
Wann, Marilyn. *Fat! So?: Because You Don't Have to Apologize for Your Size!* Berkeley, CA: Ten Speed Press, 1998.
Weingarten, Rachel C. *Hello Gorgeous!: Beauty Products in America, '40s–60s.* Tigard, OR: Collector's Press, 2006.
Weyr, Thomas. *Reaching for Paradise: The Playboy Vision of America.* New York: Times Books, 1978.
Wilson, Elizabeth. *Hidden Agendas: Theory, Politics, and Experience in the Women's Movement.* London: Tavistock, 1986.
Wolf, Naomi. *The Beauty Myth: How Images of Beauty Are Used Against Women.* New York: Morrow, 1991.
Yalom, Marilyn. *A History of the Breast.* New York: Ballantine Books, 1998
Young, William H. and Nancy Young. *The 1950s.* Westport, CT: Greenwood Publishing Group, 2004.
Zimet, Jaye. *Strange Sisters: The Art of Lesbian Pulp Fiction, 1949–1969.* New York: Viking Studio, 1999.
Zimmerman, Bonnie. *The Safe Sea of Women: Lesbian Fiction, 1969–1989.* Boston, MA: Beacon Press, 1990.
Zuckerman, Mary Ellen. *A History of Popular Women's Magazines in the United States, 1792–1995.* Westport, CT: Greenwood Press, 1998.
Zukin, Sharon. *Point of Purchase: How Shopping Changed American Culture.* New York: Routledge, 2005.

INDEX

actresses: as models of beauty 15; *see also* Doris Day; Betty Grable; Grace Kelly; Sophia Loren; Marilyn Monroe
advertisements: in black periodicals 111–13; for breast augmentation 38–9; for diets 77, 86
AMA *see* American Medical Association
American Medical Association: on breast augmentation 39, 45; Investigations Bureau 39–40
Anderson, J. Morris 109
anorexia nervosa 14, 147
Arden, Elizabeth 79–81, 121
Association of Life Insurance Medical Directors of America 59
athletes/athletics: guarding femininity 82, 118–20; tennis 83, track and field 118–19; *see also* Olympics

Bacall, Lauren 36
Balenciaga, Cristobal 21
Banner, Lois 5–6, 14, 26
Barbie 150–1
BBPS *see* Build and Blood Pressure Study
beauty culture: democratization of 5–6
beauty ideals (nineteenth century) 13–14, 109; *see also* Gibson girl; steel-engraving lady
beauty pageants: black pageants 113–14; *see also* Miss America; Miss Black America
Ben, Lisa 136

Black Power movement 110
black women: athletes 118–20; body esteem 149; diet 118, 120; fashion 121–3; hair 6, 111–12, 122; skin color 112–13
Blume, Judy 2, 38, 41
BMI *see* Body Mass Index
body build 58–9, 61, 63, 96
Body Mass Index 70, 148, 150; *see also* Ancel Keys; Lambert Adolphe Jacques Quételet
body shame 109; of breasts 48; of fat 129–30
body weight: as gauge to health, beauty, and character 15
bosom *see* breasts
Bow, Clara 15
Bradley, Dorothy 1–2
Breastaplasty 45
breasts: augmentation surgery 42–3; building products 39–40; compression 15, 32; emphasized (1950s) 33–5, 97; implants 45–6
Breslow, Lester 69
Bruch, Hilde 120
Brumberg, Joan Jacobs 5, 10, 14, 37, 76
Build and Blood Pressure Study 61–2; flaws in methodology 63, 65
build-up diets 76–7

Cahn, Susan 118–19
Campbell, Jules 102

cancer 42, 60, 78
cardiovascular disease 4, 61, 68–9, 72, 78
cheesecake photography *see* pin ups
Chicago Defender 101, 110, 120, 123
childhood: weight gain 78
Civil Rights Act (1964) 147
clothing: ready-to-wear 16–17; *see also* Christian Dior; fashion; "New Look"
Cohen, Ellen Naomi *see* Cass Elliot
Cold War *see* Soviet Union; Olympics
Conover, Harry 18–19
cosmetics/cosmetic industry 5–6, 16
cosmetic surgery *see* plastic surgery
Courrèges, André 137
Craig, Maxine Leeds 109, 117
Crosby, Caresse 32
Cult of True Womanhood 13, 17

Dandridge, Dorothy 6, 109, 113, 117–18
Daughters of Bilitis 135–6
Day, Doris 23, 72
diet industry 79, 147–8
diet pills 86–7, 130
diets/dieting 84–5; statistics on 4, 78, 82; *see also* build up diets; fad diets
Dior, Christian 3, 19–21, 25, 27, 123; *see also* "New Look"
domesticity 17, 121
Dublin, Louis I. 8, 59–65, 69, 72, 78, 87–8, 148
Duke magazine 115–16

Ebony magazine 111–13, 120–2; cheesecake photography 113–14
Elliot, Cass 138–42; death of 140; *see also* Mamas and the Papas
Ellis, Havelock 109
Esquire magazine 33, 35, 40, 91–2, 94, 96
Equal Employment Opportunity Commission 148
exercise: isometrics 81; passive 81–2; reducing salons 79–81; *see also* Elizabeth Arden; Slenderella International; Helen Rubinstein

Fabrey, William 133
fad diets 84–5, 120
falsies 40–1; *see also* breasts
fashion: democratization of 3, 17; designers 19–21, 25; diet and 27–8; Hollywood's influence on 21
fashion models *see* models and modeling
fat: health and 59, 61, 78; job discrimination 131–2; men and aversion to fat women 98–9; national threat 3, 71, 82; stereotypes of 88, 132–3, 147
Fat Acceptance 133, 136–7, 142; *see also* fat activism
fat activism: origins of movement 133–4; *see also* Fat Underground; National Advancement to Aid Fat Americans
fat admirers 133
fat camps 80
Fat Power 133–4
fat spas and resorts 80
fat studies 142
Fat Underground 133–5, 142; *see also* fat activism; National Advancement to Aid Fat Americans
femininity 18–19, 81, 98, 125, 136; athletics and 82–4, 104, 118–20; breasts and 43, 45–6, 49, 51; men and 98, 103–4
feminism: lesbian feminism 135; radical feminism 134
femme fatale 35
Fishman, Sara Golda Bracha 134
fitness *see* exercise
flappers 15, 27, 43, 102
Franklyn, Robert Alan 44–6, 81, 98
Freespirit, Judy 134; *see also* Fat Underground; Sara Golda Bracha Fishman
Friedan, Betty 17
Funicello, Annette 24, 38

Gibson, Althea 119
Gibson, Charles Dana 14
Gibson Girl 14, 16
gigantomastia 43
"girl-next-door" 91, 94, 102, 104, 116
Go Ask Alice 76
Godey's Lady's Book 13–14
Gorman, Margaret 15–16; *see also* Miss America pageant
Grable, Betty 23, 36, 94–5, 100

Haiken, Elizabeth 43, 109
hair styles and care: Afro 109, 122; straightening 111–12, 122
Handler, Ruth 150
Harlow, Jean 16
Hayworth, Rita 23
Head, Edith 21, 40
health *see* medical views and advice
Health at Every Size 148
Hefner, Hugh 36, 91–4, 102–3, 115–16;

see also Playboy magazine
height and weight tables 25, 66, 68, 120; critiques of 69–70; origins 58–61; *see also* Metropolitan Life Insurance Company
Hepburn, Audrey 21–3, 34, 44, 52
Hollywood: decline of 23–4; dissemination of beauty ideals 15–16, 22; influence on breast size 34; influence on fashion 21
Horne, Lena 6, 109, 113, 117–18
housework, housewives 77–8; *see also* domesticity
Hornby, Leslie *see* Twiggy
Hutchinson, John 68–9

"Ideal weight" 58–9, 61, 72–3, 96, 120, 140; *see also* Build and Pressure Study; health and weight tables

Johnson, John H. 111, 113; *see also Ebony* magazine
Jones, Karen 132

Kelly, Grace 22–4, 97
Kelly, Maura 146–7
Keys, Ancel 70–1; *see also* Body Mass Index
Kinsey, Albert C. 33, 35
Koop, C. Everett 3
Kraus-Weber Tests for Muscular Fitness 71

The Ladder 135–6
Ladies Home Journal 27, 66, 72, 77, 85, 95; weight loss stories 129–31
Lane Bryant 136–7
lesbian: body image 135–6, 149
Life magazine 83, 86, 111
Loren, Sophia 77, 99, 102
Louderback, Lew 133
Luciano Lynn 4
Lyon, Phyllis 135–6; *see also* Daughters of Bilitis; Del Martin

Mabel-Lois, Lynn *see* McAfee, Lynn
McAfee, Lynn 142
McBee Susanna, 86–7
magazines: men's *vs.* women's 98, 103–4; role of 18
makeup *see* cosmetics, cosmetics industry
Mama Cass *see* Cass Elliot 138
Mamas and the Papas 138–9
Mansfield, Jayne 22, 24, 51, 93–4, 99
Marie Claire 146–7

Martin, Del 135–6; *see also* Daughters of Bilitis; Phyllis Lyon
Mayer, Jean 70–1, 78
medical views and advice: on exercise 82; on overweight and obesity 68–9; on underweight 59; on weight loss 61, 70
men's magazines (1950s) 91–2, 103–4; *see also Duke* magazine; *Esquire* magazine; *Playboy* magazine
methodology 62–3; *see also* Louis I. Dublin
Metrecal 79, 121
Metropolitan Life Insurance Company: creation of height and weight tables 3, 58–9; flaws in middle class: black 110, 116–17, 121–2, 125; post World War II 17–18
Mike & Molly 146–7
Miss America pageant 15–16; protest 108
Miss Black America 108–9
models and modeling: 7, 18, 72, 98, 102, 149–50; black 117; measurements of 96, 148; *see also* Jules Campbell; Harry Conover; André Courrèges; John Robert Powers; Walter Thornton; Twiggy
Monroe, Marilyn 22–4, 27, 34–7, 73, 99
Monroe type 36–7

NAAFA. *See* National Association to Aid Fat Americans
National Association to Advance Fat Acceptance *see* National Association to Aid Fat Americans
National Association to Aid Fat Americans 132, 142; comparison to radical fat activism 134–5; origins 133–4
"New Look" 3, 19–21, 25, 27; backlash 99–100, 123; *see also* Christian Dior; fashion

obesity and overweight: new definition 61–2; statistics related to 61; *see also* Louis I. Dublin; fat; medical views and advice
Olympics 71, 84, 118–19; *see also* athletes, athletics; Soviet Union

Peiss, Kathy 5
penny scale 15
Pickford, Mary 15
Pin-ups 18; black 113–14; in World War II 23; *see also* Betty Grable; Rita Hayworth; Walter Thornton

plastic surgery 41–2; in black community 109–10; breast implants 45–6; justification 46–50; *Playboy* magazine 92–4, 101, 114–15; *see also* Hugh Hefner
Poiret, Paul 15, 20
President's Council on Physical Fitness 71
Project Dawn 150

Quételet, Lambert Adolphe Jacques 58, 70

radical therapy 134
Reader's Digest 4, 78
Redgrave, Lynn 137–8, 140–1
reducing diets *see* diets/dieting
Rubenstein, Helena 80–1, 109
Russell, Jane 34, 37, 97
Russia *see* Soviet Union; Cold War; Olympics

Saturday Evening Post 91, 133
Schwartz, Hillel 3, 18
Seltzer, Carl C. 69–71
Seventeen magazine 2, 25–6, 66, 87, 109, 114, 117, 121, 130; *see also* teen magazines
Shrimpton, Jean 137
silicone implants 46, 50; *see also* breasts
Slenderella International 79–80, 98
Smith, Diana 109
Society of Actuaries 61
Soviet Union 71, 84, 119
spooks 98–9
Sports Illustrated 67–8, 82–3, 102–3, 150–1
Stearns, Peter 3, 125
steel-engraving lady 13–14
Streisand, Barbra 139
Stone, Toni 119–20

Taking Off Pounds Sensibly 79, 131
Taylor, Elizabeth 21, 24, 50

teenagers: breasts and 37–8; diets 87, 130; desired weight 73–4, 124; mass media and 15; overweight and 129–31, 149
'Teen magazine 2, 47, 87, 130; *see also* teen magazines
teen magazines 2, 26, 37, 87; *see also* *Seventeen* magazine; *'Teen* magazine
television 24
Thompson, Era Bell 120–1
Thornton, Walter 18
TOPS *see* Taking Off Pounds Sensibly
Towles, Dorothea 6, 113
Tree, Penelope 26
Twiggy 25–7, 62, 84; in black press 123–4; backlash 137; in men's magazine 102, 104

U.S. Centers for Disease Control 147
U.S. Department of Health, Education, and Welfare: height-weight studies 70–1
U.S. Food and Drug Administration 38, 86
U.S. Postal Service: mail fraud 81

Van Doren, Mamie 22, 24, 36–7
Vargas, Albert 33
Vice Versa 136
Vogue magazine 21, 25–6, 43, 66, 70, 85, 137

weight loss drugs *see* diet pills
Weight Watchers 79, 131
white men: attitude about female diets 98–9; body image 4–5; ideal woman 96–7
whiteness 5, 23–4, 109
Williams, Saundra 108
Wolf, Naomi 5, 125
Women's Equality Day 142
women's magazines: role of 7, 18; *see also* *Ladies Home Journal*; *Vogue* magazine

Printed in Great Britain
by Amazon